WHITE WEALTH AND BLACK POVERTY

WHITE WEALTH AND BLACK POVERTY

American Investments in Southern Africa

BARBARA ROGERS

Center on International Race Relations
University of Denver
Studies in Human Rights No. 2

GP *GREENWOOD PRESS*
WESTPORT, CONNECTICUT · LONDON, ENGLAND

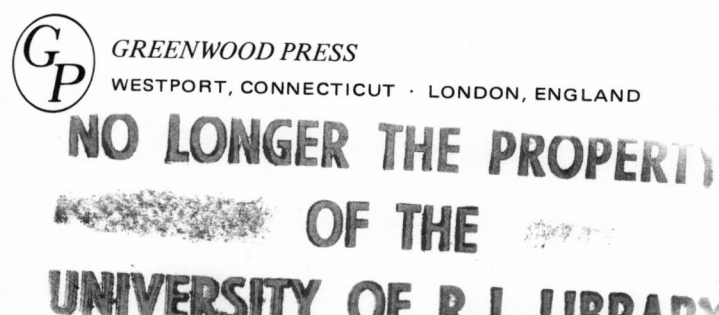

Library of Congress Cataloging in Publication Data

Rogers, Barbara, 1945—
     White wealth and Black poverty.

     (Studies in human rights ; no. 2)
     "Based on work done for a joint study, with Jennifer Davis, commissioned by
the Council for Christian Social Action of the United Church of Christ."
     Includes bibliographical references and index.
     1. Investments, America—Africa, Southern. 2. Corporations, American—
Africa, Southern.
I. Title. II. Series.
HG5850.S62R63 1976   322.6'7373'068   75-35353
ISBN 0-8371-8277-8

Library of Congress Catalog Card Number: 75-35353
ISBN: 0-8371-8277-8

First published in 1976

Greenwood Press, a division of Williamhouse-Regency Inc.
51 Riverside Avenue, Westport, Connecticut 06880

Printed in the United States of America

CONTENTS _____

PREFACE _____

In the months following the completion of this book, events have moved rapidly in southern Africa. Suddenly, white supremacy no longer seems the permanent fixture that it has been assumed to be since World War II.

Apparently on the expectation that the United States would be behind them, the South African Cabinet members made the decision to intervene openly in the Angolan civil war: first invading Angola to place troops around the Kunene dam area, and then organizing an armored column that advanced rapidly from the Namibian border toward Luanda, threatening to overwhelm the capital on the eve of independence in November, 1975. It was this action that triggered the massive increases in Soviet and Cuban arms supplies, and the direct participation of Cuban troops on the side of the MPLA. Unfortunately for South Africa, the United States Congress acted decisively to block U.S. involvement in the Angolan war, and without the expected intervention of United States and allied forces the South Africans were forced back to the Namibian border. This was a humiliating defeat, showing up the unpreparedness of South African armed forces for any conflict beyond that of hunting guerrillas with inferior arms and equipment. The call-up of reserve forces also damaged a number of businesses in South Africa, and it became clear that a prolonged conflict in southern Africa would have a serious impact on the economy of the Republic—which is in turn the ultimate guarantee of white supremacy, as indicated in this book.

Already, the South African economy is being seen as substantially weaker than has hitherto been thought. The rapid fall in the gold price at the beginning of 1976 has endangered all the ambitious plans of the South African government; following the exceptionally heavy borrowing of recent years, South Africa is also near the limits of its borrowing capacity, and its credit-worthiness is under some scrutiny. A surprisingly drastic devaluation at the end of 1975 raised questions about the continuing need to devalue the Rand in order to keep the gold mines in operation in the face of stagnant prices and mounting mining costs. Several American banks and companies have expressed unwillingness to become involved in South Africa following the Angolan episode and the gold price drop.

In Africa, the policy of "dialogue," on which the South African government depends in order to expand its export markets, has been badly damaged by the South African invasion of Angola. Southern Rhodesia is in increasing difficulties, both military and economic. The Angolan war focused attention on the illegal occupation of Namibia by South Africa. Western European governments are increasingly trying to dissociate themselves from the white minority regimes.

In this context, U.S. policy needs very careful scrutiny. With the large investments made by U.S. multinational corporations in southern Africa, there is clearly pressure for intervention there on the part of the administration, although Congressional opposition seems to be assured. The U.S. government took the drastic step during the Angolan war of imposing a total economic boycott on the MPLA in Angola, even forcing the cancellation of contracts for Boeing aircraft sales, and the suspension of operations by Gulf Oil in Cabinda. The declaration of economic warfare in this case gives the lie to claims that the U.S. government is unable to influence the nature of U.S. investment and trade with southern Africa. Instead, there are moves to increase the facilities available to American concerns in southern Africa through the Export-Import Bank.

The momentum of increasing U.S. investment in southern Africa, then, is set against the overwhelming aversion of Americans in the post-Vietnam era to becoming involved in post-colonial conflicts which are remote from their own concerns, both geographically and politically. In addition, there is a growing concern among African-Americans about southern Africa, and indentification with the African resistance to white minority rule there. The outcome of these conflicting interests may be known sooner than we could have predicted before the Angolan war.

Barbara Rogers

ACKNOWLEDGMENTS

The material in this book is based on work done for a joint study, with Jennifer Davis, commissioned by the Council for Christian Social Action of the United Church of Christ. This has subsequently been extensively rewritten and enlarged for publication for a wider audience. I am extremely grateful to Dr. George Shepherd of the Graduate School of International Studies, University of Denver, for commissioning the initial study on behalf of CCSA, and for his subsequent encouragement and support in the preparation of material for publication.

I am indebted also to Congressman Charles C. Diggs, Jr., in whose office I worked on questions of U.S. business involvement in southern Africa. Much of the writing was carried out while I was receiving a travel and study award from the Ford Foundation. Also of assistance in the course of research for this book were the United Nations and members of its Secretariat, especially in the Library; Mr. Jim Doyle of the U.S. Department of Commerce; Mr. Ed Hawley of the Graduate School of International Studies, University of Denver, who made a number of constructive suggestions; and many friends, both Americans and Africans, who have shown interest in the work and given me the benefit of their opinions and insights.

INTRODUCTION___

The question of American investment in South Africa and the whole
region of southern Africa under white minority rule has become
a highly controversial one, involving many vested interests. Increasing
criticism is being focused on the presence and activities of U.S. corporations in the area, and the attack is being met with evidence of concern
on the part of corporations as they attempt to deflect criticism, either
by attempting to modify their employment practices or, more frequently,
by launching public relations campaigns to defend their involvement.
A large-scale public relations industry has come into existence largely
to present American investment as a liberalizing influence within a
situation that is, in any case, changing for the better as an automatic
consequence of economic growth. Ford Motor Company, for example,
sent a pamphlet to all stockholders in 1973, announcing "the presence
of American-owned companies in South Africa" as a "positive factor
in encouraging economic progress and equal opportunity." Mobil Oil,
in a 1972 statement, proclaimed that "non-whites" in South Africa
needed "not disinvestment but greater investment."

Every author should make clear the philosophy behind his approach to a subject. In the present case, the writer rejects any purely ideological approach, whether this be based on the theory of "separate development" or apartheid (segregation), or any dogmatic approach to "private enterprise" as such, whether from the Right or the Left. The dominant United States approach seems to be acceptance of a "solution" of the South Africa question by means of more of the same—continued intervention in the processes at work in southern Africa by the commitment of even more resources by individuals, companies, and governments of the United States and other Western nations. However, this easy option is *prima facie* questionable, in the sense that those promoting it most actively have a vested interest in the system as it is at present.

Moreover, as a matter of principle, any controversial issue should be faced with critical challenge to all propositions and hypotheses, including—in fact, especially—those emanating from the most powerful of the interests involved. The inclination to see some easy solution to the question of investment in southern Africa is, therefore, overridden by the need for an analysis as rigorous as possible, given the incomplete and partial nature of much of the "authoritative" information available. All researchers in southern Africa are quickly faced with the problem of official concealment of key information, especially as it relates to the majority population, the Africans.

Much of the argument about investment centers around South Africa, and this has been the focus of attention in the present study. The reason for this is that most U.S. investment is concentrated there, and it provides the base for operations elsewhere in the region. South Africa is the regional powerhouse, militarily, politically, and economically; and, from the point of view of the argument, it would seem that the considerations relating to South Africa and its economy apply almost entirely to Namibia and Rhodesia, while additional arguments can be adduced in the other cases that would reinforce the conclusions bearing on the Republic itself. The question of Namibia involves the issue of illegal occupation, and the credibility of international sanctions is at stake in the case of Southern Rhodesia.

The whole southern African region presents the problem of investment in minority-ruled areas, where the economic benefits are distributed according to the decisions of the white minority and where the operation of major American subsidiaries has serious implications for the United States in the event of a serious challenge to minority rule. The rôle of multinational corporations in southern Africa is also of course an important aspect of the whole question of United States investment in countries which are dominated by undemocratic regimes, with great disparities of wealth and poverty.

WHITE WEALTH AND
BLACK POVERTY

chapter 1 ─────────────

SEPARATE DEVELOPMENT AND WHITE SUPREMACY

The South African government and its allies have been spending
millions of dollars every year on promoting the ideology of "separate development," in particular as expressed in the former "native reserves,"
dubbed the "Bantu homelands" or "Bantustans."* These "homelands"
are being presented as the vindication of the whole apartheid system and
increasingly are being used as an "alternative" to U.S. investment in the
urban centers of South Africa. To give the concept greater respectability,
the "homelands" are widely hailed as providing a platform for those
"homeland leaders" appointed or approved by the government and the
focus of either emerging African political participation in the whole
country, or alternatively as future "independent" entities in which
Africans will have their "own" political and economic structure. An
additional twist is the fact that Chief Gatsha Buthelezi, the "chief
minister of Kwazulu," is being allowed fairly strong criticism of the
"Bantustan" policy while urging, "We must carry this thing out to its

*The official term "Bantu" to describe Africans is very offensive to
them as a racial epithet and is used here only when quoting South Africans.

logical ends" in return for his much more widely publicised appeals to
foreign investors, especially in the United States, to invest heavily in
South Africa, including the "homelands."[1]

The "Bantustan" issue is so vital to South Africa's external image
that it deserves much closer scrutiny than is possible here.[2] A brief
survey will have to suffice, although the policy is basic to official
South African economic, social, and political policies. In the first
instance, the origin of the "Bantustans" is not widely understood;
they are often presented as something radically new in South Africa,
a symptom of "change" that will bring about the progressive destruction of the apartheid system. In fact they have been basic to
this system from the beginning of white conquest and settlement in
South Africa.

For the Africans confronted with white invasion and occupation,
resistance had from the earliest days involved fighting for their land
rights as pastoral people against European encroachment that imposed
a rival system of land tenure, also for pastoral purposes. Although South
Africans claim that the "Bantustans" are essentially identical with
the areas where Africans were originally settled when the Europeans
arrived in a virtually empty country, historical and archaeological
evidence overwhelmingly refutes this version of history. Even the
official Afrikaner interpretation admits that the history of white
settlement in South Africa is dominated by the violent confrontations
provoked by European arrival at the Cape (already permanently
settled by African people) and expansion northwards. The conflict
stretched over two centuries and is still continuing as Africans are
forcibly evicted from land occupied by their ancestors according to
the "consolidation," "rehabilitation," and other programs, which are
an integral part of the Bantustan policy.

As white rule was consolidated and the mining industry and
settled white farming emerged at the end of the nineteenth century,
it began to be perceived as convenient to justify and retain the
status quo in which Africans were driven back into some of the
least desirable agricultural areas, often barren mountainous or
semidesert regions, and to grant these areas a "native reserve"
status linked with policies designed to force able-bodied men into
employment by the white farmers and the mines. Thus began the
process of "underdeveloping" the native reserves, the process of

impoverishment by crowding increasing numbers of Africans into
rapidly deteriorating land which is a basic feature of the "Bantu
homelands" today. By 1916 a Senate Committee was reporting that
most of the reserves were bursting at the seams, and the land deteriorating rapidly.[3] In 1923 crop yields there were showing a
steep downward trend, while population continued to rise.[4]

The result of the increasing impoverishment was to force
large numbers of Africans onto the labor market in the effort to
support their destitute families. It is no coincidence that the 1894
legislation establishing the "native reserve" system was the creation
of the original large-scale foreign investor in South Africa, Cecil
Rhodes, the dominant figure in the development of vast fortunes
from South Africa's diamonds and gold by means of cheap "native
labor." The "hut tax" imposed on all household heads in the reserves under this legislation successfully pushed thousands of
Africans into the cash wage economy.[5] At the same time, African
urbanization proceeded at an increasing pace as the "reserves" became more and more hopeless as a subsistence base. For almost a
century, the urban African community has been probably the
fastest growing element of the South African population. There
are now more Africans in the so-called white areas (i.e., the areas
of economic activity and employment) than in the "Bantustans":
53.5 percent at the 1970 census, outnumbering whites in these
areas by 8 million to 3.7 million.[6]

The present boundaries of the "Bantustans" are defined in terms
of the 1936 Native Trust and Land Act (which simultaneously
removed African voting and other rights); this set out about 13
percent of South Africa's territory, widely scattered in several large
and hundreds of smaller pieces of land, as "native reserves." Some
of the designated areas are in fact in white hands, so that the actual
reserves occupy less than 12 percent of the total land area.[7]

Serious surveys, most of them by government commissions,
have repeatedly stressed that the reserves could never provide an
adequate basis for African society. In 1948, the Fagan Commission
concluded that the process of urbanization could not be reversed:

It would be utterly impossible to put the Native population
which is already outside the Reserves, back into the Reserves,

or even to keep the whole of the increase there in future. . . .
The spearpoint of . . . the problem of regulating the relation
between European and Native is no longer in the Reserves;
it is now in the towns.[8]

Since then, the problem has become even more acute. Population density in the "homelands" is now among the highest
on the African continent. Compared with a density of 63 persons
per square mile in Lesotho—a country geographically comparable
to the "Bantustans"—African-owned land in Natal carries a density of at least 235 people per square mile, and possibly twice as
much.[9] The increase in population density has also been extremely rapid owing to the enforced removal of many Africans whose
homes had been established in the towns and rural areas outside
the "reserves." Between the 1960 and 1970 censuses, the "homeland"
population increased from 4 million to 6.9 million.

The basis of all "development plans" is the Tomlinson Commission, which after an exhaustive inquiry reported in 1954 that
emergency measures were required to conserve the remaining
natural resources in the reserves and provide a subsistence income
for the African inhabitants, based on the resettlement *from* the
reserves of one half the population at that time.[10] However, government
policy has more than doubled the population of the reserves since these
estimates were made.

The result is clearly visible to any visitor to the "homelands."
The dominant feature of the landscape is hillside erosion both by
huge *dongas* (gulleys) and by sheet erosion, which leaves the land
bare of topsoil. A member of a scientific committee appointed in
1948 to study soil erosion has concluded:

> The indisputable and alarming fact is that there has been
> serious deterioration of the vegetation and hydrological con-
> ditions. And everywhere there has been almost terrifying
> erosion of the soil. The majority of the Committee were quite
> convinced that all the damage could be explained in terms of
> the impact of man, with his plough and his domestic animals,
> upon a land that was from the start extremely vulnerable. . . .
> Throughout the Union of South Africa soil erosion is trium-
> phantly on the march.[11]

The obvious result is increasing dependence for bare subsistence on employment in the modern sector controlled by the whites. Food production has fallen steadily while the number of people to feed has been rising rapidly. Between 1958 and 1968 the annual production of maize, the staple food, fell from 252,000 tons to 151,000 tons, a 50 percent drop in a decade, and sorghum production fell from 45,700 tons to 22,700 tons, a drop of over 50 percent.[12] As Mr. Colin Eglin, leader of the Progressive party, has observed: "The overall effect is that the real per capita income in the homelands—already the lowest on the African continent—is falling still lower.[13]

A measure of the dependency of the reserves on migrant labor for the whites is that the proportion of total income derived from migrant labor increased from 53 percent in 1960-1961 to 58 percent in 1966-1967.[14] The portion of domestic income actually derived from agriculture is almost negligible in most areas. A 1959 inquiry into the rural economy of the Ciskei concluded that only 6.8 percent of the average income was derived from agriculture.[15] Further evidence from this same area indicated that as impoverishment increased, child mortality and life expectancy were deteriorating noticeably.[16]

An inadequate subsistence base in the "Bantustans," and their increasing impoverishment, are basic to the economic structure of South Africa. They force household heads to work for whites, who control the productive farmland, mines and industry (even where these are physically located in "border areas" next to the reserves, or inside the reserves themselves). Since Africans have absolutely no alternative, the whites can hire them for as little as they like, with no regard for a minimum subsistence level, since the "homelands" themselves offer no alternative. The sociologist Pierre van den Berghe has concluded:

> Africans have not only lost most of their land to the Whites; they have also been forced out of their remaining Reserves, not fundamentally because of the "lure of the city," or opportunities for higher wages, but rather because migration was an imperative necessity for sheer physical survival. The "push" factor away from the Reserves was certainly much more basic than the "pull" factor towards the cities.[17]

Another important function of the "homelands" should be pointed out, one that is related to the export of "labor units" to the benefit of white employers. The "homelands" have become a focus for what is euphemistically referred to as "resettlement," the forced deportation of literally millions of men, women, children, old people and the growing army of unemployed Africans. The word "resettlement" was also the euphemism used the the Nazis for the deportation to concentration camps and forced labor of millions of Jews, Slavs and others. This new feature of the "Bantustan" system distinguishes it from the older "reserve" pattern, where Africans had been establishing a viable alternative in urban areas. It means the forcible separation of African communities, the separation of the "labor unit" from wife, children and extended family, and the wholesale deportation of those who are not of economic use to the whites. As Mr. Froneman, deputy minister of Justice, Mines, and Planning, explained in 1969: "Superfluous Bantu ought to be removed because their presence in the white homeland is not justified and promotes integration."[18]

Between 1960 and early 1973 a total of 1.6 million Africans had been deported from urban areas and white farms and sent to the "homelands," and the program was being stepped up;[19] Mr. Froneman estimated in 1969 that another 3.8 million "superfluous Bantu" were to be moved.[20] Most of them were described as disabled, old, women with young children, or people in some way not suitable for work. One visitor to a "resettlement area" reported that the people there referred to the removal as being sent to the "scrap yard."[21] Many of the removals had been achieved by the use of force or some form of coercion.[22] Dr. Koornhof, the deputy minister of Bantu Administration, has hailed the deportation program as "a tremendous achievement."[23] The international community, however, has compared it with the forcible deportation of civilians in Nazi-occupied Europe, which was established as a war crime at the Nuremberg Tribunal. In General Assembly Resolution 2775E (XXVI) of 1971 the assembly voted overwhelmingly (110 to 2, with 2 abstentions), with U.S. support:

> *Noting* General Assembly 95 (I) of 11 December 1946, which affirmed the principles of international law recognized by the Charter of the Nuremberg Tribunal and the judgment of the Tribunal;
>
> *Noting further* that under the aforementioned resolution crimes against humanity are committed when enslavement, deportation

and other inhuman acts are enforced against any civilian population on political, racial or religious grounds;

. . . *Again condemns* the establishment by the Government of
South Africa of the Bantu Homelands (Bantustans) and the forcible removal of the African people of South Africa and Namibia
to those areas as a violation of their inalienable rights, contrary to
the principle of self-determination and prejudicial to the territor-
ial integrity of the countries and unity of their peoples.

The situation is however growing worse as the deportation program is advanced. The people being removed from productive areas
to the "homelands" are not as a rule provided with any land at all,
but allocated to transit or resettlement camps, or "closer settlements,"
which are rural townships inside the "homelands" with no agricultural land attached. Mr. Froneman has announced that the state
feels under no obligation to prepare the "homelands" for the deportees:
"The removal of these superfluous Bantu from the White Homelands is
not dependent on the development of the Bantu Homelands."[24]
People in the camps are totally dependent on absent migrant
workers, who are under no obligation to support them, or else are
completely destitute. Rations have been provided for these people, although according to the Institute for Medical Research the diet is dan-
gerously lacking in essential nutrients, and even calories. The inevitable
result is very high child mortality, and a feature of the camps is the
large number of tiny graves.[25] A recent attempt to shift "responsibility" to the "homeland governments" demonstrates the way in
which they are being used. The financial burden of providing rations
has been shifted to these nominal "governments," despite the fact
that they have repeatedly begged for a stop to the policy of dumping
totally indigent people in their "homelands" where there are absolutely no spare resources of land, jobs, or other source of income.[26]
Since the hand-over, conditions of at least one camp, Dimbaza in
the Ciskei, have become desperate. The local Episcopal minister, Rev.
David Russell, told the press at the end of 1973:

The vast majority of families of Dimbaza, who had previously
depended for their livelihood on rations given out every two weeks

by the authorities, have received nothing for the whole of October.
Hundreds of people are affected and are desperate for food. . . . In all
the time I have been going to Dimbaza I have never been so shocked
and torn as I was that day in the presence of such numbers of hungry
people.[27]

Conditions in the camps have prompted one member of Parliament,
representing Port Natal for the United party, to warn of the consequences
for whites of uprooting thousands of people:

The attitude in the townships which we have created is frightening.
The slums and ghettoes we have created are breeding bitterness
which is a threat to our security.

Frustration is leading to bitterness, bitterness to hate and hatred to
crime and the breakdown of law and order. In our mania to separate
we have created scars in every city and in the minds of the people.[28]

The government, however, has pronounced itself well pleased with the
camps and "settlements"; in the words of the deputy minister of Bantu
Administration: "Each of these places is a manifestation of the successful implementation of the policy of separate development."[29]

If these massive deportations seem to indicate the introduction of
major elements of instability and insecurity to the African population
in the economically productive "white areas" of South Africa, this is
only the beginning of the intervention and forced removal policy getting under way in the name of "Bantu homelands." Probably far more
people are being evicted from their homes and lands *inside* the "homelands" in the name of the programs of "consolidation" and "rehabilitation."

"Consolidation" arises out of the attempt to rearrange the Bantustans,
most of them in tens or even hundreds of small, scattered fragments to
make the map of the supposedly "independent states" look less absurd.
This is important for the promotion of "separate development" abroad.
A major "consolidation" program was announced in 1973 that appears
likely to become a dominant element in the pattern of population removals. The budget allocation for these shifts have been described by
Dr. Diederichs, the minister of Finance, as "an enhanced provision for
homeland development,"[30] although in fact the money is spent on

purchasing white farms at high prices. The consolidation tears people away from their land, houses, and crops to an area completely undeveloped, requiring duplicative investment of effort, time, and money to arrive at the previous level of subsistence although frequently on much worse land. This can hardly be described as "development," especially as the imminent threat of removal is the most effective known method of inhibiting development of land on which people are living. In South Africa, this is compounded by the widespread conviction that any improvements to the land, whether they be planting trees or even food crops, will immediately prompt the white man to seize it for his own benefit. Where "consolidation" has been launched on a major scale, Africans report that it is to remove them from the more fertile valleys to the barren and hitherto unpopulated hills.[31] In fact, the "consolidation" plans offer no prospect of security for Africans; will leave the "homelands" almost as fragmented as they are now; are subject to constant revision as the white farmers revise their demands; and are likely to last indefinitely, as long as the fiction of "homeland development" continues. Government spokesmen have not specified how long the current program will take, but unofficial estimates put it at twenty to twenty-five years, at a cost of millions of rands.[32] The number of people affected will bring the total number of deportations to around 3 million.[33] No consultation was held about the plan with the "homeland governments," a few of which have protested, as in the case of "Kwazulu," that the plan deprives them of whatever good land they still had, and called it "white avarice gone mad."[34]

There has been very strong resistance by many communities faced with removals under this program, notably in Zululand; some of them are facing their second or even third removal after promises of a secure "homeland" where they would have absolute rights.[35] To bolster the police action often required to remove these communities, a bill was recently passed giving the government the power to move any African community or individual from anywhere, removing the right of appeal.[36] This completes the elimination in South Africa of any security of tenure even in the supposed "homelands" and directly contradicts the theory that these are the original ancestral homes of the Africans, who just happened to be in these poverty-stricken areas when the whites arrived to take over South Africa.

Exceeding even the disruption caused by "consolidation" is that un-

der the program of "rehabilitation," or "planning." The program contains elements of policies designed to promote rational agriculture, by
surveying, culling of excess cattle, and enclosure of land. For this, removal
of the population from their homes is a basic requirement—the idea being
that the traditional scattered *"kraals,"* or households, are irrational, and
that people can be managed better if put together in new settlements with
separate growing and grazing areas. This kind of attempt is hazardous in the
best of circumstances, as attempts at crash programs of "economic develop
ment" according to a grand design imposed from outside have demonstrate
throughout the developing world. However, in South Africa it is seen in th
context of attempts to cram more and more people into poverty-stricken
areas with diminishing resources; government agents and their collaborator
are viewed with extreme hostility, and the favoritism and use of coercion
involved in the program make it a major cause of violence and disruption
inside the "homelands." Available evidence indicates that such attempts
to impose rationalization are economically counterproductive; in addition,
it is a direct cause of the extreme violence that is a major, although largely
unreported, aspect of life in the "homelands" today. At the end of 1971,
official figures showed that between half and three-quarters of the "homelands" had already been "planned," meaning the rearranging of 3-4 million
people.[37] In the same year, the author in interviews with medical personnel in these areas was repeatedly informed that the commonest complaint, even given very high incidence of malnutrition and disease, was
trauma, or wounds of various kinds mainly from "faction fights" and
clashes with the police.[38] These "faction fights," frequently associated
with stock theft, often arise out of the allocation of land and other concessions to communities that collaborate readily with the authorities.

Reports of "terrorism" and violent opposition to the government nominees are frequent complaints of the "homeland governments." In the
Ciskei, one of the "ministers" claimed that there were several organizations that were trying to overthrow his "government" by violence and
subversive action. In the Transkei, according to the "minister of Agriculture," "they slashed the tyres of the drilling machines, and tried to burn
them out. Fences were destroyed and the lives of agricultural officers
[who mark out the new land "plans"] threatened."[39] Even the plots of
land available on the major irrigation schemes at Qamata and Ncora were
lying idle because people could not be persuaded to farm on a govern-

ment scheme (possibly from fear of retaliation by less privileged people who refused to collaborate). The many pockets of resistance to "rehabilitation" are often the same areas where resistance to the creation of the Bantustan was originally centered.[40] Far from being a refuge from the conflicts inherent in white supremacy, the "homelands" seem to be the areas where these conflicts are coming most strongly to the surface.

It would be misleading to conclude from this that there is effective opposition to the whites in the "homelands." Violence is diverted from the whites so that Africans fight each other, a basic strategy of colonial and minority rule; and popular hostility is directed at the "homeland governments" appointed as surrogates by the whites. Far from uniting the people in opposition to the real power, they deflect the political and violent energies of the people onto their own token institutions.

In the Msinga Reserve area of "Kwazulu," Chief Buthelezi has announced that "criminals" now rule the district, and that there have been 69 murders, 31 faction fights, 213 serious assaults, and 529 cases of stock theft in 1971 alone.[41] A state of emergency was declared there, along the lines of that prevailing in the Transkei since the massive resistance to the creation of the first "Bantustan" there in 1960-1961, and that imposed for the same reason in the "Owambo" Bantustan of Namibia (South West Africa) to suppress all opposition in February 1972. The proclamation of states of emergency can be issued in terms of Section 25 (1) of the Bantu Administration Act, No. 33 of 1927, which empowers the state president to repeal or amend any laws applying to any "Bantu" district and to make new laws applicable to that district.[42] This piece of legislation alone makes a mockery of claims that the "homeland governments" have any authority. In fact they have less authority in their own areas than the most minor rural council in South Africa.

INVESTMENT IN "HOMELAND DEVELOPMENT"

The Tomlinson Commission, and government policy statements since then, have repeatedly asserted that industrial development would have to solve the problem of impoverishment that the "native reserve" policy had created in these areas. The major channels for this are the Xhosa Develop-

ment Corporation (XDC) for the Transkei and Ciskei and the Bantu Inve
ment Corporation (BIC) for the rest. Although set up to channel develop
ment finance to the "homelands," the "governments" there have no control and do not even participate in their management. The administration
has been criticized as inept,[43] and there have been numerous allegations
that their funds are being misappropriated.[44] Such financial resources as
there are go not toward creating new economic potential, but largely toward buying out whites on very generous terms for "consolidation," whi
Africans are summarily evicted; building elaborate headquarters for the
real authorities in the "homelands," the white commissioners-general,[45]
while leaving the much publicized "governments" working out of tempor
ary accommodation; funding the ubiquitous "resettlement," "consolidati
and "rehabilitation" programs, keeping Africans constantly in a state of
insecurity and therefore inhibiting normal economic activity; and buildin
facilities for the white businessmen who, it is hoped, will operate in the
"homelands" on an agency basis through the development corporation.[46]

The South African government, retreating from the commitment to
the Tomlinson Commission's program with its absolute minimum estimates for providing an economic base for the "homelands," has been cutting back on expenditure in the areas,[47] and has called on private industr
and especially foreign investors, to come in and fill the void.[48] South
African businessmen, however, have been very reluctant to operate in the
Bantustans.

The "reserves" are tending to function as a protected reserve for gover
ment supporters, while even self-financed African entrepreneurs are firml
discouraged from investing capital in them. A minor scandal was caused b
the award of an account worth R50 million ($80 million) a year by the
West Rand Bantu Administration Board to Volkskas, a bank whose personnel are closely linked with government personalities and institutions.
Nearly all the twenty-nine new boards were also moving their accounts
to Volkskas. In the Transkei the XDC and other "homeland government"
accounts (managed by white nominees of central government) all moved
to Volkskas despite much better terms and services offered by other com
mercial banks and the explicit opposition of the "homeland governments."[49] Meanwhile, more minor white interests have in many cases
successfully opposed the granting of trading licenses to Africans who
might compete in the "homeland" areas as far as essential commodities

are concerned, and succeed in lowering prices there. They have even blocked essential infrastructure projects, such as the extension of the railroad in the Transkei, which would interfere with their control of the market in undeveloped areas.[50] There is no sign that the central government is dissatisfied with the practical effect of its "Bantu homeland" policy; Mr. Botha, minister of Bantu Affairs and Development, has said: "We are honestly doing each day, today, tomorrow and next year, as much as they can absorb, as much as our means, manpower, time and intellects enable us to do."[51]

For several years, great stress has been laid on "decentralization" of industry to the "border areas" on the edge of the reserves. The program, which is based on the restriction of investment in urban areas where there is more than a certain level of African employment relative to white jobs, was announced by the former prime minister, Dr. Verwoerd, in 1959: "industries owned by white people and employing the Bantu labor coming from the Bantu areas . . . [who] can be absorbed there in the service of the white people."[52] Industry has proved very unwilling to invest in these border areas, however, apart from a few areas that are so close to the industrial heartland that the "decentralization" is in name only. The major impact of the program may well have been the discouragement of African labor-intensive investment altogether, thus contributing to African unemployment. A small fraction of the projected employment target for the border areas has been achieved, much of it simply in jobs transferred from other areas. There has been a sharp decline of interest among industrialists in the border areas, applications falling from 146 in 1969 to 73 in 1971 and 29 in the first half of 1972,[53] together with loud complaints of "extreme and unnecessary difficulties" of all kinds, revolving around the poor coordination of advertised decentralization facilities by the government.[54] Funds authorized by the Industrial Development Corporation for business ventures in border areas were cut by more than one-half between 1971 and 1972, and in 1974-1975 the pressure to move out was quietly relaxed.[55]

This is partly due to the fact that the white unions were so successful in preventing what was to have been the rationale for "border industry"— large-scale African employment near the "homelands" together with opportunities for them to achieve positions of responsibility in their "own" areas. This is also the advertised objective of development inside the "homelands," which is being blocked equally successfully by the white unions. The color bar has been enforced both by limits on the ratio of African to white workers and by the continued reservation of better jobs for whites. As expressed by the president of the Trade Union Federation: "Everyone must be made to realize that a border area remains a white area and that the development of border areas aims only at the decentralization of industries." After a major controversy over mine jobs in the "homelands," the powerful Mine Workers Union succeeded in blocking the proposed allocation of "reserved" jobs to Africans. The situation, as summed up by the *Financial Mail* of Johannesburg, is therefore that: "There is no difference between a mine in the homelands and a mine in the white areas as far as job restrictions . . . are concerned. . . . The colour bar in mining, by far the biggest industry in the homelands, is still there . . . because the Mineworkers Union wants it that way.[57] Contrary to the official objective, the combination of restrictions on the use of African labor together with tax and other fiscal incentives has resulted in particularly capital-intensive industries showing interest in the "homelands"—including some American firms such as ITT, GM and the Chase Manhattan Bank (David Rockefeller explained, "people I have talked to are of the opinion that foreign investment here is advantageous to all concerned"[58]). Experience in Britain and elsewhere has shown this to be a fairly predictable result of fiscal "decentralization" measures for depressed areas. One of the largest investments in the "homelands" is a chemical plant in the Transkei, starting production in February 1974; costing R1.6 million ($2.2 million) with 50 percent of the finance from the XDC, it will provide only 200 African jobs.[59] The cost per job, at R8,000 ($11,200) each, is in fact below the average for all jobs created in the "homelands" between 1962 and 1968, which was R11,500 ($16,000).[60]. Given the government's refusal to allocate larger sums for "development finance," therefore, the prospect of creating significant employment in the "homelands" under the present policy, which relies on the leadership of companies, is not credible. Between 1962 and 1972 about 8,500 new jobs were created annually in the "homelands" and border areas combined, while between 60,000 and 70,000 workers seeking employment were coming onto the labor market from the "homelands" each year, forced out by agricultural impoverishment.[61] At that rate, the "decentralization" program was providing for only 13 percent of the annual new demand for jobs from the "homelands" alone, quite apart from the unemployed Africans being deported there from the "white areas."

In addition, it has been argued that the presence of growth points near or at the edge of the "homelands" contributes to their continued overall economic decline. It has been argued that wages are spent in the nearby "white area," and that skills, labor, and investment that might otherwise be available to the "homeland" itself is drained away by these growth points within the existing economic system of the white-controlled towns. Professor Lombard has concluded:

> Unfortunately these large Bantu towns, the major potential growth poles of their respective hinterlands, have thus far remained satellites of their economically much further advanced white poles. Instead of giving rise to multiplyer effects on further domestic employment in the homelands, as Dr. Verwoerd expected they would do, incomes from labour are, for the most part, "leaking back" to the Republican poles of activity.[62]

Dr. A.S. Jacobs, also a pro-apartheid economist and former adviser to the prime minister, has also admitted:

> It is often said that the border areas have a negative influence on the development of the Bantu areas. I have a lot of sympathy with this point of view, because the border areas are situated close to the Bantu areas and yet the Bantu are not allowed to do skilled work.[63]

Faced with this miscalculation at the base of "decentralization," the South African government has made a major incentive for local and foreign investment in the "homelands" the provision that African labor there may be paid even less than in South Africa as a whole: all minimum wages for Africans have been suspended in the Bantustan areas. It has also put responsibility for this measure firmly on the shoulders of their approved "homeland leaders." Chiefs Buthelezi, Matanzima, and others, widely promoted in the United States as the "leaders" of the African people, are depicted in prominent advertisements urging American investors: "We'll supply all the required labour. At very reasonable rates. . . . This is your chance to make a lot of money out of being a philanthropist."[64] A handout from the "Transkei government" cites proclamations perserving non-African minimum wages, but abolishing those for Africans: "Wage legislation: advantageous adaptation. The Industrial Reconciliation Act [sic] has been suspended. . . . All wage determinations are suspended."[65] The campaign has been directed so pointedly at overseas investors—primarily at Americans—that the head of BIC has been accused by local industrialists of using this as a ploy to force them to follow the foreign companies into the "homelands." Local investors are otherwise reluctant to enter these areas, which are so totally undeveloped and cut off from economic centers, markets, and supplies.[66]

The "homeland governments" are in a situation where they have little alternative to exposing their own people to exploitation. The South African government has pointedly left it to them to fix their own minimum wages,[6] in the full knowledge that they can then be held accountable rather than the whites since, as the *Financial Mail* has commented: "With little but low-cost labour to attract industry, it would be surprising if the Homeland authorities adhere to the minimum wage agreements."[68] The selective hand-over of "responsibility" to approved African officials is analogous to the hand-over of the "resettlement camps"; the absence of any alternative ensures that the policies chosen will be the most disastrous for the African people affected. Meanwhile the odium attached to these major aspects of the implementation of apartheid will be diverted from the central government, which decides the overall framework, to the "homeland leaders" who have decided, for various reasons including in some cases a genuine desire to get "crumbs for my people" (Buthelezi's phrase), to collaborate with the "Bantu homeland" policy.

The effect of removing minimum wage determinations for Africans is not necessarily to make labor costs competitive, since whites can demand and get special bonuses for "hardship" posts. It will certainly not offset the cost of investment at a distance from all the other inputs that have made the "homeland" and "border area" decentralization program so distinctly lacking in momentum. Investors decide to go to border or homeland areas for quite different reasons, whether for the fiscal benefits to curry favor with the government or, in the case of U.S. companies, to present themselves back home as being "enlightened" investors magnanimously complying with the wishes of the "homeland leaders." Once there, however, they appear to exploit the absence of minimum African wages enthusiastically. An example of the effects of removing wage determinations has been documented by the Garment Workers Union in the first "homeland" township of Temba, actually in the Pretoria area; based on this experience, the union concluded that the prospects for African workers were grim even by South African standards: "Low wages will be paid, no regular increase will be granted, hours of work will be long and employment conditions in general will be far worse than those for workers covered by an industrial council."[69] In border areas, African wages have been estimated at 64 percent below those paid in the major urban areas[70] —where, as we indicated in Chapter 2, they are well below minimum subsistence levels.

It is worth noting that apart from the theoretical discretion allowed to "homeland governments" to enforce or waive minimum wages for their people, all major aspects of investment in the "homelands" are firmly in the hands of the South African central government. Under current legislation, all foreign investment or the much debated "aid" to the Bantustans must be negotiated with the South African government, even if the "homeland governments" have played a role in attracting the capital. Far from relaxing this control, which promoters of investment in the "homelands" suggest is imminent, it is being consolidated. In a press interview at the end of 1972, the prime minister indicated that "homeland governments" would not be allowed to raise capital independently, even if they became nominally "independent."[71] One of the first moves of the new director of Homeland Affairs, Mr. C.J. Grobler, appointed at the end of 1973, was to announce that "homeland governments" would have to channel requests even for outside advice or the employment of consultants at their own expense, through his office.[72]

There is an increasing volume of support within the United States for promoting investment in the "homelands." However, in a quiet hearing with reference to the conditions prevailing in any such investment, a spokesman for the U.S. Department of Labor commented: "I am certain that if we were asked by firms if they should develop industry in those areas, we would probably recommend against it."[73]

NOTES

1. Quoted in the *Washington Post,* February 11, 1973.

2. *See*, for example, Barbara Rogers, *South Africa Bantustans* (London: International Defence and Aid Fund for Southern Africa, 1976). 1972).

3. Beaumont Commission, 1916; *see* G.M. Carter, T. Karis, and N.M. Stultz, *South Africa's Transkei: The Politics of Domestic Colonialism* (Evanson: Northwestern University Press, 1967), p. 63.

4. Mrs. J. Bowbrick, "The Agricultural Problems of African Resettlement" (unpublished paper).

5. Randolph Vigne, *The Transkei: South Africa's Tragedy* (London: Africa Bureau, 1969), p. 16.

6. Figures from the 1970 Census. For further details, *see* Barbara Rogers, *South Africa*, pp. 38-9.

7. Sheila van der Horst, *Separate Development: Is a Consensus Possible?* (Johannesburg: South African Institute of Race Relations, January 1972).

8. Republic of South Africa, *Fagan Commission Report; U.G. 28/1948* (Pretoria: Government Printer, 1949).

9. Lawrence Morgan "The Strategies of Bantu Resettlement," *Black Sash* 13, 4, (February 1970), p. 16.

10. *Tomlinson Commission Report.*

11. D.F. Kokot, "Desert Encroachment in South Africa," in Peter R. Gould, ed., *Africa, Continent of Change* (Belmont, Calif.: Wadsworth, 1961).

12. Republic of South Africa, *South African Statistics* (Pretoria: Government Printer, 1970), pp. J-6, J-8, J-10.

13. Quoted in *The Star* (Johannesburg), week of 3 February 1973.

14. *Financial Times* (London), Supplement on South Africa Part I, 22 June 1970.

15. P. de Briey, "The Productivity of African Labour," in Gould, ed., *Africa, Continent of Change.*

16. Francis Wilson, *Migrant Labour in South Africa* (Johannesburg: South African Council of Churches and Spro-cas, Johannesburg, 1972), p. 102.

17. Pierre van den Berghe, *South Africa: A Study in Conflict* (Berkeley & Los Angeles: University of California Press, 1970), pp. 188-9.

18. Mr. M.C. Botha, Minister of Bantu Development in Republic of South Africa, *House of Assembly Debates (Hansard)*, 19 May, 1971, col. 7066.

19. *Financial Mail* (Johannesburg), 15 June, 1973.

20. *Debates*, 4 February, 1969.

21. Wilson, *Migrant Labour*, p. 89.

22. *See* Ibid., and Fr. Cosmas Desmond, *The Discarded People*, African Library Series (London: Penguin, 1971). The latter gives details of many of the camps and resettlement areas.

23. Dr. P.G.J. Koornhof, Deputy Minister of Bantu Administration and Development, in *Debates*, 4 February, 1969.

24. *Rand Daily Mail* (Johannesburg), 8 June, 1972.

25. For a description of the conditions, *see* Desmond, *Discarded People.*

26. *Survey of Race Relations,* 1972, p. 204.

27. Press release by Rev. David Russell, King Williamstown, October 31, 1973.

28. Speech in the House of Assembly, cited in *Rand Daily Mail,* 24 May, 1973.

29. *Debates,* February 4, 1969.

30. Speech in the House of Assembly, cited in *The Star,* week of 31 March, 1973.

31. Interviews by the author with people moved in this way, and observers, in Zululand, Natal, June 1971.

32. *The Star,* week of 5 May, 1973.

33. *X-Ray on Current Affairs in Southern Africa* (London: Africa Bureau, July 1973).

34. Chief Buthelezi, cited in *The Guardian* (London), January 18, 1973.

35. This applies particularly to Bantustan "development areas" such as Newcastle, "Kwazulu," where employment creation has been much less than planned. People already moved there have been removed again to the camps. This information is from observers resident in the affected areas.

36. *Rand Daily Mail,* 31 March, 1973; *The Star,* week of 5 May, 1973.

37. Figures for the end of 1971 given by Mr. Botha, minister of Bantu Affairs and Development, in the House of Assembly; see *The Star,* 24 and 25 October, 1972. Percentages range from 46.4 percent in Bophuthatswana and 46.9 percent for Kwazulu to 100 percent in Basotho Qwaqwa. The Transkei is 64 percent planned (1972 figure).

38. Interviews by the author in Zululand, the Transkei and Ciskei, June 1971.

39. *The Star,* week of 31 March, 1973.

40. Ibid.

41. Ibid., week of 5 May, 1973.

42. Ibid., week of 21 April, 1973.

43. *Financial Mail,* 15 December, 1967.

44. T.G. Hughes in *Debates,* March 11, 1968, cols. 1890-2.

45. *Rand Daily Mail,* 7 August, 1968; Answer by the Minister of Bantu Administration and Development to a question by Mr. E.G. Malan, in *Debates,* June 18, 1968, col. 7519.

46. Desmond, *Discarded People,* pp. 228-34.

47. Ibid. See discussion in appendix 2, which was compiled by a management consultant; also Rogers, *South Africa.*

48. M.C. Botha, minister of Bantu Affairs and Development speaking at Butterworth, Transkei; *The Star,* week of 30 September, 1971.

49. *The Star*, week of 11 and 18 August, 1973.

50. H. Hobart Houghton in W. Backer, ed., *The Economic Development o* *the Transkei* (Lovedale, Cape Province: Lovedale Press, 1970); also Merle Lipton, "The South African Census and the Bantustan Policy," *The World Today*, (June 1972), p. 267.

51. *Debates*, March 19, 1968, cols. 2464-5.

52. Verwoerd in *Debates*, June 29, 1959, col. 9432.

53. *The Star*, week of 18 November, 1972.

54. Col. G.H. Boestra, president of the Northern Transvaal Chamber of Industries: cited in *The Star*, week of 2 December, 1972.

55. *The Star*, week of 18 November, 1972.

56. L.J. van den Berg, president of the Koordinerende Raad van S.A. Vakverenigings, 1969: quoted in Muriel Horrell, *South Africa's Workers* (Johannesburg: Institute of Race Relations, 1969), p. 42.

57. *Financial Mail*, 15 July, 1970.

58. Republic of South Africa, *South African Scope* (Pretoria: Department of Information, January 1974).

59. *Financial Mail*, 7 September, 1973.

60. M.C. Botha in *Debates*, February 20, 1968.

61. John Sackur in *The Times* (London), 27 April, 1971.

62. *Sunday Times* (Johannesburg), 4 December, 1970.

63. *Financial Gazette* (Johannesburg), 4 December, 1970.

64. Chief Matlala, "Chief Minister of Lebowa," advertisement in the Sunday Times, February 18, 1973.

65. Quoted in *The Star*, week of 12 January, 1974.

66. *Survey of Race Relations, 1972*, p. 74; *The Star*, week of 31 March, 1973.

67. Mr. M. Viljoen, Minister of Labor, in the Senate of the Republic of South Africa, *Debates* (Official Records), 19 May, 1972, col. 4101.

68. *Financial Mail*, 28 November, 1969.

69. *The Star*, week of 21 November, 1969.

70. Prof. H. J. Reynders, Pretoria University, quoted in *Rand Daily Mail*, 18 May, 1971.

71. Quoted in *Survey of Race Relations, 1972*, pp. 188-9.

72. *The Star*, week of 22 December, 1973.

73. Donald M. Irwin, U.S. Department of Labor, in testimony to the House Foreign Affairs Subcommittee on Africa, December 6, 1971; quoted in U.S. Congress, House of Representatives, Committee on Foreign Affairs, Subcommittee on Africa, *U.S. Business Involvement in Southern Africa*, Part II (Washington, D.C.: Government Printing Office, 1972), p. 167.

chapter 2 _____

WEALTH
AND POVERTY
IN SOUTH AFRICA

SOUTH AFRICA'S PROSPERITY

South Africa is a wealthy country, the second richest in terms
of income per capita on the African continent, after Libya. This fact hardly
needs to be stressed, nor does the fact that the South African economy has
recently seen a period of unprecedented growth. The annual rate of growth
between 1946 and 1966 was over 8 percent at current prices. In the decade
of the 1960s, the growth rate rose even higher. Gross domestic product
(GDP) at constant prices increased at an annual average of over 6 percent. Total output increased at an average rate of nearly 10 percent a year. Company
profits doubled within the first five years of the decade. The chairman of
the state oil corporation, SASOL, Dr. P.E. Rousseau, was able to claim in
1969 that South Africa's economic growth rate was second only to that
of Japan and more than twice that of the European Free Trade Area (EFTA)
countries. Gross national product (GNP), he recalled, had increased six times
over in the last twenty years.[1]

The high rate of return on investment during the 1960s was due partly
to the fact that South Africa was going through a phase of rapid industrial

development based on import substitution.[2] The manufacturing sector, in which U.S. investment was concentrated, increased its share of total output very rapidly. Between 1947 and 1951, manufacturing accounted for 16.5 percent of national output, and by the mid-1960s, this share reached 21 percent. Manufacturing and construction together now produce over one-quarter of total output. From an economy based primarily on mining and agriculture before World War II, South Africa turned into an urbanized nation with an extensive and sophisticated industrial base.[3] This has taken place largely as a result of government policy, and under the government's strict guidance and regulation, particularly as concerns the development of new industry and the regulation of African labor in both public and private sectors. As Mr. M.C. Botha, minister of Bantu Affairs, has said, the government achieved its tight industrial ship by taking over total control of African labor—a procedure necessary to supply employers with labor wherever it was wanted.[4] The implications of this control will be examined in detail later.

GOVERNMENT PARTICIPATION

Industrial growth in South Africa has not occurred spontaneously, nor in contradiction to the racial policies of the successive governments. On the contrary, South Africa's racial policy has been a vital element in the scenario developed to its fullest extent by the National party government since 1948. The level of economic growth, as well as its distribution, has been largely due to the direct participation of the government in the economy, including the imposition of tariff protection for emerging industries, stringent exchange control measures, establishment of vital public corporations, and the network of administrative procedures through which the government is able to control every sector and every corporation. Growth was planned to continue in the 1970s on the same level as the booming sixties. The extent to which the Economic Development Plan's ambitious targets are met will depend on the willingness of private capital, especially foreign capital, to underwrite the government's policy. This is by no means automatic, as indicated by the regional director of the London-based Economist Intelligence Unit, Mr. R.B. Olliver:

It is worth remembering that a great deal of buoyancy of the '60s stemmed from Government measures. Some were by force of circumstances, e.g., restrictions on capital outflows and import control, giving the stimulus of a mild form of siege economy. In contrast, the local content programme for the motor industry was a deliberate measure to expand and diversify industry.

This phase is over now; entrepreneurs are not aggressive visionaries; they wait for good weather.[5]

Before World War II, the state was already involved in the South African economy, through protective policy and nationalized industry, as well as the application of coercions or privileges to sections of the labor force. Since the 1940s, however, its role has become central in the "active guidance, encouragement, and regulation" of the economy as a whole: stimulating industrial rationalization, regulating imports and exports, securing foreign investments and foreign loans directly, countering cyclical economic tendencies, and the like. The Industrial Development Corporation, established in 1940, was the first of a series of bodies employing public funds to catalyze or finance sectors regarded as crucial to economic health and expansion, industrialization in particular.[6] Giants such as ESCOM (electricity), ISCOR (iron and steel), and SASOL (petroleum) are complemented by such strategically placed bodies as the Uranium Enrichment Corporation, the Arms Development and Production Corporation (ARMSCOR), and the Nuclear Fuel Corporation (NUFCOR). In terms of assets and turnover, ESCOM, ISCOR, and SASOL are among the biggest corporations in South Africa, outranking even Anglo-American and de Beers, the largest private corporations.[7]

Public sector expenditure as a percentage of GDP increased from 16 percent to 18 percent in 1960 and to 37 percent in 1970.[8] Investment by the public sector grew from 41 percent of fixed total investment in 1954 to 46 percent in 1970, and the public corporations showed the fastest rate of growth. During the 1960s, their gross fixed investment grew at an annual average rate of 13.3 percent, compared with 11 percent in the private sector, and their capital outlays rose by about 9 percent a year, against the private sector's 41.5 percent.[9] Almost half the total white labor force is employed in the public sector—about 43 percent in 1972, an increase from 37 percent three years earlier.[10]

The government is, in fact, one of the worst employers of African labor, and through its dominance of the labor market, sets a low standard for private industry.[11] Mr. M.C. Botha, minister of Bantu Affairs, has said that the idea of equal pay for equal work was the product of "integrationist thinking and did not form a part of the Nationalist government's policy.[12]

A maze of official restrictions on private industry, which allow the government to intervene at any point, dominates the economic picture. Since, theoretically, most commercial practices would be so restricted by the regulations as to be unworkable, the situation is one of rule by exception—the exemptions obtainable only by currying favor with officials, from the most minor bureaucrat to the top ministers in the government. This applies particularly to industries with a large labor force, where dependence on exemption from the many labor regulations is heavy, and also to those threatened with being moved to a "border area" without essential facilities and communications. The situation works extremely well, as far as the government is concerned, since at the slightest hint of criticism or "integrationist thinking," any company can be subtly pressured by the enforcement of a regulation damaging to it, or even by the mere hint of enforcement. As described by the *Guardian,* there need be no problem for foreign investors in South Africa, "if the South African government badly wants it; if it is big enough to argue with the government; and if it does not mind where it goes and can import its own skilled workers. It would be a great help if the imported workers spoke Afrikaans and were enthusiastic supporters of South African government policies."[13] It also helps, of course, for the foreign capital to be devoted to building up local self-sufficiency.

A further priority that has been emerging recently is the automation or mechanization of various sectors of the economy, regardless of the strictly economic rationale, to eliminate Africans from the work force or to compensate for artificially created labor shortages. For example, white farmers are increasingly using aircraft for such processes as sowing, fertilizing, applying weed-killers, and so on, rather than employing hand labor.[14] The manufacturing industry, which has been the growth leader since World War II, has also led the trend toward capital-intensive production. Until the 1950s, the major growth sectors in these industries were import-substitution and raw materials processing which were comparatively labor-intensive; since then, however, partly as a result of government policy, the growth points have been in more capital-intensive areas: automobiles and accessories, chemicals, pulp and paper, military hardware, capital goods, electronics and computers. This, of course, is also the area where U.S. investment is concentrated—an outstanding example of foreign capital carrying out the declared policy of the South African government to the disadvantage of Africans.

Capital-intensity has been fostered, not by allowing African wages to rise and so making the substitution of capital for labor economically justifiable (the normal trend in the United States and in Europe), but by government regulation of the supply of labor at a near-constant wage, the supply being cut off or reduced as an incentive to further capital investment. To the extent that labor costs rise to an unacceptable level, this is a result of white labor shortages and inflated wage demands. Since the white unions, backed by the government, have been adamant about enforcing strict ratios of black to white workers, any attempt to substitute capital for expensive white labor has necessarily resulted in the reduction of African labor. Even in the border areas and "Bantustans," the original idea of labor-intensivity has not been carried out, largely because the white wokers have insisted on reserving a certain proportion of the jobs for themselves, having the effect of reducing overall employment. As the U.S. Department of Commerce summarizes, "The Government has been encouraging the development of capital intensive, labor saving facilities to offset labor shortages and to increase South African exports."[15]

NATIONAL WEALTH AND AFRICAN POVERTY

Although there is a great shortage of official statistics of African incomes, it is possible to think in terms of quantifying a correlation between economic growth in South Africa and the welfare of its majority population. For the sake of clarity, the African group (almost 70 percent of the population) will be examined in terms of changes in the ratio of African to white worker incomes; comparison of African incomes in South Africa to those of Africans in much poorer countries of independent Africa; the trend of absolute as well as relative poverty of the Africans; and the degree to which the use of African labor can be corrected with changes in its economic status, in terms of wage employment and in terms of the African population as a whole, of whom the great majority are not in wage employment.

To start with perhaps the most widespread myth, that African incomes in South Africa are the highest on the continent, we can conjecture that this notion arises from the statistical abstraction represented by South Africa's *average* income per head as the second highest in Africa. The average has no meaning whatever in this context, because of the wide gap between white and African incomes—probably the greatest income differential of any industrial country: roughly 13:1 in favor of the whites. This happens to be approximately the ratio of incomes in the richest countries in the world to those in the poorest. The fact that extreme wealth and extreme poverty can coexist within one nation, divided strictly according to race, is the fact that makes South Africa unique, even though the problem of wealth and poverty are worldwide.

The whites, who in 1969 comprised only 19 percent of the population, received 74 percent of the total income, while the Africans—then 68 percent of the population—received under 19 percent of the income. Average income per capita was R95 ($133) a month for whites and R7 ($10) a month for Africans.[16] Far from improving their relative position, the African share of total income fell substantially during the 1960s—the time of highest growth rate of the economy—from 23 percent in 1959-1960 to 18.8 percent in 1967-1968.[17]

As a result of this unprecedented inequality in income distribution, Africans in South Africa are considerably poorer than many of those living in independent African countries which, although poorer overall, have no large white-settler population to siphon off the wealth. A survey conducted by *Business International* has confirmed that several African countries pay higher wages to Africans in industry than does South Africa.[18]

Even in a country like Botswana, until now one of the poorest in Africa and one of the least developed in the world, a close comparison reveals that African workers are better off than in South Africa. Rural per capita incomes in Botswana average about R31.5 p.a., exclusive of remittances from migrant workers, many of them in the South African gold mines.[19] This compares with figure of R25.4 for rural Africans in South Africa, only four-fifths of the Botswana figure.[20] Nor is it possible to assume that South Africans have easier access to employment in the mines; it seems that the Chamber of Mines has for a long time had a deliberate policy of focusing recruitment efforts outside of South Africa and severely limiting the number of job applicants from the South African "homelands," as part of the "outward looking policy" designed to increase the dependence of neighboring countries on the South African government and to undermine the power of African workers to organize in their own interests.[21] Wages in Botswana are generally comparable to those in South Africa in most sectors or, if anything, slightly higher. Economic activity is restricted largely by the South African government's policy of discouraging foreign investment in Botswana and other neighboring countries, where it would compete with South African interests. This is, of course, a much more basic reason for the large numbers of foreign African workers in the South African mines and other industries, rather than the allegedly attractive standard of pay. Official policy has ensured that there is no practical employment alternative.

It happens that the income levels of Africans in South Africa appear higher than they actually are, relative to those in independent Africa, because of the unusually large proportion of the African population that is urbanized in South Africa (over 30 percent) as compared to the next most urbanized, Zambia, with 10 percent.[22] Although cash incomes are higher in urban areas, so are costs, with the result that the figures for South Africa are probably exaggerated as a measure of living standards. Even so, the statistics show African incomes in South Africa are lower even than the *average* for independent Africa, which was put at $110-120 a year in the late 1960s.[23] The South African figure at the same time was only $108 per year.[24] These figures must be treated as very rough approximations since the cost of essential items, and irregularities in exchange rates, make an accurate comparison impossible. However, it is clear that because of the maldistribution of income the majority population of South Africa, the wealthiest country in sub-Saharan Africa, is probably worse off than the majority of people on the continent as a whole. Taking into account the large number of Africans in South Africa living in urban areas, with incomes about three and one-half times those in rural areas, then it would appear that the population of the "homelands"—the supposed equivalent of the traditional African subsistence economy—is among the poorest in Africa. One estimate puts the income of "homeland" Africans at about $45 a year, which is less than 40 percent of the average income on the African continent.[25]

TRENDS IN AFRICAN LIVING STANDARDS

There are two definitions of poverty in current usage: the first is a relative concept used, particularly in the United States, to describe the level of deprivation of the goods and services that are available in a consumer society. The level of poverty is therefore related to the general standard of living of the country. In these terms, Africans in South Africa are among the poorest in the world and are rapidly becoming more deprived relative t the affluent white society.

The second definition of poverty is based on various calculations of basic human subsistence requirements, assuming that no money is spent on anything other than food and, sometimes, a few other essentials. The concept originated with the British industrialist and philanthropist Rownt and has become very popular in South Africa to measure the absolute mini mum at which Africans are thought by outside academics to be able to sur vive. These are essentially theoretical figures, allowing nothing for wastage or incidental items, and often not even for adequate clothing, medicine, housing, education, or basic items in a real budget such as beer and cigar ettes. A population such as that in South Africa, suffering from a high in fant mortality rate, malnutrition, and socio-economic diseases such as tu berculosis, and where basic education is an unreachable luxury, would have to be considered poverty-stricken in an absolute, as well as a relative, sense. The measurement of this will have to be in terms of the "Minimum Effecti Level" and the wholly unsatisfactory "Poverty Datum Line," in the absenc of any other standard.

Attempts to establish the absolute minimum level at which health can b maintained on a very short-term basis, and allowing for none of the normal expenditures of an African family's budget, produced the Poverty Datum Line (PDL). This standard has, in fact, been widely criticized as unrealistic as an assessment of poverty. Professor Batson, who originated the techniqu in the early 1940s, has described it as "a line below which health and decer cannot be maintained. . . . It is not a 'human' standard of living. . . . It doe not in any sense describe even a minimum ideal."[26] Bearing in mind that th PDL, popularized as an acceptable standard for African wages, is in fact widely recognized as much too low, the fact still remains that the majority of Africans in the urban areas earn wages below this level: in 1967, 68 perc of the Africans in Johannesburg were below the PDL.[27] Further, when the PDL was used as a standard in the first national survey of African wages by the Productivity and Wage Association in 1972, it was estimated that 80 percent of all Africans in the private sector in South Africa were below the poverty line.[28] One-third of them earned less than half of the PDL. The es timate was considered to be an overestimate, indeed, since the companies that responded to the survey were likely to be those with above-average wages and conditions for Africans. Wages in the public sector, which were not covered, tend to compare unfavorably with those in the private sector.[29]

An alternative, equally arbitrary, "minimum," which Professor Batson has proposed as one which may offer the possibility of maintaining normal health for an average-size family, is the Minimum Effective Level (MEL). This is fixed at one and one-half times the PDL for the area concerned. On this basis, in 1970, African average earnings in all sectors were below the level in most sectors.[30] Obviously, the minimum wage in all cases was far below the MEL. Some sociologists have objected that the MEL is quite inadequate in practice, even given the most careful and time-consuming housekeeping, and have suggested that the "basic minimum income" would be at least twice the PDL. On this basis, it would be surprising if 5 percent of all African urban families were receiving the basic minimum.

In practice, the mother of a family is forced to work full time, at rates considerably lower than those even for African men. Her efforts will help, but most probably will not bring the total family income up to the basic minimum level. In many cases, she will be the sole wage-earner. The result is an acute impoverishment of the children's environment, deprived of any parental care or educational stimulus, and going all day without food, since many hours of the day will be wasted by the parents in commuting to and from the "township."

If urban African families are split up, and living below any acceptable income level, the situation is worse for Africans in rural areas. African farm laborers surveyed in Natal were described as living in "incredible poverty"; the report, in a Durban newspaper, described them as the most exploited and powerless people in the country. The whole family, including the children, work six months a year for little or no payment at all. They have no rights and are exposed to beatings by employers or immediate eviction to "resettlement" areas.[31] Workers on forestry and other plantations have also been described as living in abject poverty. One survey of a government project estimated that the standard wages paid these workers were well below half the Poverty Datum Line for that rural area.[32] Africans outside the wage economy fare even worse. The problem of those confined to the "homelands" without land or other means of subsistence is mounting rapidly, even outside the camps—where many are totally dependent on the erratic "daily rations." A survey in two districts of the Transkei showed that in 1968 the "unemployment" of men and women over sixteen years of age was 22.5 percent. The "unemployed" included those neither working at the time of the survey, nor having worked for the previous four months; those owning no land and having no right to land use anywhere; those neither working as farming assistants, nor even doing household tasks—in a word, those with no means of subsistence at all.[33]

It is impossible in a study of this kind to give an adequate picture of the meaning of such poverty in human terms. It is also difficult—not to mention illegal—for the reader to visit African areas of South Africa to witness it for himself. The situation remains one of bare statistics: for instance, one-third of all Africans born in Port Elizabeth, where Ford and General Motors operate, die before their first birthday.[34] Conditions are worse in the rural areas where child mortality can reach as high as 50 percent.[35] Statistics, largely non existent, are perhaps of little relevance. A recent letter to a welfare organiza from the secretary of a Dutch Reformed mission hospital in the Transvaal stated: "It is impossible to estimate our requirements. The people here are terribly poor and malnutrition is the rule. We have a high occurrence of tuberculosis, kwashiorkor and marasmus. The children suffer the most." The secretary of another mission in the Transkei added that deprivation was also a result of the enforced separation of wage-earners and their dependents by the "migrant labor" system: "The people are called back to the homelan and they come to find there is no work here, the families are 'dumped' and husbands go off to the Cape to work on the farms where they soon forget their responsibilities in Cala, thus leaving their wives and children to starve." Observations on the South African scene, while acknowledging the existence of African poverty, tend to be very optimistic about the prospects for improvement. The press, U.S. government officials, and interested parties in the investment debate, including many critics of business practices, maintai stoutly that things are getting better and will continue to do so, depending on the rate of economic growth. The theory has by now become so engrain in the argument of both sides that it is almost heresy to challenge it. Nevertheless, close scrutiny of the economic situation of Africans in South Africa does not support the claim of constant African economic advancement along with national economic growth; on the contrary, the majority has been growing worse off since World War II, and this deterioration appears to be accelerating.

A recent theoretical analysis of the effect of South Africa's unequal income distribution, by Sean Gervasi, suggests that it is likely to result in the African population growing increasingly deprived in real terms. The study focuses on whether the expansion of the economy as a whole makes more real resources of per capita income available to the poor and suggests that in cases of highly unequal income distribution, stimulated by the growth of purchasing power available for the luxury market will therefore far exceed that available for essentials; the tendency therefore will be for investment to shift continuously toward the production of new items for the wealthy, rather than increasing production of basic essentials. This is not likely to do much more than keep pace with the growth of numbers. Costs will be relatively high, as the cost-cutting benefit of new investment will go directly to items at the top of the scale. While there is, of course, considerable overlap between the items bought by the rich and the poor, the composition of their budgets will be sufficiently differentiated to have a market effect along this theoretical model. Gervasi concludes, "There is no real possibility in South Africa of the poor rising above the level of poverty as long as the distribution of income remains unchanged."[37] In fact, the figures for the decade 1957-1967 show a tendency for the differential between the average white and African wage to increase rather than decrease. The percentage increase in white wages was 61.4 percent and that of Africans was 59 percent. This meant an increase in the actual difference between the average wages from R120 a month to R194 a month (from $168.00 to $271.60)—an increase of 61.7 percent over the ten years.[38]

A South African economist, Arndt Spandau, has examined economic trends from 1920 to 1968. He adduced evidence that long-run factors relating to supply rather than effective demand are the main determinants for the "growth performance of the South African economy" (a view compatible with Gervasi's), and showed that there is a very perceptible correlation between an increase in the role of investment, increased economic growth, and increases in indices of inequality. He explained these results by the fact that the whites have a much higher propensity toward saving. Therefore, a high degree of inequality in the distribution of income maximizes the potential for savings and investment. Finally, then, while Gervasi pointed to the perpetuation of inequality as a result of growth in the South African economic structure, Spandau indicated that this is also a necessary condition of such growth. On the basis of his empirical findings, Spandau concluded that,

WHITE WEALTH AND BLACK POVERTY

South Africa is still confronted with the incompatibility between the distribution and growth goals . . . a redistributive policy would be detrimental to the growth performance of the economy, since any curtailment of
the income commanded of high income groups . . . would slow down the
long-term growth rate of the economy.[39]

The basic problem, as Gervasi has suggested, is the rising cost of basic
essentials, especially food. Food prices are maintained at a high level to assist marginal white farmers, and excess food production is destroyed by the
various Control Boards, where it threatens to reduce prices. The same is
true of the food manufacturers and processors, who have unused capacity
that they frequently are asked to bring into use; however, they find it convenient, according to one survey, to "restrain supply to keep prices up."[40]
A similar process is at work in the protection of domestic industry, which
has been the feature of the economy of the 1960s. Import substitution was
concentrated in areas of African demand, such as cloth, footwear, iron goo(
and cheap consumer items generally.[41] This is a very common phenomenon
among newly industrialized nations; the consumers of these products have
to pay higher prices for the protected, locally produced goods than they
have previously paid for imported ones. It is the local investors who benefit at the expense of the impoverished majority. There has always been a
strong preference for imported goods among the higher income groups in
South Africa as elsewhere, and these goods are much less affected than basi(
necessities by the government's import policy. It is not surprising, then,
that prices of goods produced in South Africa have shown a higher rate in
increase than imported items; in the nine months from June 1972 to March
1973, the former rose by 16.5 percent, as opposed to 13.3 percent for the
latter.[42] The government has made it quite clear that there is no intention
of taking action to limit the rise in prices of locally produced goods, nor
to control the dividends, profits, and white wage benefits that are driving
up the prices of these essentials.[43]

There is an increasing volume of press reports about steep rises in the
prices of items that Africans use: suburban rail fares from the segregated
"township" to the city; fuel; medical supplies and expenses; educational
costs; clothing; housing; bread; "Bantu beer"; mealie meal—the staple food
of most Africans—and other grains; vegetables, milk, tinned food and many
other grocery items. Consumer prices have shown an overall acceleration—

the consumer price index rose by 2.4 percent in 1969, 4.1 percent in 1970, and 5.7 percent in 1971.[44] Between June 1972 and June 1973, the rate shot up to 10 percent, with wholesale prices leading the way.[45] In the year ending February 1975 the annual rate was 15 percent, and seemed unlikely to slow down.[46]

Wholesale prices of goods for domestic consumption rose by 7.3 percent in 1971-1972 and by another 13.3 percent in 1972-1973. In that year, the prices of domestically produced goods rose by 23.7 percent.[47] Food prices overall rose by 16 percent from December 1973, as compared to the index for all items of 10 percent.[48] For the year ending July 1974 the food index rose by 22.1 percent, compared to the cost of living rise of 14.9 percent.[49] The problem of food prices has become so severe, even for whites, that the Department of Commerce launched an investigation in 1974 into allegations of collusive price fixing by grocery markets and food manufacturers.[50]

Perhaps the most difficult, though also the most important, estimate to be made is the increase in the African cost of living. The consumer price index is based on a 1966 calculation of a white family's budget, which contains an entirely different selection of items from those purchased by Africans. Despite repeated requests from various quarters, the South African government has declined to issue statistics for an African consumer price index. As compared to the rate of increase in the price index for the principal urban areas, the cost of living for Africans has been estimated to have risen 50 percent faster than that for whites during the period from 1938-1939 to 1953-1954.[51] Another study has indicated that between 1967 and 1969, the African cost of living rose 12 percent, over twice the rate for whites, 5.5 percent.[52]

From 1944 to 1954, the cost of living for urban Africans increased about 8 percent per annum.[53] The PDL seems to have risen by just under 5 percent between 1957 and 1964.[54] It then dipped to about 2.3 percent per annum from 1964 to 1966, and 2.5 percent from 1966 to 1969.[55] From 1969 to 1971, the annual increase rose to 6.2 percent.[56] Using a different estimate, that of the Johannesburg Chamber of Commerce, the increase between May 1971 and May 1972 was 8.4 percent.[57] The *Financial Mail* reports the Soweto PDL rising by 11.4 percent from November 1971 to November 1972, compared to a consumer price index rise of 7 percent.[58] The Urban Bantu Council, also of Johannesburg, estimated the rate of increase in a standard budget in one of the poorest areas to have been 24.5 percent in two years, or 12.3 percent a year, between 1971 and 1973.[59] For 1973-1974, several different estimates are available: an 11.3 percent increase in Soweto for the year ending May 1974, according to the Johannesburg Chamber of Commerce; 16.1 percent for Africans in Durban, according to Natal University's Department of Economics, for the year ending March 1974; and a variety of different levels in various cities for the year ending May 1974, according to the Bureau of Market Research, the highest being 15.8 percent and 15.4 percent for Africans in Johannesburg and Pretoria respectively. The greatest increase is in taxation (41 percent increase in Johannesburg, 45.2 percent in Durban), despite the fact that the income is assumed to be rising no faster than the PDL.[60]

This is an indication of the structural nature of the rapid rises in the African cost of living, being a direct result of white supremacy and not any chance occurrence. It has long been government practice to tax blacks at a higher rate than whites, despite their much lower incomes, and to cut their essential services to provide for other areas of government spending required to maintain the structures of minority privilege and power. It is similarly in the interest of the white minority to place severe restrictions on African businesses in African "townships," so that blacks have to buy from white stores. Soweto, which with a population of over a million is South Africa's largest city, has no supermarket, pharmacy, bakery, or motor dealer; one bank, and very few other stores. There is no real economic infrastructure or even a business center, and very few of the houses have electricity or indoor plumbing. It is difficult or impossible for an African storekeeper to expand, diversify, or borrow money because of the morass of restrictions and the requirement that his or her pass be stamped every month, and the trading license renewed every year provided the whites consider him or her "fit and proper." The result is very high prices, and major shortages of basic consumer items.[61]

If overall family incomes are used as the basis of calculation, then the average income increase per capita between 1948 and 1970 is just under 5 percent—almost exactly the same rate as the rise in African cost of living over the same period. However, this is not the same as saying that African average wages kept pace with the cost of living; in fact, they fell far behind. The difference is made up by the number of wage-earners per family. Statistics on this are incomplete, but figures for 1958-1966 show average family incomes in Soweto rising at about 4.5 percent per annum; given the rise in the number of wage-earners per household, however, the increase is reduced to 2.6 percent per annum, which is well below the rise in cost of living. Estimates for all South African cities between 1954 and 1968 show a rate of increase in family incomes of 3.2 percent per annum.[62] Assuming the same rate of increase in wage-earners per family, this would be reduced to 1.1 percent.[63] These annual average figures, of course, conceal areas of great shortfall, where there is only one wage-earner per family, especially in the frequent cases where a woman is the head of the household.[64] In Durban, a study indicated that 70 percent of the household heads had earnings below the PDL.[65]

Total African cash incomes, according to government statistics, rose from about R730 million ($1,022 million) in 1958 to R1,020 million ($1,228 million) in 1970, an increase of 65 percent. In the same twelve years, however, the number of African wage-earners increased by over 25 percent. Average cash incomes per capita, therefore, increased by about 3.3 percent per annum during the period, compared to a rise in the African cost of living of just under 5 percent. Income in kind has also fallen. In the "white" rural area, African real incomes in cash and in kind are often below the level of sixty years ago.[66] In the "homelands," estimated total income per capita has dropped from R25.8 ($36.12) in 1954 to R22 ($30.80) in 1969, most of it in kind.[67] Although different bases of calculation were used, making the estimates inexact, the drop in real income over those fifteen years seems to have been over 30 percent, or 2 percent annually.[68] It is clear, from the data available, that African incomes overall have fallen in real terms. One observer estimated the decline at about 1.7 percent a year in the twelve years ending in 1970, taking into account an increase in total income of wage-earners and subsistence farmers combined of about 20 percent in real terms, the increase in the consumer price index, and an increase in the total African population of about 40 percent.[69] The decline actually is more pronounced than this suggests, given the cost of living for Africans is increasing at between one and one-half and two times as fast as the consumer price index, at least in the major urban areas.

The static or deteriorating standard of living of Africans, including in particular those in the urban areas who are most visible to whites, is fairly widely recognized in South Africa, although it tends to be omitted from publications for overseas consumption which stress only rising cash wages and fail to mention rising prices for Africans. The recent pay "boost" following strikes in Natal is a classic case. It is generally assumed in the United States that the Africans there won a sizeable victory; however, Lucy Mbuvelo, an African trade union official involved in the affected industries, said: "The increases were so small—usually between 25c and R1 a week—that they have barely covered the rise in cost of mealie meal, bread, milk and coal, and these are basic commodities." This was confirmed by a white businessman who reported that Africans receiving wage increases were spending every cent on basic goods: "Most of their increases are being absorbed by the rising cost of living. There's precious little left over."[70]

The Johannesburg City Council has admitted that "the general mass of Bantu have not improved their positions financially in the two decades 1946-1966."[71] The *Financial Mail* emphasized that this is not confined to Johannesburg, but is a national phenomenon, as shown by the countrywide surveys of the Trade Union Council.[72] Even in Cape Town, where Africans should be better off than elsewhere because of a severe labor shortage, a detailed survey concluded that although the position of Africans appeared to be improving in the early part of the 1960s, there had been a marked cline in the second half of the decade, and that the decline was accelerating.[73]

These trends toward impoverishment of the African majority is in direct contradiction to the ideology of apartheid, which maintains that "separate development" of all the races will benefit everyone. A staunch supporter of the apartheid system has commented:

> This is most unfortunate and disconcerting to South Africans like myself, who sincerely believe in the superiority of White leadership. . . . The fall in the Africans' real earnings is a particularly nasty blot on White South Africa, for this deterioration has taken place during a period of unparalleled good fortune in the Union and unparalleled progress throughout the world.[74]

THE IMPORTANCE OF AFRICAN
LABOR TO THE ECONOMY

During the whole course of South Africa's industrialization, Africans have formed an increasing proportion of the labor force. The participation

of blacks, as a whole, in the work force rose from 64 percent in 1946 to
77 percent in 1970. Africans are moving into employment now at the highest rate in twenty years, at about 4.5 percent a year.[75] About one-half the
319 million economically active Africans in 1967 were "employed in essential services ministering to all racial groups," according to a comprehensive
survey at that time.[76]

Of all Africans employed in 1970, the largest number (31.8 percent) were
in agriculture. In the "services and other" category were 31.4 percent; 22.5
percent were in mining.[77] As a proportion of the total work force, Africans
were most numerous in agriculture (82 percent) and mining (90 percent),
with 67.3 percent in construction, while in services and manufacturing,
their strength was 54.7 percent and 51.7 percent respectively. In 1970, only
about 5.9 percent of the total African population was employed in manufacturing, as compared to 9.6 percent of the whites.[78] In this light, the constant stress laid on raising wages in the manufacturing sector is clearly not of
key importance in the overall economic situation for the African population.

By sheer weight of numbers, blacks provide the major proportion of the
manpower in all nineteen main industrial sectors, with the sole exception of
printing, where they are just under 50 percent of the work force.[79] There are,
of course, specialized subsectors where very high technology and capital-intensive automation is involved, such as computers, automobiles, oil, and other
specialized manufacturing, where U.S. investment is concentrated. Here, white
workers predominate, together with a relatively high proportion of Coloureds and Asians.

Africans are not only increasingly used as a growing proportion of the
labor force, but are also being "used" in the sense that their wage increases are kept well below their increase in productivity. It has been estimated that between 1957 and 1962 alone, the physical output of the
African labor force rose by 30 percent.[80] This is well in excess of the
actual increase in the size of the African labor force over the same period. The inference is clear that productivity per worker increased substantially, while at the same time, wages per worker increased very
little, and real earnings actually declined.

The deterioration in real conditions for Africans is confirmed by a
study of the years 1946-1962, covering wages in the manufacturing industry. The study shows that real white wages rose, while real black
wages were static or falling (using the white consumer price index),
and "producers' gross profits in manufacturing showed a positive sec-

ular trend."[81] The same trends apply to other major sectors of the e-
conomy, according to a further study of black wage rates that states:
"In many sectors of the economy wages paid are probably less than
marginal revenue produced (which is exploitation)."[82] The importance
of keeping black wages lagging behind productivity is evident to the business community as it is currently organized. The *Financial Mail* commented in 1971 that "in South Africa it is undeniable that the relatively
high returns on capital invested are due, at least in part, to South Africa's
discriminatory non-White labour policies, which . . . perpetuate wage
levels well below those justified by productivity."[83]

It would be useful at this point to consider the contentious question
of "job fragmentation," or the process by which many Coloureds and
Asians are taking over semiskilled jobs vacated by whites who are moving to white-collar positions. This is particularly true of Asians and Coloureds in more valuable "production" jobs in industry and elsewhere.
Certain categories vacated by them are then filled with Africans.[84] The
Reynders Commission reported in 1972 that "at present there would
appear to be very little statutory constraint on the employment of
Coloreds and Asians in the various job categories. With regard to Bantu,
however, various types of restrictions on the occupational and geographical mobility of this group exist. . . ."[85] In effect, then, Coloureds and
Asians are taking over some of the more valuable jobs in production,
while the whites either cease to contribute directly (working as "supervi-
sors"), or fulfill "managerial" functions also not directly related to production. The relative positions of the various categories of workers naturally remain the same; as the Ford Motor Company's industrial relations
manager, Mr. F.H. Ferreira, described it, "There is an upward movement
of the whites as they make way for the progression of non-whites."[86]

The whole process of upgrading "black" labor is seized on by proponents of the "more of the same" theory as proof of economic advancement for the majority and the progressive destruction of apartheid. The
ambivalence about the term "black" in South Africa is used to disguise
the actual situation. Almost no members of the actual majority group,
the black Africans, are involved in the replacement of white workers in
specific job categories. In the first place, such a process almost inevitably
means either the "fragmentation" or "downgrading" of a certain piece of
work, so that its job title is categorized as suitable for "blacks," includ-

ing, in some cases, Africans. The new category will carry a much lower wage than the previous "white" category. The average skilled white is paid over three times as much as the average skilled black, and the differential is even greater in manufacturing.[87] The white employer, then, benefits—by paying less money for as much or more work, since black workers are often more efficient as the employers have more power over them. The white worker also benefits—by receiving a higher grade job, often an easy desk job, together with higher pay. This is perhaps the crux of the whole issue, and the means by which "job fragmentation" is, in practice, a depressant to average African living standards, although a very small minority may benefit.

The process of job fragmentation can take place on a worthwhile scale only with the consent of the white unions, which are highly sensitive to any possibility of "white" jobs being taken over by blacks at cut rates. It will, therefore, normally be tolerated by the unions only in cases where there are absolutely no whites wanting the job in question. This is highlighted by the case of the state-run South African Railways (SAR), which have, in fact, long been an area of sheltered employment for unskilled whites, and have recently led the way in job reclassification. The minister of Transport stated in 1968: "My policy is very clear, namely that with the approval of the staff and on condition that wages, status and standard of living of the whites are protected, I am already employing non-whites in work previously done by whites."[88] Far from contradicting government policy, then, the process of job fragmentation is spearheaded by the government. By the end of 1972, SAR employed over 3,000 blacks and Coloureds in jobs formerly held exclusively by whites, although at lower rates.[89] In 1970, the minister of Labour told the National Party Congress that "nonwhites" would be allowed to do jobs previously done by whites, in the interests of economic growth, provided that no white workers could be found; that "nonwhites" must not replace whites willing to do the job; that whites and "nonwhites" should not do the same jobs together; and that whites must not work under "nonwhites".[90] This provides a system of protection for white workers as complete as any trade union official could desire.

The unions, therefore, are conceding nothing in their negotiations with employers on job fragmentation. In return for their agreement, however, they are demanding very real benefits for their members, usually including major wage increases. Innumerable examples can be found: in the building industry, white artisans received major increases in wages and fringe benefits in return for the creation of a new "nonwhite" job category between laborers and artisans; in the engineering field, the Industrial Council in 1970 gave a 20 percent increase to white artisans at the same time that it gave exemptions to firms to allow Africans to perform one category of work at one-half the non-African rate, and meanwhile, job reservation was reinforced by the exclusion of Africans from other categories.[91] In the case of SAR, the very substantial wage increases for white workers, in return for the employment of more "nonwhites," was sufficient to cause an immediate 20 percent tariff increase on the railroads, which not only boosted the general cost of living, but brought a sudden sharp rise in cost of living to Africans, who are forced to spen a considerable proportion of their incomes on commuting to work.

The general pattern, then, is for a few "nonwhites"—mainly non-Afri cans—to take over new responsibilities, while at the same time, existing jobs may be taken away, mainly from Africans. These few nonwhites assuming greater responsibilities will probably receive a higher wage than before, but the majority will be unaffected, some will be downgraded, a all may be afflicted by an increase in cost of living. The *Financial Gaze* described the process:

> The important handmaiden of fragmentation is what is known as "downgrading." We might see jobs as spread out on a ladder. As the different racial groups move up, progressing to higher skills, the ladd is also being made longer by fragmentation. But as the ladder gets longer, wages get spread more thinly over it, *except at the top*. Whea a new job is created by being taken away from the artisan, it is place lower down on the ladder, and a lower wage is paid for doing it. Also when a job comes down on the ladder, *those below it are often mov down a rung.* This is a system that employers have abused to a poten tially dangerous extent. It is the frequent result of a round of bargai that a *non-white doing a job on the middle of the ladder finds over night that the rate is severely cut,* although the work remains the sai . . . The whole process makes financial sense for a particular employ In any given bargain with the trade union, he will usually raise the skilled workers' pay considerably, but will recoup this loss by spend

less on other jobs, by downgrading them. He often ends up by saving on his total bill. [Emphasis added] [92]

It should be noted that such transactions *never* involve sacking any of the white employees. Since they receive a substantial pay boost, and since the total wage bill is often lower, it is obviously the "non-white" workers, and especially the Africans, who suffer a direct cut in income. The limited number of Africans who benefit from any kind of upgrading is evident in the fact that 62 percent of the economically active Africans have never been to school; many of those who have some education never reached a level of functional literacy because of the very high initial dropout rate; and only 0.3 percent, or 3 in 1,000 has finished high school. [93]

In return for upgrading a tiny minority of blacks, usually non-Africans, the whites receive pay increases that are well in excess of their productivity. The president of the Chamber of Mines stated recently that "in order to maintain our White labour force at its present strength, the mining industry has already been compelled to increase the wages of skilled men at about twice the rate of the increase in productivity." [94] The *Financial Mail* summed up the situation in bargaining: "As a result of these (skilled labour) shortages, employees, and particularly white employees, realize that they are in a position of absolute exploitation and are beginning to use this." [95] In terms of protection of the most desirable range of jobs, the monopolistic position of the whites is increasing rather than declining through these "concessions" of semiskilled jobs they no longer want. Filling these jobs helps to promote the automation of production, which makes skilled and management personnel indispensable. The Government Plan estimates that, by 1980, 5 percent of all skilled jobs will be vacant. The increasing demand for skilled workers is also an aspect of the increasingly capital-intensive nature of production encouraged by official policy, which is cutting out large numbers of jobs for unskilled workers at the bottom of the hierarchy. This is quite deliberate, as outlined by government economist P.J. Riekert: "Present Government policy is aimed at utilizing both approaches of encouraging more capital-intensive methods of production as well as augmenting our skilled manpower supply from the non-white groups." [96] Consequently, as a handful of Coloureds take over jobs no longer wanted by the whites, much larger numbers of unskilled Africans are deprived of jobs by means of the same process.

At the same time, the inflationary pressures exerted by escalating white wage scales—part of the increases negotiated in return for "job fragmentation"—are depressing the real incomes of the African majority as a whole. The increase in white salaries and wages was already approaching 30 percent a year in early 1973 and is continually escalating.[9] The South African Reserve Bank has estimated this to be the major element in South Africa's unprecedented inflation in recent years.

As noted, the average income of Africans in South Africa has deteriorated substantially for many years, and this deterioration is now accelerating under the impact of the steeply rising African cost of living. Job fragmentation, far from counteracting the trend, is exacerbating it, through its links with increasingly capital-intensive and labor-displacing production, the practice of reducing lower grade job wages when adjustments are made, and the massive inflationary pressure of white wage increases. To the extent that a handful of Africans may be benefitting from the process, this simply means that the average is concealing very substantial impoverishment at the lower end of the scale. The process can be seen directly in various industries, though in the sector where job fragmentation is most common—the construction industry—the gap between white and African wage levels is most striking, except for that in mining, where special conditions prevail.[98] The same is true when one considers other sectors where Africans are increasing their proportion of employees—apparently breaking down the other major aspect of the color bar, the fixed ratio of white to "nonwhite" workers—where the reduced number of white employees is correlative to the rapidly widening gap between white and African pay scales.[99]

It may also be observed that as Africans have increased their overall percentage in the labor force in the South African economy, their real wages have declined. At the same time, they are contributing more to the economy, not only by the productivity increases cited earlier, which are far greater than any cash raises, but also by their overall level of work, illustrated by the fact that the proportion of African workers described as laborers (the lowest category) in the Department of Labour surveys for nonmining industrial occupations has dropped steadily: in 1936, it was 89.5 percent, falling to 84 percent in 1960, and thereafter dropping fairly steeply down to 68.2 percent in 1970.[100] Africans are becoming more valuable contributors to the white economy, while the benefits they derive from it fall continuously. As concluded by a British observer in a recent review in the London *Times* of the job fragmentation picture in South Africa: "It is a mistake to see this process as a breach of *apartheid*; indeed, it is the essence, because job reservation is a flexible instrument for maintaining white supremacy in a changing industrial economy."[101] To see the process as somehow "breaking down" apartheid and creating viable opportunities for African progress is a misreading of the whole South African situation in terms of myths about the rigidity of the white power structure. In fact, white power is maintained by constant manipulation of the economy and constant policy adjustments—even contradictions—in the interest of white supremacy and white prosperity.

Government policy statements have consistently stressed that Africans are to participate in the South African economy solely on the basis of contributing their labor, with no rights to participate in the benefits as equal citizens. The basic theory was put forward in official form in 1921, when the Transvaal Local Government Commission, known as the Stallard Commission, recommended "the native should only be allowed to enter the urban areas, which are essentially the white man's creation, when he is willing to enter and to minister to the needs of the white man and should depart therefrom when he ceases so to minister."[102] The idea of the African as nothing more than a "labor unit" is a basic theme running through South African economic and political development; the 1921 motif was echoed, for instance, in 1955 by the minister of Bantu Affairs:

> I see the future economic pattern of South Africa being that there will always be thousands of Bantu on the white farms, in the mines, in industry and also as servants in the white homes. The difference, however, will be that the natives will be there, not as a right but at the bidding and by the grace of the whites.[103]

In 1967, Mr. Botha reiterated: "It must be understood very fundamentally that the Bantu who are working in the industries in South Africa on the basis of our policy are not here on an integrationary basis . . . to become equal workers, equal entrepreneurs, or equal partners."[104] In the following year, Prime Minister Vorster repeated the theme:

> It is true that there are blacks working for us. They will continue to
> work for us for generations. . . . The fact of the matter is this: We
> need them, because they work for us . . . but the fact that they work
> for us can never—if one accepts this as one's own criterion one will
> be signing one's own death sentence now—entitle them to claim poli-
> tical rights. Nor now, nor in the future. It makes no difference whether
> they are here with any degree of permanency or not . . . under no
> circumstances can we grant them those political rights in our terri-
> tory, neither now nor ever.[105]

In recent years, the policy has been restated and emphasized with increasing frequency by top government representatives. Mr. Botha repeated in 1972:

> . . . the Bantu *are present here for the sake of their labour.* That la-
> bour is regulated by statute; they cannot simply accept work at ran-
> dom and at will; no, it is regulated properly in the interests of the
> Whites as well as the Bantu. Therefore, they cannot come here and
> take what is offered to them here in the social, economic, and all
> kinds of other spheres. That is why on many previous occasions I
> have said that the Bantu are here in a loose capacity *exclusively on
> the basis of their labour.* They are not here in a permanent capa-
> city to acquire what you and I can acquire in the sphere of labour,
> and the other spheres. [Emphasis added.] [106]

The major instrument by which this policy is carried out is a nation-
wide network of legislative and administrative structures that enforce
"influx control"—control of the movements of the entire African population in the interests of regulating the labor supply for white farms,
mines, and industries. As summarized by a progovernment analyst, this
means that

> every Bantu born in the Republic of South Africa or in South West
> Africa who reaches the age of sixteen years, must be in possession of
> a reference book, and may not be employed if, 1) he is not in posses

sion of a reference book, 2) it appears from such a reference book that the Bantu concerned is not permitted to be in specific area, and 3) his reference book does not show the termination of previous contracts.[107]

The last provision is designed to prevent competition among employers for African workers, which would, of course, tend to raise the overall level of wages. An African, in effect, belongs to his employer for the duration of the contract; an attempt by another employer to hire him would be regarded in the same light as stealing his possessions. Any African who leaves his employer for any reason before the termination of his contract, or who is otherwise "illegally" present–by virtue of being unemployed– in an urban area, is subject to penal sanctions, including forced labor. Under Article 6 of the Bantu Laws Amendment Act of 1970, he may be sent to a rural village, settlement, or other place indicated by the authorities, and may be "detained thereat for such period and perform such labour as may be prescribed by law in terms of which such rural village, settlement, rehabilitation scheme, institution or place was established." In the case of Africans theoretically in their "own" areas, the "homelands," it is also a criminal offense to refuse to accept work. In terms of the Bantu Labour Regulations (Bantu Areas) Act, No. 74 of 1968, registration with the local Labour Bureau is compulsory for all Africans in the "homelands"; if they refuse to accept any job offered by the bureau, they may be subject to penal sanctions.[108] The two laws cited above do not change the situation in which an African has no right to take employment without his reference book or "pass" in order, and wherein he has no right to be in areas where the jobs are located–the "white" areas (though blacks predominate there as elsewhere)–without employment. Recent legislation has simply refined and strengthened the power of the government over Africans as "labor units." Under the Bantu Laws Amendment Act of 1964, white officials have almost unlimited power to "endorse out" Africans from the towns; the act allows unemployed Africans to be detained in "youth camps" or "labour depots," resulting in constant police harassment and raids in African "locations," with 300,000 to 400,000 arrests and convictions each year. As described by the Episcopal bishop of Kimberley, this law "amounts to slave labour."[109]

Although the "pass" system primarily acts as the means of the govern-

ment to control African movement, it provides great opportunities for un
scrupulous employers to exploit the workers under their personal control
as if they, too—like the government—"owned" them. The Black Sash, a
voluntary organization that assists Africans with "pass" difficulties, reported in 1972 that a disastrous impact on the lives of its clients had
been effected by the "thoughtlessness, sometimes even the deliberate
malice, of employers." In many cases, employers made no effort to register their employees in accordance with the "pass" law requirements; in
others, they threatened to "spoil" passbooks or to refuse to allow employees to leave their jobs, knowing that if the "F" card is not sent in,
registration for new employment will be refused. There are also employe₁
who "used the pass laws in order to exploit a worker." Men in the position of hoping to qualify for "permanent residence" in the "white area"
were dependent for qualifying on staying with one employer for *ten
years*—clearly a situation conducive to employers taking advantage of the
complete power this gives them over the workers.[110]

The system of the pass laws is currently being tightened up, with special reference to the deportation of "surplus appendages like wives and
children," who are not working for the whites.[111] A government spokesman told the House of Assembly in 1968, "We are trying to introduce tl
migratory labour pattern as far as possible in every sphere, that is in fact th
entire basis of our policy as far as the White economy is concerned. . . .'
Mr. Botha again summarized the objective: "As far as I am concerned, th
ideal condition would be if we could succeed in due course in having all
Bantu present in the white area on a basis of migratory labour only."[113]
He called the deportation of families "the right thing to do," and repeatedly emphasized that the idea "should become an obsession with all of
us."[114]

Out of a total of 3,071,000 registered African workers, at least 892,0(
can be positively identified as "migrant" workers. This figure omits thou
sands more in the fields of domestic service, construction, manufacturing
and accommodation and catering services who are, in fact, migrants.[115] It
has been estimated that half of all Africans in the labor force are migran
who are separated from their families.[116] The migrant labor system was
originated for the benefit of the gold mines and has subsequently proven
most convenient as a source of cheap and rightless labor for white settle₁
on the land and in myriad other concerns. The mineowners collaborated

to form a monopolist cartel for labor recruitment, eliminating competition among themselves, which enabled them to keep wages for Africans far below even the South African average for Africans.[117] The ratio of white to African wages in mining is 16:1, about four times higher than in sectors not using migrant labor to the same degree. The migratory system is a major factor in depressing African wages and subsidizing white increases. Its abolition would be a serious threat to the mining industry.[118]

Far from being a dwindling relic of the past, migratory labor is being reinforced and expanded into sectors previously relying very little on it. It has been argued, in fact, that there is a symbiotic relationship between migratory labor and the color bar—intended, of course, to reserve skilled and highly paid jobs for whites, while keeping blacks unskilled. This, in turn, has meant that possible savings accruing from a stabilized, skilled African work force could not apply and that the cheapest form of casual, unskilled labor—migrant labor—could be exploited. By depressing African wages, the financial burden of the color bar is reduced. The economist, Dr. Francis Wilson, concludes that, given the twin priorities of economic growth and white supremacy "the contradictions inherent in the simultaneous pursuit of the twin goals can be resolved only by entrenching the pattern of oscillating migration at the heart of the economy, so that . . . more and more people are involved in perpetual motion between their rural homelands and their urban places of work."[119] Far from withering away, as it is in the general economic pattern elsewhere, migratory labor in South Africa will continue to expand, and "its maintainence will depend increasingly not on the balance of economic pressures but on the force of law."[120]

This is precisely the objective—with its consequent depressing effect on overall African wages, since the migrant worker cannot choose his employer according to the wages offered or any benefit criterion—that government spokesmen are calling for. Under the 1968 labor regulations, no new contract workers can qualify to remain in an urban area under any circumstances, since they may not reside there continuously for more than one year; hence the fiction that they are residents and "citizens" of some "homeland" they have never seen and the annual compulsory "return" there. The regulations effectively mean that any new African workers brought into the economy—for example, by new American investment—by definition have no security, being condemned to perpetual migrant labor under fixed, nonnegotiable contract and with no choice of employer. They will be en-

tirely at the mercy of the employer, forcibly separated from their families, with no means of negotiating wage increases other than by illegal
strikes. They will be dumped in one of the camps or left landless in a
"homeland" as soon as their usefulness expires. This is the meaning behind the claims of investors that they "provide employment" for Africans.

Apart from its systematic depression of African wages, the migrant practice is a powerful force in the disruption of the whole social fabric of Africans in South Africa. It destroys the family unit by physically removing
the father, or other primary wage-earner, from it in the struggle for subsistence. As one government official put it, the Africans—especially in the
"homelands"—have "nothing but their labour to sell."[121] The result, in
destroying the culture and social well-being of entire communities, is not
unlike that of slavery, in that marriage, family, social and cultural mores
were ignored there, also, in the effort of the whites to split up and disin-
tegrate families and cultures for their own profit and convenience.

In terms of human suffering, the effects are almost impossible to assess because of government classification of such matters as "national
security" issues and because of the freeze on access by researchers to the
"homelands." It is fairly clear, however, that the system promotes bigamy
and illegitimacy, the evasion of kinship obligations, the complete destitu-
tion of families deprived of a breadwinner, the breakdown of traditional
authority, a debasement of the role of women, mental breakdowns and
the traumatic experience of loneliness and bereavement, and an intensifica-
tion of poverty and social deprivation. For every single African wage-
earner—to whom an employer can point as an example to "progress"
since he has income to spend on consumer goods—there will be a whole
extended family, including the very old and very young, which is desperate for the income he left home to earn—and on the verge of starvation. Ironically, the fact that some workers are not supporting their
share of the majority of Africans not directly earning money in the "white
areas," is used by employers to justify a refusal to adopt even the wholly
inadequate Poverty Datum Line as a basic minimum wage. Even Dr. Wilson,
who has studied in the most detail the effect of the splitting-up of African
families by the migratory labor system, is at a loss: "I cannot convey ade-
quately the sense of hurt rage of Black South Africans at what is being
done to them."[122]

Since the migrantization of an already urbanized labor force is, in effect, forcibly reversing the dominant demographic trend of this century, it is evidently being accomplished only by the use of coercion and special police powers, by the deportation of hundreds of thousands of Africans from their homes and breadwinners to the camps and rural slums of the "homelands." Chief Buthelezi, appointed head of the Kwazulu "homeland," described these places as "cesspools of poverty, ignorance, and disease."[123]

A few observations should be made about conditions for Africans in the urban areas. The first concerns the question of the color bar, or "job reservation," which tends to reinforce, rather than reduce, white privilege in the labor sphere and white percentage of total wages. There is still the common argument, however, that the white unions, by pressing the slogan of "rate for the job," have changed sides and are promoting African interests as parallel to their own. It is therefore important to record that the role of the government in directly reserving certain jobs for whites is minimal; such determinations affect less than 3 percent of all jobs in South Africa, and most of these are exempted.[124] The available powers are essentially for contingencies; the fact that they are not much used is an indication of the strength of the color bar without direct government intervention. The color bar has always been enforced, with the backing of the government, by the white unions, whether by "closed shop" agreements (the exclusion of nonunion members precluding Africans, who are not allowed to join unions, from working in closed shops), or by union insistence on the "rate for the job" principle as a basic means of protecting white privilege in the labor market.

Since the whites—originally skilled immigrants—had a monopoly on "journeyman" skills and on access to apprenticeships and training facilities, it was very much in their interest to maintain high rates for these occupations and to prevent employers from hiring less skilled "nonwhites" at much lower wages. They therefore stressed the "rate for the job" principle on the assumption that if it were not possible to undercut the rate, an employer would naturally prefer to employ a conventionally trained white. The "rate for the job" dictum was adopted by the Pact government in 1924, which relied on white workers' support and faced serious problems of "poor white" underemployment. Along with the allocation of work went a fixed determination of wages under the "civilized labour policy" embodied in the Industrial Conciliation Act of 1925, and in all such acts from then on. It was stipulated that no discrimination or differentiation on the basis of color or race could be made in determining *wages* in industrial council agreements; the result was that certain *categories* of work were accepted as "white," wit fixed and immutable rates of pay attached, so that competition from those prepared to work for less was effectively outlawed. A government publication explains: "The White person with his high standard of living finds it di ficult to compete with the non-White . . . and there are employers who read exploit the position by employing non-Whites at low rates of pay."[125]

The "rate for the job" demand has been supplemented at various stages other measures applied by white workers and their unions in agreements wi the employers and often backed by government recognition. For example, Bantu Laws Amendment Act of 1970 enabled the minister of Bantu Affairs to prohibit the work, or continued performance of work, by a "Bantu" in a specified area, specified class of employment, specified trade, or in the service of a specified employer or class of employers. Used as a central issue fo white unions during their major struggles with employers, before the nation government guaranteed them virtually anything they wanted, the "rate for job" slogan died down a little under the Nationalist government but has rec ly reemerged. Far from signifying a fight for African interests, it is being us principally to stop employers from quietly taking a job out of the "white" category and reducing the pay attached, unless this is part of a deal with the white unions. As we have seen, these job fragmentation package deals are directly detrimental to the interests of African workers.

The same is broadly true of the current debate on allowing Africans to join registered unions, which several of the white union leaders are now advocating. They feel potentially threatened by the various possibilities that cheaper African labor in the "homelands" could make these areas competitive with the present industrial areas and even undermine their own jobs; that African unions will be formed in the "homelands" in competition with white unions; that strikes by Africans are as much a threat to the white unions as to the employer; and that the tiny minority of skilled Africans could undercut white union members. The white unions are therefore violently opposed to allowing Africans to register their own unions, since this would seriously undercut the white monopoly of bargaining with employers. The progovernment paper, *Die Vaderland,* which has condemned this policy of the unions as directly contradictory to the policy of separate development, has described it as offering "fourth rate membership for the Bantu in mixed trade unions with approximately one-quarter of a say."[126] However, the policy has been found by the unions to be a sound way of dealing with competition from "nonwhites." As a representative of the Trade Union Council of South Africa (TUCSA) explained to a parliamentary committee:

> Up until 1927, we refused to have Indians in the Typographical Union. They then commenced negotiating separately and practically eliminated the European printer from Natal. We then took them into our union to stop that. The result is that I suppose one could count on the fingers of your one hand the number of skilled Indian printers in Natal. They have been almost eliminated. That happened because we took them into the Union.[127]

It is through this historical experience that TUCSA has now arrived at a policy that Africans doing the same jobs as whites should be allowed to join their unions, although the overwhelming majority—those doing unskilled work and demonstrably in the greatest need or organization—"would probably remain unorganized, as they are now," according to TUCSA's general secretary.[128] Other white unionists have stressed the need, following the wave of African labor unrest, for white unions to negotiate for African workers.[129]

There is a great deal of vociferous debate about African membership in trade unions, but no significant change. The main trade union groupings, the Confederation of Labour and TUCSA, have failed to agree on the objective.[130] The government is backing the Confederation in complete opposition to African unionism.[131] Meanwhile, talk of "starting" African labor organization ignores the fact that African unions were once relatively active, with substantial membership, and enjoying a basic minimum protection against harassment. The trend has been for the victimization of African union leaders, the liquidation of the unions, and draconian legislation to prevent Africans from organizing, registering their unions (the key to legal protection), or striking. In 1957, the government even abolished the right of African workers to obtain an investigation of their conditions and wages by an official Wage Board—a form of activity that had provided a limited means for African unions to promote their members' welfare.[132]

Strikes by Africans are illegal and carry heavy penalties of up to R1,000 ($1,300) or three years imprisonment, or both. Furthermore, the definition of "communism" in the Suppression of Communism Act, No. 44 of 1950, is wide enough to apply to any strike by Africans. At the beginning of 1969, nearly 1,000 Africans were in jail under this act, the Unlawful Organizations Act and the Terrorism Act, under which many strikes can be defined as "sabotage." Violations can carry the death penalty.[133] It is hardly surprising that, when Africans strike in desperation over falling real wages, no spokesmen are ever available to negotiate with employers and the police. The "works committees" established by individual companies to provide a means of "communication" proved "completely out of touch with the workers," according to one top industrialist hit by an unofficial strike.[134] The prospects for more representative bodies, however, are not good, since the government regards them as potential vehicles of political expression:

> There are always organizers who prefer to use those Bantu trade unions as a political instrument for their particular political aims rather than as an economic negotiating instrument . . . It is important that we keep on saying that the Government believes that on the basis of experience gained in this country with Bantu trade unions in the past, and the way in which these were also applied as political instruments, it is not in the interest of South Africa that Bantu trade unions should be recognized.[135]

The conditions under which Africans work, then, is to be determined, as before, by the government, the white unions, and the employers. None of these have any concern for promoting African interests, still less in preventing the strengthening of the migratory labor system. While depressing African wages and conditions and destroying the fabric of African life, migratory labor is useful to the government in giving it complete control over the African labor force, as well as allowing the removal of large numbers of "surplus" Africans to places out of sight of the white population. Further, it allows employers to pay lower wages to Africans than to whites since African workers have no choice of contract nor the freedom to leave before it terminates, and it protects white workers from competition from a settled and organized African labor force. The system is, therefore, as outlined earlier, becoming immovably entrenched.

One element in this institutionalization of the migratory system is the mass program of "hostel" building in the major cities, in addition to the "compounds" built by the mines, municipalities, and private employers. According to a recent estimate, there are already almost one-half million Africans, both men and women, many of them married, living in these new hostels; massive new blocs are being established in Alexandra, near Johannesburg, and elsewhere. The "compounds," or barracks, are frequently overcrowded, with few basic facilities and, in many cases, without heating. Because of the fiction that African workers are in the area of employment on a "temporary" basis, private employers have been allowed to construct the cheapest sort of temporary buildings to reduce costs. Even the Post Office built insufficient accommodation, between 1969 and 1971, with the amount of space-per-man at one-half the legal minimum. Conditions in the compounds and hostels greatly exacerbate the socially destructive effects of the migrant labor system: Africans have no alternative choice of accommodation; wives and children are banned from entering and must live in another hostel; many compounds are surrounded by prison fences and barbed wire, and the newest hostels have special automatic steel doors to seal off sections in case of riots.[136] The overcrowding and poor conditions, according to a committee of nongovernment experts, are in positive correlation with high morbidity and mortality rates, violence, crime, prostitution, mental disorders, marital problems, and suicide. The forcible separation of families settled in the towns causes alcoholism, faction fighting, rioting, sex crimes, assault, and theft.[137]

The situation on white-owned farms is still worse, and Africans invariably choose to work in urban areas if that option is offered, as it generally is not. Once having worked on a farm, an African's "pass" is marked so that he can work only in agriculture. There are more than 2 million Africans working on farms—90 percent of all farm labor, and the percentage is growing. Two laws lay down the basic conditions: the Masters and Servants Act of 1856, still very much in force, and the Native Contract Act of 1932. Under them, the employer has no contractual obligations as far as minimum wages or conditions are concerned. The laborers, on the other hand, commit a criminal offense if they violate their contracts by "desertion," taking steps to change their jobs, or failure to carry out orders.[138] The farmer may punish any disobedience himself, without trial, by fines or beatings. There are frequent reports of serious physical injury as a result of punishments, and of exorbitant fines for minimal offenses.

These have the effect of putting the farm worker and sometimes his children into bondage to the farmer for the rest of their lives.[139]

Migrant labor is becoming an increasing factor in the agricultural labor force; recruitment of women is regarded as undesirable in "white areas," since they are potential "incubators of labour" in the wrong places. The old system of labor "tenants" is also being demolished. These people were settled on nominally "white" farms, using the land and, in return, performing six months work for no pay. It seems that the eviction of "labour tenants" is partly the result of pressure from farmers who wanted more contract labor and regarded the Africans feeding themselves on a subsistence basis as a waste of potential labor for themselves. [140] The same is true of farms once owned by Africans and labeled "black spots" by the government; so labeled, a farm's owners may be forcibly evicted.

White farmers have a natural interest in eliminating much of the subsistence agriculture; the overcrowding of the "homelands" has largely achieved this for them there, and the eviction of "labour tenants" from white farms, often to the landless villages of the homelands, has also contributed to the inability of many African families to feed themselves. As a result, they are obliged to earn cash wages as best they can and are then obliged to spend them on high-priced food, produced largely by their own labor, on land the whites expropriated from them over the period of invasion and occupation of the country or more recently seized by eviction.

The establishment of mining and industry in South Africa, as elsewhere, is dependent on a surplus of agricultural production, as well as a surplus of labor. When the new market for agricultural goods first opened up, white farmers found themselves challenged by low-cost peasant procedures. A crucial part of government activity in the early years, therefore, was the subsidization of white farming, construction of transportation networks to white farm areas, and the establishment of a "whites only" Land Bank to provide credit. Eventually, prices for white farm products were guaranteed by a system of producer-controlled marketing boards. All this, of course, coincided with the taxation of African peasants to drive them into mine labor and the progressive impoverishment of their agricultural and other resources. As one noted sociologist concluded, "local Africans have been dispossessed of their lands to a greater degree than in any other part of the continent."[141]

The logical conclusion of this process is the widespread use of prison labor on the farms. In the effort to escape the conditions of the farm contracts, with minimal wages, fourteen-hour days and seven-day weeks Africans attempt in large numbers to gain access to urban employment centers; the prevalence of "illegal" residents is estimated to make Soweto, for instance, double its "official" size. If "illegal" residents are caught in a police raid, they can then be sent back to the farms as forced labor. Long-term prisoners are organized in a major system, established by the Nationalist government as soon as it came to power in 1948. According to a report on prison labor in the Western Cape, a major agricultural region, farmers group together in associations to build prison outposts and take shares on a certain number of prisoners. The prisoner allocation is frequently advertised as part of the farm's assets if it changes hands. In some cases, shares may be resold at a negotiable price. The prison officials charge the farmers a fixed daily amount for use of the prisoners and stipulate that they are responsible for guarding them. The convicts, of course, receive nothing. Obviously, the prison-labor system has a directly depressant effect on the wages of Africans on contracts.[142]

Practices such as these lie at the very heart of the South African economy. It is not so much widespread use of prison labor, or abuses of employer power, or the white unions, or the migratory labor system that is the root of the problem; it is the legal, administrative, and economic structure of South Africa as a whole. The declaration by Cecil Rhodes in 1894 still applies today: "We want to get hold of these young men and make them go out to work. . . . It must be brought home to them that in the future nine-tenths of them will have to spend their lives in daily labour, in physical work, in manual labour."[143] This ideal, put into practice over a century of consolidating white power in South Africa, is still behind the refinements to the labor system that have been added since the Nationalist government came to power and coincide with the major period of economic boom of the 1960s and early 1970s. The network of resulting legislation has been carefully analyzed by an ad hoc committee of the International Labor Office (ILO—a body set up primarily to establish basic minimum standards of employment and with great expertise in the field of forced labor). Reporting on the situation as early as 1953, the committee concluded:

> With regard to the economic aspect of its terms of reference, the Committee is convinced of the existence in the Union of South Africa of a legislative system applied only to the indigenous population and de-

signed to maintain an insuperable barrier between these people and the inhabitants of European origin. The indirect effect of this legislation is to channel the bulk of the idigenous inhabitants into agricultural and manual work and thus to create a permanent, abundant and cheap labor force.

Industry and agriculture in the Union depend to a large extent on the existence of this indigenous labor force whose members are obliged to live under the strict supervision and control of the State authorities.

The ultimate consequence of the system is to compel the native population to contribute, by their labour, to the implementation of the economic policies of the country, but the compulsory and involuntary nature of this contribution results from the peculiar status and situation created by special legislation applicable to indigenous inhabitants alone, rather than from direct coercive measures designed to compel them to work, although such measures, which are the inevitable consequence of this status, were also found to exist.

It is in this indirect sense, therefore, that in the committee's view, a system of forced labour of significance to the national economy appears to exist in the Union of South Africa.[144]

The ILO itself, largely due to the support and leadership of the U.S. delegation, in 1964 adopted a policy strongly critical of South Africa's "degrading, criminal and inhuman" labor policies, which are in violation of the Forced Labor Convention, 1930; the Abolition of Penal Sanctions (Indigenous Workers) Convention, 1955; the Abolition of Forced Labor Convention, 1957; the Freedom of Association and Protection of the Right to Organize Convention, 1948; the Right to Organize and Collective Bargaining Convention, 1949; and the Discrimination (Employment and Occupation) Convention and Recommendation, 1958. Violations of a very wide range of other international conventions are involved: for example, the use of forced labor in goods for export is contrary to the General Agreement of Tariffs and Trade (GATT), as well as the U.S. Tariff Act. The violations involve basically, the blatant discrimination against Africans on grounds of race, and the exploitation of their labour in conditions that can be described as "indentured" labor—"placed under contract to work for another over a period of time. . . . Generally, indentured servants included . . . victims of religious of political persecution . . . and paupers"; or as outright "slave" labor—"persons, especially a large group, forced to perform labor under duress or threats . . . any forced, coerced, or poorly remunerated work."[145]

It is this systematic abuse of 15 million people in their own country by a small minority with a monopoly of power based on race that constitutes the uniqueness of the South African situation. It may be the most flagrant breach, on a national scale, of the Universal Declaration of Human Rights, a document adopted in response to the racial supremacy theories of Nazism and Fascism that led to World War II:

> Whereas recognition of the inherent dignity and of the equal and inalienable rights of all members of the human family is the foundation of freedom, justice and peace in the world,
>
> Whereas disregard and contempt for human rights have resulted in barbarous acts which outrage the conscience of mankind. . . .
>
> Whereas it is essential, if man is not to be compelled to have recourse in the last resort to rebellion against tyranny and oppression, that human rights should be protected by the rule of law. . . .
>
> Article 1. All human beings are born free and equal in dignity and rights. . . .
>
> Article 2. Everyone is entitled to all the rights and freedoms set forth in this declaration, without distinction of any kind, such as race, colour, sex . . . national or social origin . . . or any other status. . . .
>
> Article 7. All are equal before the law and are entitled without any discrimination to equal protection of the law. . . .
>
> Article 13 (1). Everyone has the freedom of movement and residence within the borders of each state. . . .
>
> Article 16 (3). The family is the natural and fundamental group unit of society and is entitled to protection by society and the State. . . .
>
> Article 21 (1). Everyone has the right to take part in the government of his country, directly or through freely chosen representatives. . . .
>
> Article 23 (1). Everyone has the right to work, to free choice of employment, to just and favorable conditions of work. . . . (3). Everyone who works has the right to just and favorable remuneration ensuring for himself and his family an existence worthy of human dignity. . . . (4). Ev-

eryone has the right to form and join trade unions for the protection of his interests. . . .

Article 25 (1). Everyone has a right to a standard of living adequate for the health and well-being of his family, including food, clothing, housing and medical care. . . . (2). Motherhood and childhood are entitled to special care and assistance.

"ECONOMIC GROWTH WILL BREAK DOWN APARTHEID"

Employers, especially American investors, have a tendency to blame the government of South Africa for all discriminatory measures; the government blames the employers, pointing out that there are no restrictions on maximum pay for Africans; occasionally, the finger of blame is pointed at the unions. Rather than supporting one or another of these competing accusations, however, it should be noted that the actual situation, regulated by the government, benefits *all* the white interest groups They all have a vested interest in the preservation of the system's major elements; their interests overlap to a large extent, and where they do not, there is a trade-off process that maintains a kind of equilibrium among them.

Perhaps the dominant feature of the Nationalist government since 1948 is its reliance on the support of workers who feel constantly threatened by competition from African labor. As Prime Minister Vorster has said, "We know only one person to whom we owe an explanation and that is the White worker in South Africa who has brought the National Party to the position it occupies today and will keep it in that position in the future."[146] White workers have been the beneficiaries of industrialization from the beginning particularly in the import-substitution sectors that weigh so heavily on African consumers. Tariff protection has been used by successive governments as have government contracts, as incentives to employers to use white labor at "civilized" rates.[147] White workers have, in fact, been strong supporters of African migratization, since this system gives whites many competitive advantages with employers, as well as boosting their income potential by depressing the Africans' share of the total wage bill. Whites have also supported the maintenance of other political structures that give them privileged access to the state; in fact, their continued economic advantage depends on the maintenance and reinforcement of the discriminatory, or apartheid, structure of power.[148] The monopoly of the negotiating process, which employers back by the full force of state authority, can be used to appropriate concessions that in a nonracist society would go to all workers. A white TUCSA official described the unions' attitude: "Usually there is an off the cuff hand out for the white workers, and human nature being what it is, the unions have to put the interests of members first."[149] Usually these agreements include job reservation provisions and are legally binding on all parties, as well as on the African workers, who have no direct representation.

It is hardly necessary to stress the government's responsibility, since it enforces legislation that protects the privileged position of the white workers, as well as maintaining, to the benefit of the employers, the system of labor bureau and "pass" controls that make the structure of forced labor operative. There are other areas in which the government is directly responsible for the Africans' increasing impoverishment. One of these is the tax system, which is itself discriminatory. Almost all Africans pay a much higher proportion of their incomes in tax than a white with the same income, starting at a level which is less than half the PDL. Africans receive no exemptions for children or other dependents, and various standard deductions do not apply to them, while they pay additional fixed amounts that non-Africans do not.[150] Further, the government is responsible for the deteriorating standards of African education, which clearly has a direct impact on African's actual and potential earning capacity. In 1968, annual expenditure on African pupils averaged about R14.48 per capita, while for white pupils, it was approximately R228, or fifteen times as much.[151] The proportion of state expenditure on African education has fallen steadily since the mid-1950s, and it has also fallen in terms of expenditure per capita.[152] While there has been much talk recently about vocational training, little of this is for Africans: the actual number of Africans involved in the programs is negligible, with many never completing the course, and there is fierce competition from white workers, who refuse to do the training. For Africans, at least, vocational training is a farce and can hardly compensate for their deteriorating overall educational level since the introduction of "Bantu education."[153]

Those who are, perhaps, most culpable in creating African poverty—be-

cause they take advantage of the power provided them by the government-
are the employers. They can also be the most hypocritical, complaining a-
bout restrictions on "upgrading" African labor, while remaining silent a-
bout discriminatory provisions in the law where it suits them. Mr. Harry
Oppenheimer of the Anglo-American Corporation is the foremost exponen
of this art. He devoted no less than one-third of his chairman's statement
for 1973 to the question of African wages, while it was actually the white
mineworkers who were about to receive a big raise. It is also clear that he
has no intention of paying serious attention to the problems of the least
skilled workers, though he is aware of the deprivation caused by erosion of
real wages by rapid inflation: "In the short term, the scope for improving
real standards of living through increased minimum wages is strictly limited
The real advance will be achieved only in the much longer term as we progr
from the present low-wage labour intensive economy to a high-wage capital
intensive economy.[154] This is in fact a common approach of all employers:
while refusing to raise minimum wages on the pretext that this would lead
African unemployment, they are rapidly divesting themselves of African
workers in their efforts to replace labor with capital, consistent with government policy. This is particularly true on the docks, where containeriza-
tion is threatening the jobs of thousands of Africans while making heavy
investment demands.[155] The gold mines are also undergoing major programs of mechanization, with the explicit objective of reducing the black
labor force drastically.[156] In industry, 29 of the top 100 employers have
apparently reduced their African labor force between 1970 and 1972;
British Leyland, for example, in the process of investing heavily in motor assembly production, reduced its labor force from 5,500 to 4,100
during that period.[157] Mobil, Caltex, and Shell also have cut back their
black labor force, at a time of heavy investment. This trend is in itself a
refutation of the claim that every new investment creates jobs for Africans.

Employers are particularly talented at presenting their own case in
the most favorable light without much regard for the facts of the situation. For example, they claim to be raising African wages in response
to an international campaign; an analysis of government labor statistics,
however, indicates that African wages in the major employment sectors
of mining, manufacturing, and construction failed even to keep up with
the cost of living for Africans. Between 1971 and 1972, for instance, wages
in manufacturing rose by 8.6 percent, while the African cost of living rose

by either 11.4 percent or 12.3 percent, depending on the basis of calculation.[158] In fact, employers as a group, far from promoting legislative and
administrative measures to help Africans, are exerting a major influence to
prevent the legal minimum wage determinations being raised. Less than
one million of South Africa's five and one-half million African workers
are, in fact, subject to minimum wage provisions of any kind. [159] Where
they are, very strong representations are made to oppose any minimum
wage increases, often with the argument that the *employer* does not need
it, since he can obtain all the labor wanted at existing rates of pay. Cost of
living factors are ignored, except where the argument is made that employers
should be able to increase the deductions from African wages for their board
and lodging.[160]

Employers are also adept at producing excuses for the low wages they
pay, usually by claiming that wage increases for Africans would threaten their
profitability and ultimately deprive them of their jobs. Even in South Africa
this is regarded as specious reasoning; as the *Natal Mercury* commented,
"What kind of business is it that cannot pay a decent wage to its most menial employee and still show a profit?"[161] The argument is also forgotten when
it is a question of redistributing what might be considered excessive profits.
The gold mining industry's total black wage bill in 1972 was R95 million,
while profits before tax were R548 million—63 percent higher than in the
previous year. The *increase* in profits was more than double the miners'
total wage bill.[162] On the more general level, a detailed study has shown
that no matter how profitable an industry, the wages for Africans are completely unaffected: they receive the absolute minimum regardless of the
company's ability to pay.[163]

The labor system, like the whole apartheid structure of which it is a
key element, can be viewed simply as an alliance of interest groups that
fight among themselves for the major concessions available, but never to
the extent that they forget the overriding need to ally with each other to
defend the system of special privilege against the majority, at whose expense they conduct the power plays. For this reason, South Africa's a-
partheid is not an ideological monolith that responds to any outside pressure by forming a mythical *laager*; nor is it threatened by economic growth
and prosperity. On the contrary, the convergence of interests of the various white groups—employers, workers, farmers, the government— are not
seriously threatened *provided* that sufficient surplus wealth is constantly

being created, by economic growth and African impoverishment, to provide real goals and rewards for all the white groups. General prosperity of
the minority, indeed, allows the power structure to maintain itself against
threats from the dispossessed African majority by means of elaborate systems of control, mass removals, administration, police activity, the maintenance of a huge bureacracy for supervision (creating sheltered employment for whites), and the continual escalation of armed forces to deal
with any resistance or uprising.

   This is not to say that there is a conspiracy in existence to impoverish
the African population. Constant exhortations to raise African status can
be heard from all directions in South Africa—with absolutely zero effect.
The impoverishment is an inevitable result of a situation where whites are
in collusion to appropriate all the resources of the country, whether in
land, money, or jobs, and where they have undertaken the process of protecting their own status and privileges to the point where Africans have no
defense at all; where, in fact, wage agreements are made on their behalf by
white workers negotiating with white employers and given force by a government elected exclusively by and for whites. As the *Financial Mail* admitted in the early stages of South Africa's economic boom in the 1960s,
"the kernel of the matter is this: We have a completely artificial economic
society with conditions frankly and openly manipulated to protect white
privilege."[164] A sympathetic review of apartheid ideology has also pointed
out the causal connection between economic growth, resistance to the involvement of the African population, and the drive for white supremacy:

   The development of the apartheid idea was stimulated to a significant
   degree by the swift economic integration of the Bantu during the first
   40 years of this century. The Afrikaner's opposition to this development was one of the great driving forces behind the apartheid idea. Because this integration took place chiefly in the urban areas, it is evident
   that Bantu urbanization was a primary and very real factor in the development of the apartheid idea. It is true to say that the native problem is to a large extent an urban one. Without the considerable urbanization of the Bantu we would today definitely not have had anything
   of the nature of apartheid.[165]

Given this basic link between economic growth, increased African employment, and apartheid, the exponential growth of the first two may be

expected to result in the strengthening of the third. The deep fear of the *swart gevaar* (black threat) is consistently played on in Nationalist election campaigns, with great success.

It is a phenomenon of fairly recent origin—industrialization—that sociologists associate with the growth of apartheid in its current form. Another observer, with a different political orientation, has come to similar conclusions:

> The policy of apartheid which conditions the lives of all South Africans is a direct reaction to the new conditions arising from industrialization. It was industrialization, the growth of towns associated with it, and the movement of Africans to meet the labour needs of the expanding towns and industries which led to the enunciation of this policy as a political doctrine and to the attempt to impose separation between white and black in all spheres.[166]

Referring specifically to the Nationalist ideology imposed after 1948, an official U.S. government publication notes:

> After World War II the whites' reaction to the process of partial economic integration and growing urbanization of the non-white and more particularly of the African population was a crucial factor in the election victory of the Nationalist Party in 1948 and in the evolution of the apartheid policy. The party's viewpoint as expressed in the Sauer Report of 1948 was that Afrikaner nationalism and unregulated economic integration of the black man were now incompatible forces and that only separate development—that is, geographic apartheid—would provide a weapon for the whites against the mass integration of the Africans and prevent white South Africa from eventually succumbing to revolutionary Africanization.[167]

The essentially self-interested nature of the interaction among the white interest groups in South Africa belies the myth that apartheid is merely an ideological belief, rooted in the Voortrekkers, the *laager*, the Dutch Reformed Church, and the farming community. This myth is enthusiastically propagated by the Nationalist party and their allies, and taken up by many overseas groups with parallel interests in claiming that investment, industrialization and economic growth, together with a little "communication" of

enlightened Western ideas, will undermine and finally destroy the old order. It would be extremely inconvenient for the protagonists of such a view
to recognize, as academic observers have, that industrialization is the *foundation* of the current manifestation of apartheid. The fact that overseas,
as well as local, businessmen, while theoretically not subscribing to the
ideological tenets of apartheid, are nevertheless extremely satisfied with it,
has been succinctly pointed out by the sociologist, Heribert Adam:

> Business concessions to Afrikaner political beliefs seem to stem from a
> realistic assessment of the necessity of state control over the labor force
> rather than from ideological agreement with the Apartheid implications.
> Potential profit restrictions as a consequence of this policy are far out-
> weighed by considerations of internal stability and unlimited access to
> abundant cheap labor which still guarantees a comparatively high re-
> turn from investments. The political authority on the other side is no
> less interested in a continuing economic boom. Only with a booming
> economy can the danger of internal conflicts be frozen and the exter-
> nal threats of sanctions be refuted. In this the interests of the govern-
> ment and industry coincide. Ideological differences play a role only
> within the framework of the common goal: to ensure white rule.[168]

It may be useful at this point to look at the question of inefficiency in
the South African economy, since this has frequently been claimed as a
major handicap that will ultimately force the abandonment of apartheid.
The basic waste of resources in South Africa is obvious, a fundamental
part of the white power structure. It was described well by van den Berghe

> Whites, in effect, have chosen to monopolize all skilled occupations in a
> complex industrial economy. . . . The results obviously are vast under-
> utilization of non-White skills, and a corresponding over-employment
> of Whites. Both of these take an enormous toll in industrial and admin-
> istrative efficiency. . . .
>
> With no prospect of job improvement, non-Whites have little incentive
> to work better; on the other hand, the privileged, protected European
> worker likewise has little incentive to improve his performance, because
> he is assured of remunerative employment. Non-White proletarians be-

come totally alienated from their jobs, or indeed from the whole system of production, and respond to discrimination with output restrictions, passive resistance, minor sabotage, and boycotts of shops and products. . . .

Racial stereotypes may also have an indirect economic effect. . . . For example, the White view of the non-White worker as "unreliable" and "irresponsible" can easily become a self-fulfilling prophecy. A worker . . . is likely to either lose all interest in his job and perform his tasks unthinkingly and apathetically, or to exhibit his spite by deliberate irresponsibility, coupled with a punctilious obedience to the letter of stupid orders. This method can be an effective means of passive resistance and could have an appreciable effect on production. Fulfillment of role-expectation provides the non-White worker with a relatively safe and satisfying way of expressing hostility toward Europeans.[169]

He also points to other government projects that are both costly and senseless in economic terms, such as the subsidization of European immigration while deporting Africans: the geographical location of African townships ten to twenty miles from the employment centers for purely political and military reasons; the creation of Bantustans on a wholly "impracticable plan;" and the "decentralization" of industries far removed from all necessities except the cheapest and most mobile—African labor.[170]

All these contributing factors to inefficiency are at the same time vital to the preservation of white minority rule. It makes no sense economically for the white elites to take steps to reduce their own income, however wasteful the system that produces it. The waste consists largely, after all, in African potential, both human and economic. The blacks are subsidizing, in effect, the increase in white profits and wages, by receiving wage increases well below their own increase in productivity. So long as this continues, together with sufficient economic growth for distribution among all the white interests, there is no sound economic or political reason for the whites to try to change the system of production and distribution.

In a less distorted economy, the circumstances in South Africa would have resulted in a much faster increase in productivity. However, the pattern of industrialization everywhere is that management raises productivity, not as an end in itself, but only when it is forced to do so by pressures of increased labor costs arising from a lengthy struggle with trade unions. Without this stimulus, there is no incentive to rationalize an already profitable operation. In the modern American context, efficiency becomes almost synonymous with profitability, because of the cost of labor. In a cheap labor economy, this is not so. In fact, profit margins depend on keeping labor costs down, regardless of efficiency considerations. There are innumerable examples of highly profitable enterprise, both in agriculture and in mining and industry, where labor is so cheap as to be readily expendable, with no need for thought as to its efficiency. Two obvious examples of this are the pre-Civil War slave economies which were the basis for plantation agriculture in the southern United States, Brazil, and the Caribbean; and the massive industrialization program in the early days of the Soviet Union or the use of convict labor in its gold, salt, and other mines both before and after the Revolution. While slave labor is unsuitable for highly skilled technical processes, this is not an insuperable problem in South Africa because of the existence of an intermediary class of operatives, mainly Coloureds and Asians, to do these jobs, and the fact that the highly technical production fields, such as computers, oil, or the auto industry, employ very few blacks and only a relatively small number of whites, often imported from overseas.

South Africans do not need a sermon on the virtues of efficiency. They pay lip-service to it constantly, while recognizing that there are much more important concerns for them. The minister of Labour has admitted that the rate of productivity per capita in South Africa is one of the lowest in the world.[171] It also seems to be falling in a number of sectors: for example, a report on Durban harbor showed that working performance there had dropped by over 40 percent in the last eight years.[172] The labor force working for the government and its agencies leads the field in inefficiency: its productivity per person is about two-thirds that of the national average.[173] Falling productivity, concurrent with a high growth rate and rising profits, cannot be discounted as an unfortunate coincidence. In fact, gross inefficiency is a luxury South Africa can afford so long as it continues to boom economically and the whites can take an increasing share of the proceeds. The *costs* of inefficiency are borne by the Africans.

The depression of African wages is probably a necessary prerequisite for the whole process, much as in Brazil (another economy with a gross disparity between the rich elite and the poor masses). There the economic "miracle" is dependent on an authoritarian government and, in particular, on the notorious "Act No. 5" which outlaws trade union organization and any other form of organized opposition. The stability obtained in this manner ensures cheap labor; all the evidence points to falling real incomes for industrial workers, together with rising unemployment for the unskilled. This situation acts as a magnet to U.S. and other foreign investment, operating in close alliance with the dominant state corporations. South Africa, Brazil, the Soviet Union, and many other "success stories" of crash economic development are evidence of the easy path to national economic growth through the use by an authoritarian regime of the population as "cannon fodder in the fight for economic achievement," as the noted economist Kuznets expressed it.[174]

South Africa is outstanding, not so much in its combination of repression, inequality, and abuse of labor, as in the explicit racial basis for this process. It has also been uniquely favored both by foreign investment in key areas by private businesses and governments (first Britain and then the United States, in gold and uranium), and by the human and natural resources of the country. Just as the Boer methods of pastoral agriculture were highly wasteful and ecologically disastrous—but still very profitable, since there was abundant land to be taken from the natives—so the mineral wealth and import-substitution industries are wasteful, allowing ample scope for inefficiency and high profits given the abundance of cheap African labor to bear the costs.[175]

Given the compatibility of a good profit margin and what amounts to slave labor, the question may validly be asked why there is any claim that economic growth is "breaking down" apartheid. The answer may lie in the superficial plausibility of the notion, based on a widespread assumption that apartheid is an old-fashioned rural ideology, rather than, as Heribert Adam described it, "possibly . . . one of the most advanced and effective patterns of rational, oligarchic domination."[176] Another reason is the vigor with which the "Oppenheimer thesis" has been pursued as a rationalization for increased investment. This idea originates with an official of Oppenheimer's Anglo-American Corporation, Mr. M.C. O'Dowd, and is also widely known as the "Green Bay Tree" theory, after an article of that title in the London *Economist*.[177] Repeating the main theme in *Harpers Magazine*, Norman Macrae argued:

... in recent years the black workers within the industrial system seem
actually to have got a slightly larger proportionate increase in real incomes than white ones.

The urban nonwhite in South Africa today ... happens to be improving his material standard of living at a faster pace than anybody else
on his continent. ... He is also generally literate. ... [178]

The three factual claims in this excerpt alone are demonstrably false.
However, the fine details of the argument have been lost in the popular-
ity of the theory that investment automatically benefits the Africans and
is inexorably breaking down apartheid. Innumerable instances could be
cited to demonstrate the uncritical acceptance of it as a rationalization
for "more of the same." The *Financial Mail,* for example, which generally
echoes the white, English-speaking community, sums up the popular version:

> Every extra rand invested is thus another ray of hope for those trapped
> on the dark side of apartheid, every extra job created is another step
> toward the peaceful transition that the inexorable process of economic
> life will impose. And, as African living standards improve, as they be-
> come more educated, as the cultural gap closes, and as their way of
> life moves close to that of Western society, so it is hoped the fear which
> explains so much that is otherwise inexplicable in this country, will sub-
> side and a realization of the true complementarity of the White and
> Black increasingly take its place.[179]

The fundamentally expedient and willfully blind nature of otherwise
rational observers' acceptance of the "Oppenheimer thesis" is quite clear.
It has certainly played a useful role for investors in dividing and confusing
the critics of financial support for South Africa, and it has the added advantage of just the right amount of moralism to distract an opposition made
up largely of rather timid moralists. It is interesting that in the days before
the public relations "corporate responsibility" campaigns, many American
businessmen talked openly of their real concerns and dismissed the "Oppenheimer thesis" as ridiculous. They argued that economic forces would
not destroy apartheid and create an integrated society, but would merely
prevent it from reaching its superficial objective of total separation of the

races, while retaining most of its vital characteristics.[180] The sudden conversion of U.S. businessmen to the theory evidently represents expediency, not conviction.

A commentator in the London *Times* sums up the attraction of the thesis:

> The idea of economic forces overcoming the political power structure, as it were by internal subversion, is immensely attractive. It offers the prospect of change and the satisfaction of moral qualms, at absolutely no cost to anybody.

> Unfortunately, the premises of this argument are not realistic, presupposing as they do a model of society in which the economy operates independently of the interests of the groups who control it.[181]

Ironically, the idea that economic trends are the ultimate determinants of political structure is fundamentally a Marxist theory. The "Oppenheimer thesis" is easily translatable into Marxist categories by claiming that the artificially chained forces of production are not allowed their full development within an outdated institutional framework or superstructure of race laws, and therefore must inevitably (or "inexorably") lead to its antithesis by bursting apart the mode of production and, through job fragmentation, the division of labor.[182] This Marxist line is directly refuted by the evolution of Western industrial democracies, where economic redistribution has been achieved, painfully, by means of political power, acquired by means of labor organization and use of the vote by urban lower-income groups, rather than the other way around. In South Africa, on the basis of the situation outlined earlier in this chapter, the urban lower-income groups are falling further behind all the time, not only in relative but also in absolute terms. The direct responsibility lies in their political powerlessness.

In fact, the last vestiges of the franchise were taken away from nonwhites during the time of great economic prosperity, when legislation was directed against them specifically in terms of their freedom of movement, organization, speech and assembly, and above all, excluding them from the negotiating process and depriving them of the right to withdraw their labor—a key element in the fight for a living wage. There is nothing automatic about improved wages and conditions, as any American labor union official could testify. They have to be fought for, with whatever means or weapons are available. In South Africa, Africans have no weapons. In fact, they are worse off now from that point of view than before the economic boom and their greatly increased contribution to the total labor force, when Africans, Asians, and Coloureds increased in representation from 64 percent in 1946 to 77 percent in 1970.[183] The real struggle for black advancement, economic as well as political, took place in the 1950s. During this period, economic growth centered around labor-intensive sectors, and black labor had a relatively strong position (compared to the 1970s) because of that and because of the bargaining power acquired during World War II, when blacks held more strategic positions in the economy due to the absence of many whites in the army, and even managed to close the black–white pay gap.

During the 1950s, African trade unions, rural Africans in the "reserves" and in national political organizations, the African National Congress, the Pan-Africanist Congress, and others waged massive campaigns to achieve mild reforms and to redistribute political and economic assets more equitably. The ruthless government reaction included banning of black political parties, arrest or exile of the leaders, breaking up of the trade union movement for Africans, and passage of repressive "national security" legislation giving unlimited powers of supervision, arrest and detention without trial, and other measures to the security police. The 1960s, with its economic boom, coincided with the most repressive period of South African history. Of the 200 racial laws now in force in South Africa, almost half were passed in the decade 1961-1971. The determination of the government to preserve white supremacy at any cost was obviously a factor in the judgment of foreign investors about South Africa's "political stability" and the consequent desirability of investing there. Again, it is very obvious that economic developments are largely determined by political power.

Although economic growth is vital to the present balance of power in South Africa and government policy is to promote growth to the fullest extent possible, this does not mean that everything is to be sacrificed to this ideal, including the groups in power. Policy is not to maximize economic growth, but to optimize it within a certain political framework that ensures the surplus is channelled in the direction of the dominant interests, the whites. As the minister of Labour said in 1970, "Important as the growth rate may be, it is not the most important factor. It does not weigh up against the position of the White worker."[184]

Again, the Marxist concepts have obscured the issue by suggesting that the central criterion on which social, economic, and political power and status is determined is class. In fact, white workers and employers have far greater interests in common than do white workers and black workers. To quote van den Berghe again:

Of greater interest yet is the lack of salience of social class in South Africa. To be sure, there exist income and occupation strata within each of the four races, but at the same time, there is a high correlation between socio-economic variables and race. Social classes in the Marxian sense of relationship to the means of production exist by definition, as they must in any capitalist country, but they are not meaningful social realities. Clearly, pigmentation, rather than ownership of land or capital, is the most significant criterion of status in South Africa.[185]

The assumption that class antagonism between white workers and employers will inevitably promote irreconcilable interests leads to a gross overevaluation of the white political infighting in South Africa. Heribert Adam has set the record straight:

. . . the analytical perspective which focuses on the essential compatibility between economic interests and white political power comes much closer to reality than the naive belief in economic growth as the magic defeat of racial discrimination. It recognizes that the disputes between industrialists and the government's supporters are not about the abolition of white power, but the distribution of its yields. . . .[186]

The opposition United party is often thought to represent pragmatic business interests against the "ideological" Nationalist party. In fact, though the tensions between the two parties, reflecting largely the antagonisms between the English and Afrikaner groups dating back to the early settlements, are real, they are limited by a tacit understanding that, as a matter of practical politics, both have a vested interest in the white monopoly of power. The fact that the Nationalists have a built-in ethnic majority, as well as a heavily gerrymandered districting system, in their favor is not enough for the United party to advocate any basic reallocation of that monopoly so as to construct an alliance with outsiders, i.e., other racial groups. Politically, the United tionalists on the Right. They strongly support the color bar and back the Nationalists in times of "national crisis"; that is whenever there is a threat to white rule. For example, during the 1960 state of emergency, the United party supported most of the government's repressive measures. It has fairly consistently continued to do so, even when "security" measures are turned against whites, as with the Schlebusch Commission of Inquiry's investigation into various church and research organizations alleged to be "subversive." When the Congress Alliance called for a three-day "stay-at-home" strike in protest against apratheid in May 1961, almost all industrial concer carried on as usual, and many threatened strikers with dismissal, despite the fact that the demonstration coincided with the official proclamation of South Africa as a republic outside the Commonwealth, a move that the English-speaking group bitterly opposed. Van den Berghe summed it up as follows:

> The fundamental tacit rule of the game between Nationalist and English leaders is that, given agreement on the issue of White domination, the English opposition (both in its political and business form) will not resort to any "dangerous" action, such as industrial shutdown, and will keep exclusively to ineffective parliamentary action, negotiation, and restrained verbal attacks in the press.[187]

A standard work on the subject of racial discrimination in rapidly industrial societies is *Industrialization and Race Relations,* a series commissioned by UNESCO. In the keynote article, Herbert Blumer summarizes the overall emerging pattern:

> There is minimal likelihood that inside the industrial structure the dominant and subordinate racial groups will enter into competitive relations with each other. The assumption of open access in such a society to one another's occupations, lines of industrial endeavor, areas of entrepreneurial opportunities, and residential areas is not true. Understandings quickly arise, frequently buttressed by legal sanctions, as to the occupations, industrial positions, business and residential areas which subordinate racial members may enter and those which he may not enter. . . .[188]

The most outstanding observation that is forced on us by empirical

evidence is that the apparatus and operations introduced by industrialisation almost invariably adjust and conform to the pattern of
race relations in the given society.[189]

Blumer argues that if an alteration or abolition of traditional racial discrimination were to come about, it would not be economic requirements
(which adapt themselves to the political and social structure), but external political factors that would have to be invoked. The irrationality of
racial prejudice does not, in itself, result in industry attempting to coun-
ter it. On the contrary, it is a rational approach to a situation of race
prejudice to take into account the fact that employment of blacks a-
bove a certain level would affront those in control and disrupt efficient
operation.[190]

Blumer argues that from the perspective of a South African industrialist, it is "rational" and wise to base decisions on other considerations
than efficiency of the industrial operation, because there are other trade-
offs that he would regard as more undesirable and that would hit his profits harder: for example, hiring black semiskilled workers at lower pay
without the approval of the white trade unions could lead to his losing
all his white workers or facing a prolonged strike by them or the enforcement of one of the network of government administrative options
against him, which could make his business less profitable or, possibly,
cost him already granted concessions or even the permission to operate
at all. Decisions to refrain from using efficient black labor, in these circumstances, would be rational ones "which are guided just as much by
the aim of efficient operation and economic return as if they took into
account only the productive capacity of the individual racial member."[191]
Therefore, while industrialization can completely "change" the social order, the race system on which it is based would remain, and industry
would conform to or even strengthen the social pattern of white supremacy.

An econometric analysis of trends in employment and income distribution in South Africa over the last twenty-five years in manufacturing
and construction tests the Blumer and O'Dowd theses. It concludes that
the O'Dowd (Oppenheimer) thesis is incorrect: economic growth does
not break down apartheid, and that the Blumer thesis—that industrialization sets up new structures that reflect the existing racial framework—is more

accurate, given certain modifications: "industrialization in South Africa i
reinforcing the system of racial discrimination and, possibly, exacerbating
it in a more complex method than outlined by Blumer."[192]

The question that naturally arises from this situation is whether the
processes in motion in South Africa—the trade-off of white interest group
siphoning off more than the total increase in national wealth, together wi
African impoverishment and social destruction—can continue as they are
indefinitely. While the elites have a surprising capacity for adaptation and
flexibility in survival and in adjusting their ideology to their economic sel
interest, the very means by which they maintain exclusive political and
economic power are provoking conditions that, although they are widely
recognized, seem to be incapable of solution by the power structure as co
stituted at present. For example, the migratory labor system has been cor
demned by the Dutch Reformed Church:

> . . . A cancer which so rages in the lives of the African people must nec
> essarily affect the whole social and religious life of all the population
> groups in our fatherland. As a result of the laws of God, the whites wil
> not be untouched by the disease that is destroying the moral life of the
> Africans.[193]

Yet even this traditional guardian of the Afrikaner soul has had no impact
on the rapid spread of this "cancer," since it suits the economic convenience of all the whites to allow it to live. Similarly, many influential business, government, and other personalities make frequent appeals for a
closing of the wage gap "to avoid disaster."[194] None of them is prepared,
however, to give up his own privilege and power. While there is universal
agreement around the world on the need to reduce inflation, experience
shows that each group in a strong bargaining position continues to press
its own wage claims and interests. The South African situation is, if anything, worse than elsewhere in the world because of the immense power
over both employers and government wielded by the white unions. Government spokesmen have repeatedly refused even to discuss wage and
price policies that might offend these supporters.

Another trend that might be viewed with alarm is the growing number
of African unemployed. Although the African proportion of the total labor force as a whole has steadily risen, the proportion of the African pop-

ulation that is economically active has fallen, from 35.5 percent in 1960 to 33.9 percent in 1970.[195] This is one reason why the supposedly greater bargaining power of Africans is a fallacy: the number of unemployed willing to replace them in the event of a labor dispute is increasing. Official statistics suggest that there were over 400,000 Africans unemployed at the time of the 1970 census, which is about 15 percent of 15.8 million economically active Africans.[196] However, the census seriously underestimated the number of African males, presumably because many of them were unemployed and living illegally in the urban areas. It also ignores the employment of African women. Professor J.L. Sadie has calculated that there were about 1.3 million, or 22.5 percent, unemployed Africans at the end of the 1960s; the National Development and Management Foundation projected around 1.9 million unemployed blacks (most of them Africans) by 1975, or nearly one third of the total economically active. Professor Jan H. Lange who, like Sadie, has access to unpublished government data, has estimated that African unemployment is rising at the rate of 100,000 per year.[197]

With mass unemployment, especially in a situation where subsistence offers no substitute for a growing number of Africans, the result is crime and violence. As Vorster himself has warned, "The greatest danger confronting South Africa is not so much the threat from outside her border, serious though that may be, but mass unemployment and disturbed race relations." The *Financial Mail,* speaking for the employers, agrees: "A rising tide of black grief and unemployment, in town and country, is the greatest threat imaginable to the white man."[198] Ironically, the threat to whites of African unemployment is often implicit in employers' rationalizations of their substandard wages, with the claim that an increase would make labor more expensive than machinery and, therefore, lead to African unemployment. This argument continues to be advanced even though, as has been shown, it is the cost of *white* labor that leads to automation.

Unemployment concentrated in the "homelands" through deportations seems to have led to very severe outbreaks of violence, especially against government informers and against communities that collaborate with officials to obtain more than their share of land. It is highly political, although routinely dismissed by the press as "faction fighting."[199] Whole areas of the Transkei were recently reported to be starving because "faction fighting" had distracted the people from agriculture.[200] Even Chief Buthelezi, who usually

takes a very moderate and proinvestment line, has warned, "when one loo
at the South African scene, one is left with no doubt about the fact that ¹
lence is on the ascent, and that chances of a non-violent change are gettin
scantier by the day."[201]

The wave of strikes in the urban areas may be seen in much the same
light. They are certainly not carefully organized moves with specific econ
omic and political demands, as the "greater bargaining power" theory wo
suggest. Their dominant features are the short duration, the apparent spo
taneity of mass walk-outs, the absence of clear-cut objectives, the general
nature of complaints about living conditions and the inability to survive o
wages earned, and, most strikingly, the refusal of any participants to be
singled out from the security of the crowd as a spokesman for fear of the
penalties attached to "agitation," "sabotage," and "subversion." Employ
have been at a loss to know who to negotiate with or what the strikers' d
mands are. In many cases, the strikes are very short, since the strikers fac
literal starvation. Concern centers on cost-of-living allowances, and work
are often forced to return to work unsatisfied. For example, the 2,000 D
ban dockworkers returned to work after being threatened with deportati
to the "homelands," following derisory pay increases; they showed their
sentiment, however, in a near-riot in which a policeman who tried to arres
one of them was attacked.

In the first three months of 1973, there were over 100 strikes in Natal
involving 100,000 workers. While many workers did obtain pay increases
of some kind, many others were summarily dismissed and deported, and
some were arrested for various offenses under the "security" laws. In one
textile mill, 2,600 workers were dismissed as soon as they went out on
strike. While the wave of strikes met with expressions of surprise and con
cern at the low black wages from all quarters in South Africa, and there
were dire predictions of future waves of labor unrest, nothing was accom
plished apart from a new "Bantu Labour Act." This theoretically permitt
African strikes, but only after going through devious negotiation channel
controlled by white unionists, who have been increasingly concerned abo
the "dangerous racial edge" of the strikes, which they believe is directed a
much against them as against the employers.[202]

The mines have been the scene of escalating violence. At the Anglo-
American gold mine of Western Deep Levels, disturbances broke out on
September 12, 1973, over "job fragmentation" and "downgrading". Af-

rican machine operators protested that their differentials over less skilled
workers had been reduced. Company officials countered later that no
specific demands were made, that there were no spokesmen and no works
committees through which negotiations could be conducted. The grievances
erupted into a demonstration, with riot police shooting into the crowd,
killing twelve miners and wounding twenty-seven. It was not untypical of
South Africa that the wage dispute occurred at the most profitable of all
Anglo-American's gold mines, whose booming profits had not added a cent
in bonuses or increased wages for African miners. Although the police
claimed that they had fired in "self-defense," a number of other sources
maintained that they had gone on a "manhunt," deliberately seeking out
and killing unarmed Africans as a reprisal for the threatened uprising.[203]
There have since been reports of a series of "faction fights" at the various
South African mines, involving many more deaths, and there are indications
that the government is instigating some of them to expel "trouble-makers,"
especially Lesotho citizens working in the mines.[204]

The economic and political future of South Africa is obscure. During
the 1960s, there were so many cries of "wolf" about impending revolution that the idea became discredited. (In the fable, of course, the wolf
did indeed arrive when nobody took the warnings seriously any longer.)
The 1960s, however, were a period of consolidation of white supremacy
and, especially, white economic power, together with unprecedented
growth that helped to cement the alliance of white interests. The vital
gold mining sector flourished, thanks to the extremely low rate of inflation which kept costs down at a time of static gold prices. The situation now evolving is quite different, in that, although the speculative rise
in the gold price has given South Africa a temporary bonanza, the specter
of accelerating inflation is threatening the continued growth of the whole
economy, according to South African economists in both the academic
and business spheres. The argument is that with inflation higher than interest rates, cash is moving away from productive investment into nonproductive hedges, such as property or shares already listed.[205] The Reserve Bank has named inflation as one of the most pressing problems facing the country. The government faces hostility from white consumers,
members of its own party, and even higher wage claims by white unionists
to preserve the increase in their real incomes. A government spokesman has
explained that price control is not being considered, since it might curb

economic growth; meanwhile, the money supply is growing at an exceptionally high rate.[206] The problem is deeply rooted in the whole power structure of South Africa, and South Africans themselves recognize that the unproductive use of African labor, the restrictive color bar, and the absence of an adequate domestic market because of African poverty are the basic causes of the country's inflation and not conducive to normal corrective measures. Inflation reached the 10-13 percent annual level in 1973, which United party leaders claim is a "threat to peace," and 15 per cent in 1975. South Africa is not alone, of course, in suffering from a hig rate of inflation; however, its key mining sector is particularly sensitive t increases in costs, and inflation is particularly severe for the already poverty-stricken majority, as described above.

Industrial performance, both in investment and output, has been particularly poor since around 1969, well below the target levels in the Econ omic Development Plan; volume of production has stagnated at under 3 percent increase per year.[207] For the year ending June 1972, the Reserve Bank reported that output was low despite surplus capacity, and that prc ductivity generally had deteriorated.[208] At the end of 1973, critical raw materials shortages began to affect a wide range of products.[209] There was a recovery in 1974, but a serious recession made itself felt by mid-1975.[210]

Many local and overseas observers see the slowing up of economic growth as an inevitable long-term result of the extreme imbalance of income distribution. A survey by the U.N. Economic Commission for Africa emphasizes the hidden costs of migrant labor and concludes that the concentration of income in a small section of the community leads to a high rate of capital formation, but later brings the economy to a standsti because of the limited internal market.[211] The various reactions from foreign and domestic investors reflect a basic uncertainty. Harry Oppenheim for example, complained: "what we are doing to my [sic] country turns up. The long term future of South Africa is bleak."[212] The Afrikaner bus ness grouping, AHI, has also complained of "a spate of bankruptcies and liquidations such as occurred after Sharpeville in 1960," which has hit its own members, relative newcomers to the business field, especially hard.[213] The capital outflow from South Africa has resulted in a renewed trend of falling foreign exchange reserves, despite the gold bonanza, toward the en of 1973.[214] Gold pays for a diminishing proportion of South Africa's growing import bill: 41.5 percent in 1966-1968, falling to an estimated

20 percent in 1980. Its proportion of GDP has fallen from 13 percent in 194 in 1945 to 10 percent in 1965 and is expected to dwindle to 2 percent in 1980.[215] Since mid-1975 the falling gold price has caused serious balance of payments problems.

The trend is serious, since South Africa's dependence on foreign trade is one of the highest in the world.[216] Exports are particularly threatened by the phasing-out of Commonwealth Preference in the British market, owing to its accession to the European Common Market, and by the soaring freight rates for the sea-borne trade on which the country is so heavily dependent.[217] In 1973, South Africa had a record trade deficit of R890.5 million, 14 percent higher than that of 1972.[218]

Foreign investors are not the only ones giving second thoughts to a commitment to South Africa's economy. Immigration from Europe, a traditional aspect of the apartheid policy representing substantial savings on local education and training costs, fell to its lowest level in ten years during 1973—less than one-half the 1966 figure.[219]

Thus, the industrial apartheid system entrenched by rapid economic growth over the last two decades is facing new bottlenecks and new strains at a time when overall economic recession in the western world has reduced the extent to which endless new capital can be imported. This coincides with the profound political changes taking place all around South Africa's frontiers, with the decolonization of Mozambique and Angola and the crisis for majority rule in Southern Rhodesia. It is symptomatic that a Durban rally celebrating Frelimo's coming to power in Mozambique was the occasion for mass arrests of young black activists throughout South Africa in the attempt to stamp out the black consciousness movement.

Black resistance to apartheid in South Africa today is to a large extent leaderless, and often takes the form of spontaneous, even random violence —faction fights in the "homelands," murderous riots in the gold mines, or criminal violence against individuals. Official repression has stamped out moderate black political parties, and made negotiation of black interests patently impossible. It is hard to estimate the extent to which the South African liberation movements with headquarters in exile—the African National Congress and the Pan Africanist Congress—are directing the internal resistance. How then can anyone predict the nature and timing of outbreaks of serious violence against the whites in South Africa? And equally, how can any observer dismiss the potential for such violence? It is not necessary to assume a successful outcome to appreciate the possibility of revolt against the white authorities and their black collaborators.

Tension in South Africa mounts with the "removal" of the most deprived elements of the population out of sight of the whites. The possibility of observing and estimating the degree of black alienation is therefore receding the time, although it can only be assumed to be on the increase. Meanwhile however, the number of blacks in "white" cities continues to increase, with many of the blacks present illegally; this adds to pressure from the whites to step up the evictions. The prospect often promoted by overseas investors that white supremacy could somehow be modified by the relaxation of w. fear of blacks because of economic prosperity, becomes daily less credible Indeed, the minority's hold on political power is a function of its economic power; there is no question of its giving up either.

The strength of the South African oligarchy and its increased effectiveness during the period of economic growth in repressing all African resistance has been noted by military experts as a result of its "high degree of ideological commitment," as a study for the Institute of Strategic Studies puts it.[220] The American militarist, Lewis Gann, states that in South Africa "the state machinery is efficient; the ruling groups are confident. Part of this confidence derives from the extraordinary growth of the country's economic potential.[221] The "ideological commitment" has most recently been described by Connie Mulder, leading Nationalist party theoretician and minister of Information, who is widely regarded as most likely to be South Africa's next prime minister:

> . . . I demand as a White that in my White Parliament, the Whites alone will rule in all circumstances and for all time. I ask no one's pardon for that.
>
> The Nationalist Government of South Africa are prepared to do everything—even to use military force if necessary—to maintain the right of the White men to control South Africa.[222]

This is not the kind of "commitment" that is prepared to relax white power in order to alleviate African unemployment and poverty, when this would mean a reduction in foreign investment and capital inflows backed by Western governments. Nor is there any sign at all that a reduction in the white monopoly of power is to be made in answer to the limits of this growth which have now become apparent.

For South Africa, there are no easy answers to the mounting prospect
of violent confrontation. However, it is apparent that an increased American commitment to the status quo, through new investment, is far more
likely to drag the United States into the confrontation than it is to effect
any reduction in its probability.

NOTES

1. *Rand Daily Mail* (Johannesburg), October 14, 1969.

2. *Foreign Investment in the Republic of South Africa* (New York:
United Nations Unit on Apartheid, ST/PSCA/SER. A/11, 1970), pp. 1-2.

3. Sean Gervasi, *Industrialization, Foreign Capital and Forced Labour
in South Africa,* (New York: U.N. Unit on Apartheid, ST/PSCA/SER. A/10,
1970), p.1.

4. M.C. Botha, July 1970, quoted in *Anti-Apartheid News* (London),
February 1971.

5. R.B. Olliver, quoted in *The Star* (Johannesburg), 4 November, 1972.

6. Martin Legassik, "South Africa: Capital Accumulation and Violence,"
in E. Laclau, ed., *Capital Accumulation and Violence* (forthcoming).

7. "Top Companies," special survey of the *Financial Mail* (Johannesburg),
March 1968.

8. Martin van den Berghe, managing Director of Interbank, at the Congress of the Afrikaanse Handels-instituut (AHI), quoted in *The Star,* 6 May,
1972.

9. *Financial Mail* 2 June, 1972.

10. Van den Berghe in *The Star,* 6 May 1972.

11. *Rand Daily Mail,* 10 February 1965.

12. *The World* (Johannesburg), 23 September 1971.

13. *The Guardian* (London), 23 October 1970.

14. *The Star,* 5 May 1973.

15. U.S. Department of Commerce, Overseas Business Reports, *Establishing a Business in Southern Africa,* OBR 70-50 (September 1970).

16. Market Research Africa, reported by the *Financial Mail,* 18 April 1969.

17. *See* the table compiled by G.M.E. Leistner, "The Role of the Non-White
Population Groups in the South African Economy," *Mercurius* 11 (September
1970).

18. *Financial Mail* 3 July 1970.

19. P.M. Landell-Mills, "Rural Income and Urban Wage Rates" in *Botswana
Notes and Records* (Gaborone), 2, 1970, pp. 80-1.

20. Former director of the South African Bureau of Census and Statistics, in

an address to the Institute of Public Health, East London; reported in *Ra*
Daily Mail, 21 September 1968.

21. Interviews by the author in the Transkei, Ciskei, Botswana, and L
July 1971. In 1970, only 34 percent of the African labor force of the Wi
tersrand Native Labour Association, covering most gold mines and some
coal mines, were from South Africa. *Report on Apartheid to the 54th In
national Labour Conference, Geneva, 3-25 June 1970* (Geneva: ILO, 197

22. John Sackur, "Casualties of the Economic Boom in South Africa,"
The Times (London), 26 April 1971.

23. A.F. Ewing, *Industry in Africa* (London: Oxford University Press,
1968), p. 21.

24. This is using the rate of exchange of R1 = $1.40. This is the stand
exchange rate used in conversions in this book, being the prevailing rate a
the time of writing. As of late 1975, the rate was R1 = $1.50

25. Market Research Africa, reported by the *Financial Mail,* 18 April

26. E. Batson, *Reports* and studies of the *Social Survey of Cape Town
No.* SP 3 (Cape Town: University of Cape Town School of Social Science
1942). For a discussion of the various "minimum" income estimates, *see*
Survey of Race Relations in South Africa, 1973 (Johannesburg: South A
rican Institute of Race Relations, 1974), pp. 197, 200.

27. Survey by the Johannesburg Non-European Affairs Department,
quoted in *Survey of Race Relations, 1969,* p. 82.

28. *Wage Survey* 1972 (Johannesburg: Bantu Wage and Productivity
Association, 1973).

29. *Rand Daily Mail,* July 24, 1972; Institute of Race Relations, Johannesburg, *Race Relations News* 34, 9 (September 1972).

30. *8th Special Report of the Director-General of the International
Labour Office* (Geneva: ILO, 1972), p. 18; *Rand Daily Mail,* 3 December
1971.

31. *Sunday Tribune* (Johannesburg), 15 July 1973.

32. Wages Commission, University of Natal, Pietermaritzburg, "A Socio-Economic Survey into the Government of Forestry Estates," published in U.S. Congress, House of Representatives, Foreign Affairs Committee, Subcommittee on Africa, *U.S. Business Involvement in Southern
Africa, Part III,* appendix 41 (Washington, D.C.: Government Printing
Office, 1973), pp. 733-8.

33. Johann G. B. Maree, "Problems of Definition and Measurement of
the Underutilization in the Traditional. Rural Sector of an Economy with
Migrant Labour (Ph.D. diss., quoted in *Survey of Race Relations, 1973,*
p. 217.

34. *Race Relations News,* March 1971.

35. P.M. Leary and J.E.S. Lewis, "Some Observations on the State of Nutrition of Infants and Toddlers in Sekhukhuniland," *South African Medical Journal, Nutrition Supplement* (December 18, 1965).

36. *The Star,* 16 December 1972.

37. Sean Gervasi, *Apartheid and Economic Growth* (New York: U.N. Unit on Apartheid Notes and Documents, No. 30/71, July 1971).

38. Study by Anthony Davenport, quoted in *Rand Daily Mail,* 21 July 1968, and the author's calculations.

39. Arndt Spandau, "Income Distribution and Economic Growth in South Africa," Vol. 1, "Theory and Analysis," (D. Comm. Thesis, University of South Africa, 1971), pp. 287, 291, 293.

40. "Top Companies."

41. Legassik, "South Africa."

42. South African Reserve Bank, *Quarterly Bulletin* (December 1973), p. 11.

43. Dr. T.W. de Jongh, governor of the Reserve Bank, quoted in *The Star,* 25 August 1973; Dr. Diedrichs, minister of Finance, in Ibid., 1 September 1973.

44. Ibid., 14 October 1972.

45. *Survey of Race Relations, 1973,* p. 196.

46. *Financial Mail,* 25 April 1975.

47. *Survey of Race Relations, 1973,* p. 196.

48. *The Star,* week of 26 January 1974.

49. *The Star,* week of 31 August 1974.

50. *The Star,* 3 May 1974.

51. F.P. Spooner, *The South African Predicament: The Economics of Apartheid* (New York: Praeger, 1961), pp. 261-2.

52. Sackur, "Casualties of the Economic Boom."

53. *African Taxation* (Johannesburg: Institute of Race Relations, 1960), p. 24.

54. *See* Barbara Rogers, *The Standard of Living of Africans in South Africa* (New York: U.N. Unit on Apartheid, Notes and Documents, No. 45/71, November 1971), p. 9.

55. Ibid., p. 10.

56. Based on the Institute of Race Relations' PDL figures for 1969 (R59.70) and for 1971 (67113)—both from the *Surveys of Race Relations, 1969,* p. 82, and *1971,* p. 117.

57. The 1971 figure was R75.80; 1972, R82.19. Cited in ibid., *1971* and *1972.*

58. *Financial Mail,* 9 February 1973.

59. The figures are: R116.38 for 1971 and R145 for 1973; *see The Star,* week of 12 May 1973.

60. *Survey of Race Relations,* 1974, pp. 232-4.

61. *Financial Mail,* 14 February 1975.

62. For the calculations involved, *see* Rogers, *Standard of Living,* pp. 10-12.

63. Ibid., p. 12.

64. *See Survey of Race Relations, 1973,* p. 202.

65. Natal Region of the Institute of Race Relations, Memorandum on PDL values in Durban, 1967, quoted in *Survey of Race Relations, 1967,* p. 105.

66. Sackur, "Casualties of the Economic Boom."

67. Union of South Africa, *Summary of the Tomlinson Report* (Pretoria: Government Printer, 1956), pp. 74-84.

68. Sir de Villiers Graaff in Republic of South Africa, *House of Assembly Debates (Hansard),* February 3, 1969, col. 28.

69. Sackur, "Casualties of the Economic Boom."

70. *The Star,* 9 June 1973.

71. Report by the Johannesburg city engineer and the manager of the Non-European Affairs Department of the Johannesburg City Council in *Rand Daily Mail,* 29 March 1968.

72. *Financial Mail,* 2 February 1968.

73. Michael Hubbard, *African Poverty in Cape Town, 1960-1970* (Johannesburg: Institute of Race Relations, 1972).

74. Spooner, *South African Predicament,* p. 170.

75. Dennis Kiley in *The Star,* 4 November 1972.

76. E.G. Malherbe, *Bantu Manpower and Education* (Johannesburg: Institute of Race Relations, 1969).

77. Alan Van Egmond, "Economic Growth, Power, and Apartheid: The Management of Change in South Africa," (M.A.L.D. thesis, Tufts University, 1973), p. 43.

78. J.L. Sadie, "Labour Supply in South Africa" (paper read at the National Labour Conference, April 29-30, 1971) and calculations by Egmond, "Economic Growth," pp. 41-46.

79. *Labour in South Africa* (Johannesburg: TUCSA, 1967).

80. Harry Goldberg, president of the Bantu Wage and Productivity Association, in the *Natal Mercury* (Durban) 22 April 1967.

81. Ian Hume, "Notes on South African Wage Movements," *South African Journal of Economics* 38, 3 (September 1970), pp. 240-56.

82. L.B. Katzen, "The Case for Minimum Wage Legislation in South Africa," *South African Journal of Economics* 29, 3 (September 1961), p. 201.

83. *Financial Mail,* 18 June 1971.

84. Republic of South Africa, Department of Labour, *9th Bi-Annual Manpower Survey*, April 30, 1971, cited in *The Star*, 17 February 1973.

85. Republic of South Africa, *Reynders Commission Report, R.P. 69/1972* (Pretoria: Government Printer, 1972), pp. 394-5.

86. Quoted in *Fortune* (July 1972): 52.

87. *The Star*, 24 March 1973.

88. Mr. B.J. Schoeman, Minister of Transport in *Debates*, March 20, 1968, cols. 2480-1.

89. *The Star*, 2 December 1972.

90. Marais Viljoen, minister of Labour, at the National Party Congress of the Cape Province, November 11, 1970, quoted in *Cape Times* (Cape Town), 12 November 1970.

91. *Power, Privilege and Poverty* (Johannesburg: Spro-Cas, Economica Commission, 1972), pp. 68-9.

92. *Financial Gazette* (Johannesburg), 10 December 1971.

93. Spro-cas, *Education*, p. 28; figures from the 1960 census.

94. *The Star*, 22 June 1971.

95. A.J.M. de Vries, acting head of the Stellenbach Bureau for Economic Research in the *Financial Mail*, 16 October 1970.

96. P.J. Riekert, *The Economy of the Republic*, Council Papers on Separate Development, R.R.19/70 (Johannesburg: Institute on Race Relations, 1970), p. 16.

97. "Top Companies."

98. Leistner, "Role of Non-White Population Groups."

99. *Financial Mail*, 26 March 1971.

100. Sadie, "Labour Supply," p. 20.

101. Sackur, "Casualties of the Economic Boom."

102. Stallard Commission, *Transvaal Province Report of the Local Government Commission* (Pretoria: T.P.I., 1922), para. 267.

103. Cited by Alex Hepple, *South Africa* (London: Pall Mall Press, 1966), p. 188.

104. *Debates*, February 6, 1967, col. 744.

105. Ibid., April 24, 1968.

106. Mr. M.C. Botha in *Debates*, February 3, 1972, col. 298.

107. P.J. van der Merwe, "Manpower Policy in South Africa," *Finance and Trade Review* 10, 2 & 3 (December 1972/June 1973), p. 104.

108. *Memorandum on the Application of Pass Laws and Influx Control* (Johannesburg: Black Sash, 1971), pp. 4-5.

109. Quoted in *The Times*, 2 April 1964; also Pierre van den Berghe, *South Africa: A Study in Conflict* (Berkeley & Los Angeles: University of California Press, 1970), pp. 193-4. A more complete description of

88   WHITE WEALTH AND BLACK POVERTY

the "pass laws" and their operation is available in the Black Sash's *Memorandum: see also* the publications by the U.N. Unit on Apartheid; Alex Hepple, *Workers Under Apartheid* (London: Defence and Aid Fund, 1969); and Muriel Horrell, *South Africa's Workers* (Johannesburg: Institute of Race Relations, 1968).

110. *Advice Office Report* (Johannesburg: Black Sash, 1972), quoted in *Survey of Race Relations, 1972*, pp. 164-5.

111. Mr. Froneman, deputy minister of Justice, Mines, and Planning, quoted in the *Rand Daily Mail*, 28 March 1969.

112. Mr. G. F. van L. Fronemen in *Debates*, February 6, 1968, col. 90.

113. *The Star*, March 7, 1970.

114. Mr. M.C. Botha in *Debates*, June 18, 1969, cols. 8379-80.

115. *The Star*, 27 January 1973.

116. Francis Wilson, *Migrant Labour in South Africa* (Johannesburg: South African Council of Churches and Spro-cas, 1972), p. 196.

117. For details, *see* Francis Wilson, *Labour in the South African Gold Mines, 1911-1969*, African Studies Series (Cambridge: Cambridge University Press, 1972), p. 184-5.

118. van den Berghe, *South Africa*, p. 193.

119. Wilson, *Migrant Labour*, pp. 156-8.

120. Ibid., p. 165.

121. Dr. P.G.J. Koornhof in *Debates*, 19 May 1971, col. 7066.

122. Wilson, *Migrant Labour*, Preface.

123. Opening address by Chief Buthelezi at the Conference "Towards Comprehensive Development in Zululand," organized by the Institute for Social Research, University of Natal, Durban, February 9-11, 1972.

124. Survey of Race Relations 1971, p. 189-90.

125. *Work Reservation*, (Pretoria: Department of Labour, 1960).

126. *Die Vaderland* (Johannesburg) August 25, 1972.

127. Quoted in Adrian Guelke and Stanley Siebert, "South Africa's Starving Work Force," *New Statesman*, London (23 March 1973), pp. 408-9.

128. Quoted in Frene Dinwala, *African Workers Strike Against Apartheid* (New York: U.N. Unit on Apartheid, Notes and Documents, No. 14/73, June 1973).

129. *See* for example the comments of the general secretary of the South African Electrical Workers Association, *Rand Daily Mail*, 16 March 1973.

130. *The Star*, 2 June 1973.

131. *See* for example Mr. Viljoen, minister of Labour, *The Star*, 9 December 1972.

132. Hepple, *Workers*. For a useful analysis of the African labour movement *see* Stanley Siebert, Adrian Guelke *Is State Control of Labour in South Africa Effective?* (London: The Mandate Trust, October 1973).

133. Reply to parliamentary question by Mrs. H. Suzman, in *Debates*, May 30, 1969, col. 6948.

134. *See* "Looking Ahead," discussion by six leading South African industrialists, in "Top Companies."

135. Mr. M. Viljoen, Minister of Labour in *Debates*, February 20, 1973, col. 1071.

136. Wilson, *Migrant Labour*, pp. 40-43, 52-53, 71.

137. Committee of sociologists, psychologists, town planners, *etc.* in a memorandum quoted in *X-Ray on Current Events in Southern Africa* (London: Africa Bureau, July 1973).

138. Mohamed Awad, *Apartheid—A Form of Slavery* (New York: U.N. Unit on Apartheid Notes and Documents, No. 37/71, August 1971).

139. *Masters and Serfs* (London: Defence and Aid Fund, 1973), pp. 26 and 31-33.

140. Wilson, *Migrant Labour*, pp. 21 and 91.

141. Van den Berghe, *South Africa*, p. 190.

142. Cape Western Regional Office of the South African Institute of Race Relations, *Report on Prison Labor,* cited in *Survey of Race Relations, 1972,* pp. 89-90.

143. Cecil Rhodes, speech in Parliament, Cape Town, 1894.

144. *Report of the Ad Hoc Committee on Forced Labour* (Geneva: International Labor Office, 1953), paras. 372-375.

145. Definitions from the *Random House Dictionary of the English Language.*

146. Mr. J.B. Vorster, 1956; quoted in Tim Smith, *The American Corporation in South Africa: An Analysis* (New York: Center for Christian Social Action, United Church of Christ, 1971), pp. 32-3.

147. Siebert and Guelke, *State Control*, pp. 4-5.

148. Legassik, "South Africa."

149. *Rand Daily Mail*, 4 March 1969.

150. *Financial Mail*, 15 March 1973.

151. Spro-cas, *Education*, p. 24.

152. Muriel Horrell, *Bantu Education up to 1968* (Johannesburg: Institute for Race Relations, 1968), also U.N. Document E/CN. 4/949, p. 149.

153. *The Star,* 7 April 1973 and 2 February 1974; "Top Companies."

154. *Financial Mail*, 8 June 1973.

155. Republic of South Africa, *Report of the Working Group Investigating New Cargo Handling and Packing Methods* (Pretoria).

156. *The Star,* week of 23 November 1974; also *Wall Street Journal* (New York), 4 November 1974.

157. "Top Companies."

158. For calculations, *see,* Republic of South Africa, *Bulletin of Statistics* (Pretoria, September 1973).

159. *The Star,* 2 June 1973.

160. *Financial Mail,* 9 February 1973.

161. *Natal Mercury,* 31 January 1973.

162. *Financial Mail,* 9 February 1973.

163. Arndt Spandau, "South African Wage Board Policy: An Alternative Interpretation," *South African Journal of Economics,* 40, 4 (December 1972): p. 385-7.

164. *Financial Mail,* 2 August 1963.

165. *Apartheid: A Socio-Historical Exposition of the Origin and Development of the Apartheid Idea* (Cape Town: Haum, 1960), p. 244.

166. Sheila van der Horst, "The Effects of Industrialisation on Race Relations in South Africa," in Guy Hunter, ed., *Industrialisation and Race Relations* (London: Oxford University Press, 1965), p. 102.

167. Irving Kaplan et al., *Area Handbook for the Republic of South Africa* (Washington, D.C.: Government Printing Office, 1971), D.A. Pamphlet 550-593, p. 570.

168. Heribert Adam, "The South African Power Elite," *Canadian Journal of Political Science* (March 1971): p. 88.

169. Van den Berghe, *South Africa,* pp. 197-200.

170. Ibid., pp. 200-2.

171. *Die Vaderland,* 1 August 1973.

172. Evidence from a shipping agency, cited in *Report of the Working Group.*

173. Dr. Cronje, cited in *The Star,* 10 March 1973.

174. Simon Kuznets, "Economic Growth and Income Inequality," *American Economic Review* (March 1955): p. 25.

175. For elaboration of this view, *see* van den Berghe, *South Africa,* pp. 183-216.

176. Heribert Adam, *Modernizing Racial Discrimination: The Dynamics of South African Politics* (Berkeley: University of California Press, 1971), p. 16.

177. M.C. O'Dowd, in an unpublished paper entitled, "The Stages of Economic Growth and the Future of South Africa."

178. Norman Macrae, "What Will Destroy Apartheid?" *Harper's Magazine* (March 1970), pp. 40-1.

179. Editorial in the *Financial Mail,* 11 September 1970.

180. Interviews by Tim Smith, *American Corporation in South Africa,* p. 3

181. Sackur, "Casualties of the Economic Boom."

182. For expansion of this idea, *see* Adam, *Modernizing Racial Discrimination,* p. 146.

183. *Time to Withdraw* (Geneva: World Council of Churches, 1973), p. 9.

184. Quoted in Cosmas Desmond, *The Discarded People* (London: Penguin Books, 1971), p. 20.

185. Van den Berghe, *South Africa,* p. 267.

186. Adam, *Discrimination,* p. 153.

187. Van den Berghe, *South Africa,* p. 208.

188. Herbert Blumer, "Industrialisation and Race Relations," in Hunter, ed., *Industrialisation and Race Relations,* p. 236.

189. Ibid., pp. 240-1.

190. Ibid., p. 233.

191. Ibid., p. 233.

192. J.G.B. Maree, "Industrialization, Income Distribution, and Employment in South Africa" (M.A. thesis, University of Sussex, Institute of Development Studies, January 1971).

193. *Report of the Committee on Current Affairs,* adopted by the General Synod of the Nederduitse Gereformeerde Kerk (October 1966), pp. 50-1.

194. *See* for example Mr. D. Etheredge, manager of the Gold Division of the Anglo-American Corporation, *Rand Daily Mail,* 19 January 1973. Mr. Etheredge said in the same speech that there was a strong case for persisting with minimum wages below the PDL for some time to come, citing the "danger" of unemployment.

195. Egmond, "Economic Growth," pp. 37-39; calculated from *Some Notes on the Economically Active Population 1960 and 1970,* R.R. 78/73 (Johannesburg: Institute of Race Relations, 1973).

196. *Cape Times,* 15 December 1972.

197. *Rand Daily Mail,* 10 May 1973.

198. *Financial Mail,* 24 April 1970.

199. Interviews by the author in the Transkei and Ciskei, July 1971. Most people are reluctant to discuss such a sensitive issue, but some well-informed sources confirmed that armed resistance to government authority is often organized by such clandestine groups as "The Hill" and others involved in the Transkei uprisings of 1960-61.

200. *Mission hospital reports to the welfare organization Kupugani,* reported in *The Star,* 16 December 1972.

201. Address by Chief Buthelezi on the unveiling of the tombstone of Chief Albert Luthuli of the ANC, July 23, 1972; reprinted in U.S. Congress, House of Representatives, Foreign Affairs Committee, Subcommittee on

Africa, *The Faces of Africa,* appendix 21 (Washington, D.C.: Government
Printing Office, 1972).

202. *The Star* (editorial), 6 December 1972.

203. There has been much published on the 1972-1973 African strikes;
space does not permit an account here. For more details, *see: The Durban
Strikes, 1973* (Durban: Institute for Industrial Education with Ravan Press,
1975); Frene Dinwala, *African Workers; The Crisis in Labour Relations,*
(Johannesburg: Spro-cas Dossier 1973); Dr. Barakat Ahmad, *Significance
of Recent Strikes of Black Workers in South Africa* (New York: U.N. Unit
on Apartheid Notes and Documents, No. 2/73, February 1973).

204. Press reports and interviews by the author in November 1973 with
officials of the government of Lesotho, which conducted its own investigation following the deaths of several citizens in the shootings.

205. Ibid.; also *The Star,* 20 April 1974.

206. *The Star,* 3 February, 12 May, 25 August, and 23 June 1973.

207. Ibid., 26 May, 21 July, 1 September 1973 and 23 February 1974.

208. "South African Survey," *Financial Times* (London), July 17, 1972.

209. South African Reserve Bank, *Annual Economic Report, 1972*
(Pretoria: Government Printer, 1973).

210. *Financial Mail,* 25 July, 1975.

211. *Viewpoint,* F.C.I. journal, quoted by Michael Chester, financial
editor, *The Star,* 9 December 1972; also, *Financial Mail,* 24 August 1973.

212. *Economic and Social Consequences of Racial Discriminatory
Practices* (New York: U.N. Economic Commission for Africa, 1963).

213. Harry F. Oppenheimer, quoted in the *Melbourne Herald,* 22 April
1970.

214. AHI, quoted in *The Guardian,* 29 March 1971.

215. *The Star,* 26 January 1974.

216. Etienne Rousseau, chairman of FVB and SASOL, quoted in the
Financial Mail, 1 May 1970.

217. *Report of the Working Group.*

218. *The Star,* 19 January 1974.

219. *Financial Mail,* 12 October 1973; *The Star,* 23 February 1974.

220. Anthony Wilkinson, *Insurgency in Rhodesia 1957-1973* (London:
Institute of Strategic Studies, 1974), p. 41.

221. Lewis H. Gann, "The Military Outlook: Southern Africa," *Military
Review* (July 1972), p. 68.

222. Connie Mulder, at an election meeting in Vereeniging, quoted in
The Star, 4 November 1972, and at a public meeting in Ladysmith, quoted
in *Civil Rights Newsletter* (Cape Town, December 18, 1972).

chapter 3 _____

THE SPECIAL ROLE OF
FOREIGN INVESTMENT IN
SOUTH AFRICA'S ECONOMY

The inflow of foreign capital into South Africa has been associated at every stage of the country's economic growth with the opening of new and vital sectors of the economy, which could never have been launched without the capital, and even more, the expertise, of overseas investors. The South African industrial and mining economy is at its present stage of prosperity because of the massive intervention of foreign capital at crucial stages in the country's history. This is true of gold, uranium, platinum, and other mining, the manufacturing sector, and emerging sectors such as "defense" industries, the auto industry, and nuclear power. After the initial, pioneering stage, the foreign enterprise tends to take on a local coloration and becomes more identified with the general economic interests of the South African white community.

The history of gold mining is the outstanding example of this process. For technical reasons both diamond mining and, more particularly, gold mining (emerging in the 1880s) required inputs of capital on a scale beyond the resources of the existing white settlers. This was particularly the case for the deep-level gold mines that began to be developed in the early 1890s. The investment capital for this purpose came from Britain and Europe, prompted by the international demand for gold as currency. This

investment was instrumental in the creation of a highly centralized structure of control in gold mining; its ownership was outside South Africa,
but its management was largely in the hands of the newly rich South Africans or European immigrants who saw their personal future in a "white
South Africa." Ownership, then, meant passively receiving dividends from
a system controlled by local segregationist interests. One of the major objectives of the mining conglomerates (de Beers in diamond mining, Rhodes
Consolidated Gold Fields in gold mining) was to reduce drastically the cos
of African labor, partly to offset the wages necessary to attract skilled
European workers. The centralization of recruitment in the Chamber of
Mines, made possible by the alignment of the various foreign interests
in the hands of a cartel of local managers, was the essential element in
the degradation of African wages in the mines. In the latter years of the
1887-1913 gold rush, over 85 percent of the shares in the industry were
in foreign hands.[1]

The control of the industry passed gradually and smoothly into local
hands, which were sufficiently cohesive to ensure that a large proportion
of capital accumulated as a result of foreign investment remained in South
Africa. One result of this tendency was the formation in 1920 of the South
African Reserve Bank, taking over from foreign mineowners the right to
sell gold and gradually establishing control over monetary policy to support local interests. By the 1930s, the local share ownership in gold mining had increased from 15 percent to 40 percent. One important element
in this was the formation of the Anglo-American Corporation by the South
African Sir Ernest Oppenheimer, in which the catalytic capital was from
the American financier John Pierpont Morgan. This corporation is now the
single largest interest group in the South African economy.[2]

ROLE OF THE STATE

From an early stage, the state played an important part in the centralization of control of capital and of labor, channelling foreign inputs according to the dictates of the dominant white interest groups. The state
corporations were founded at a surprisingly early stage in the economic
growth period: in 1923 ESCOM was formed for electricity generation,
gradually displacing the privately-owned corporation founded by the mine

The state-owned iron and steel corporation, ISCOR, was legislated into existence despite protests by foreign-allied and mining interests, after unsuccessful efforts at private production. Coal mined by cheap African labor benefitted ISCOR and ESCOM greatly. ISCOR took over major elements of foreign enterprise, acquiring control of its major competitor, Union Steel, establishing subsidiaries for ferroalloys and heavy engineering, and, since the Second World War, expanding into a huge complex, incorporating both foreign and local private capital. ISCOR and ESCOM are now major recipients of export credits (especially from Britain, in connection with ISCOR's takeover of British Steel Corporation interests in South Africa). They are also receiving large loans from the United States and Europe, through consortia set up by the European—American Banking Corporation. This follows a trend established in the interwar period, when state investment as a whole drew quite extensively on foreign—mainly British—loans.[3]

Local industrial development has also been characterized by the absorption of foreign capital for the benefit of local white interests. A series of takeovers by the state corporations of Afrikaner-based institutions was one means of bringing foreign interests under local control: Alcan Aluminum and American Motors are among the foreign interests taken over by "Afrikaner" capital, often to the benefit of their American shareholders, since these institutions enjoy privileged status in South Africa. As major new sectors are opened up, often with the U.S. government playing an important role in collaboration with U.S. private interests (in the case of gold mining and purchasing, uranium mining and treatment in the 1950s, platinum mining and key industries), the state moves in at an increasingly early stage, usually through state corporations such as the Bantu Investment Corporation, the Bantu Mining Corporation, the Industrial Development Corporation, the Nuclear Fuels Corporation, and many others. Once locked into the situation in South Africa, American companies involved in major projects can quite genuinely claim that they do not control the operation that they are financing.

The trend, overall, has been toward greater centralization of capital control, toward the interpenetration of the various sectors, and toward a partnership between foreign and local capital in all sectors. At the same time the trend of investment is clearly toward a growth in the high technology, capital intensive sectors that will make the country internationally

competitive. It is in these sectors that American investment is concentrated, and it is for this reason that the employment benefit of such investment is often very minor, and sometimes even negative as labor-intensive
production becomes uncompetitive.[4]

FOREIGN CAPITAL AND GROWTH

Foreign investment is therefore qualitatively significant, indeed vital,
in that it has determined the direction of South African economic growth
and provided the essential momentum, capital, and technology at the for-
mative stage of each major new economic sector. Even today, however, it
is also quantitatively important. The unprecedented industrial expansion
in South Africa since World War II has been associated with an equally
unprecedented inflow of foreign capital. This is often associated with the
inflow of technology, in which case even minority participation can be
decisive in an industry. The more successful local firms started to call on
a measure of foreign participation to introduce the latest technology and
production methods. Overall, the amount invested in South Africa since
the war is over three times, in monetary terms, the estimated cumulative
total of overseas investment in the whole of previous South African history.[5] Between 1946 and 1950, the average net inflow (excluding undistributed profits of foreign-owned shares) amounted to the equivalent of
almost two-fifths of gross domestic investment, with a record of nearly
three-quarters in 1947. Subsequent years showed a declining tendency as
the economy became more self-sustaining. There was an actual net outflow of capital in 1957 and 1959, which was greatly increased by the withdrawal of foreign funds after the Sharpeville massacre in 1960. The net
outflow continued up to 1964—although the United States was a significant exception to this trend, and American investors greatly reduced the
impact of this crisis.

The outflow was reversed after 1964 as a result of the exchange controls
imposed in 1961, which reduced the outflow of capital, and the attraction
of a very rapid rate of growth, which both required and attracted foreign
funds to supplement domestic savings.[6] Between 1967 and 1970, foreign
capital inflows financed 11 percent of gross domestic investment, and its
share of new investment in industry increased from 24.4 percent in 1956
to 33.7 percent in 1970.[7] During the 1960s as a whole, foreign investment

was increasing at a rate of about 5 percent a year, which is higher than the rate of increase of domestic savings in many countries providing the investment in South Africa.[8] Without this diversion of international funds toward South Africa, the unusually high rate of growth could not have been achieved.

The London *Financial Times* in 1972 outlined the importance of foreign capital to South Africa's growth: "South Africa . . . cannot, despite its mineral advantages, generate sufficient internal savings to back the growth of which it is capable. The need for foreign funds will endure for many years yet."[9] The South African Reserve Bank has itself admitted this continued and even increased dependence:

> In the long run, South Africa has to a large extent been dependent on foreign capital for development purposes . . . it is still highly dependent on foreign capital, particularly risk capital, to achieve a relatively high rate of growth.[10]

> The relatively high rate of growth experienced by the South African economy during the last three years [1969-71] was, therefore, only achieved with *an increase in the relative importance of foreign funds* in the financing of gross domestic investment.[11] [Emphasis added]

The official Franzsen Commission's third report shows that 40 percent of South Africa's industry is directly controlled from overseas, and that this degree of foreign involvement is increasing.[12] Another recent report from the Afrikaner Chamber of Commerce (AHI) states that foreign capital controls, directly or indirectly, 80 percent of all industrial production.[13]

Some major commentators have suggested that without a continued and increasing inflow of investment capital to supplement the stake already there the whole system could be in trouble. Dr. van Wyk, in *Management*, has said: "It's clear we cannot continue developing at the necessary rate without an *increasing* inflow of foreign money. [Emphasis added]"[14] Professor Friedman of the Maxwell Graduate School of Syracuse University comments:

> Foreign investment in South Africa bears an ascribable responsibility for apartheid. By no means the exclusive underwriters of apartheid, foreign investors are nonetheless to be counted among the bankers and pro-

viders of know-how for the present version of apartheid. Their roles are
to be identified directly with a major cornerstone of racial containment,
namely, economic exploitation as reflected in the high rate of earnings,
profits being repatriated regularly or ploughed back into plant expansion or new enterprises.[15]

It is a truism that throughout the world, foreign investment tends to
strengthen the government under which it operates; the tax payments a-
lone made by foreign investors amount to a substantial income for the
host government. In South Africa 41 percent of company profits accrue
directly to the state, while numerous other financial benefits are also involved, as well as the power inherent in large-scale investment that can be
directed or controlled by the state and the associated dominant local interests. It is a basic feature of U.S. government policy to encourage investment for political reasons in countries it considers allies, as a means of
building up the political strength of the governments involved. The U.S.
"aid" policy, export credits, insurance of overseas private investment, and
overall trade and investment policy are based on the belief that investment
strengthens the political structure (in many cases, it may be noted, an undemocratic structure). Among the benefits to a local system that are frequently cited are:

Bringing in new equity, production and distribution skills, market intelligence, and new and otherwise prohibitively expensive technology;

Skill in recruiting skilled personnel, abroad if necessary, and in effect-
ing modern management techniques;

Access to the world money market and sources of credit that would not
be easily available to host country entrepreneurs;

Significant increases in the productive capacity of the host country;

The continuing benefits of expensive research and development programs

The exchange control policies adopted by the South African government
since 1961 have ensured that foreign investment and its resulting benefits
are not only "locked in," but also through restrictions on their local borrowing, are forced to import fresh capital from outside to finance the expansion needed to retain competitiveness, or the expenses involved in fol-

lowing government regulations, such as the local content regulations for passenger cars, or relocation in "border areas." American companies may borrow on the Eurodollar market as well as in the United States, further promoting Western European commitments to South Africa. Many of them may operate in South Africa through British or other subsidiaries in the first place and transfer funds from these. The official restriction on local borrowing also encourages the retention of earnings in South Africa for reinvestment there, instead of repatriating all or most of the profits as dividends. Generally, therefore, government policy has obliged foreign investors to increase their stake in the country, once established there, and to import fresh sources of foreign exchange through investment and loan funds. The regulations tend to become increasingly stringent over time.

As a supplement to direct investment, loan finance has been increasingly important to South Africa since 1965,[16] and the government itself has raised very large amounts abroad to cover its budget deficits. West Germany, Italy, Switzerland, and the United States, alone, lent the government over R80 million ($112 million) between 1964 and 1968. There were also even larger amounts in unrequited intergovernmental transfers.[17] In 1970 the total government foreign debt more than doubled, from R100 million to R229 million. It nearly doubled again in 1971 to R416 million, and in February 1972 it rose to R445 million.[18] South Africa is among the top ten borrowers in the world's capital markets, and in some of them among the top five. Several U.S. banks are close to the statutory limits beyond which they may not lend to any one foreign borrower.[19]

THE IMPACT OF FOREIGN INVESTMENT ON SOUTH AFRICA'S BALANCE OF PAYMENTS

The value of South Africa's imports and exports are each equal to approximately one-quarter of gross domestic product (GDP), a relatively high figure and one that demonstrates the reliance of South Africa on foreign economic links. Foreign trade could not be much reduced in South Africa without severe dislocation to the whole economy, and exports could not easily be redirected to the domestic market, given the extreme maldistribution of purchasing power. This applies in particular to agricultural products, where despite the desperate need among the majority in

South Africa, there is no cash income with which to pay the officially regulated prices. The same is true of manufactured goods for consumer use, which, together with processed raw materials, form an increasingly important proportion of exports. Here, it is becoming difficult to find sufficient new markets because of political factors. The *Financial Times* has pointed out the significance of

> the trade boycotts and political antipathy that have shattered the dream South African industrialists used to have in the 50's of their country becoming the workshop of Africa. Even the much-vaunted outward-looking policy . . . has been singularly unsuccessful in arresting the serious downward trend in trade with Africa outside the southern sub-continent.

> Trade with African countries north of Angola, Zambia, Malawi, and Mozambique . . . has stagnated over the past ten years with exports actually declining from R24m. in 1961 to under R20m. in 1970.[20]

South Africa therefore has little flexibility in its overseas trade relations, particularly as regards imports. Those that were nonessential to the economic and political structure have been largely excluded by protectionist import controls. By 1959, the bulk of imports was already composed of manufactured goods, machinery, and transport equipment. Between then and 1968, over half of the increase in imports was made up of machinery and transport equipment alone. During the 1960s South African industry began to operate on an import-intensive basis, highly dependent on the continued supply of capital goods for the increasingly high technology and capital-intensive operations. Much of the essential equipment came from the United States, some of it backed by Export-Import Bank credits. Imports of raw materials are also becoming increasingly vital to South African industry, oil being the most obvious but by no means the only essential commodity import.

South Africa runs a chronic and growing balance of trade deficit: between 1961 and 1969, total imports increased by over 100 percent and exports by only 50 percent. There was also a significant and increasing deficit for services. Gold exports, traditionally the basis of South Africa's international economic strength, financed no more than 40 percent of imports in 1969 as compared with over 50 percent in 1961. Although obscured by steep increases in the price of gold in the early 70s, the expected fall in gold production during the decade, together with rapidly rising imports, will reduce this proportion further, and gold sales will be less and less adequate for covering the trade deficit. That this is a long-term problem not conducive to superficial relief measures was emphasized by the financial editor of *The Star* at the end of 1972: "Basically, the balance of payments situation remains haunted by the structural imbalance of the South African economy."[21]

The outlook for the second half of the 1970s appears to be one of increasing trade deficits. In 1973-1974 there was a deficit of R361 million ($505 million), following a surplus in the previous year of R503 million ($704 million). The increased trade deficit was compounded by a net outflow of capital.[22]

Apart from the structural need for capital inflows, foreign capital is in many cases tied to the purchases of the sophisticated goods necessary for South African industry, and so is quite irreplaceable from domestic sources.[23] The very thought of foreign investment faltering or drying up is enough to produce a degree of panic in the South African business community. The *Financial Mail,* for example, pointed out that in 1971 "the only thing that saved South Africa from bankruptcy was an incredibly high R385m. of capital from abroad that underpinned total foreign reserves. . . . [24] It has also warned of the danger to the South African economic structure of

> further anti-South African feeling among those businessmen upon whom South Africa heavily depends for its foreign markets and capital needs. And don't be misled by all the proud talk about this country no longer needing foreign capital. Over the past five years we ran a current deficit on our balance of payments of R563m. Where would we have been without the foreign capital to finance it? . . . Foreign capital aside, South Africa is still vitally dependent on the goodwill of foreign businessmen for its export market. . . . South Africa cannot afford to lose even its smallest markets.[25]

FOREIGN INVESTORS' REACTION
TO THE SHARPEVILLE MASSACRE

Sharpeville, the massacre of a peaceful crowd demonstrating against the pass laws in 1960, was one of a series of events in 1960-1961 that seemed at the time to mean the end of white supremacy, but that eventually was countered by a wave of repression of dissent, and recovery of the economy, that

have led some to believe that there could never be any successful resistance
The episode can perhaps be compared with the unsuccessful 1905 revoluti
in Russia, when for a time the whole structure of society was in jeopardy a
both peasants and workers staged a series of uprisings. In South Africa the
was also serious and widespread unrest in 1960-1961, which lasted longer i
the countryside than in the urban areas. If the Russian experience is valid,
would seem that economic recovery was basic to the reinforcement and ad
ditional repression by the regime for a time; its "solution" was threatened
only by a lengthy and disastrous war that destroyed the economic prosperi
built up prior to 1914.

For a while, at the height of South Africa's disturbances and the ensuin
economic crisis, the government came close to making major concessions t
popular demands. Paul Sauer, deputy prime minister and acting prime min
ister after the attack on Dr. Verwoerd, announced that the time had come
for a rethinking of South Africa's racial policies. South African (though
not, apparently, foreign) investors were reported to have been "putting
pressure on the government to make some concessions to the Negro population" to head off further disinvestment that could bankrupt the economy.[26]

The flight of capital was almost entirely due to the withdrawal by foreign shareholders in the stock market or the money market.[27] South Africa's foreign exchange reserves were cut by almost 50 percent as about
$271 million of private capital left the country in 1960 and a further $63
million in early 1961.[28] However, companies that participated directly by
establishing or expanding plants in South Africa continued to support the
economy and even made special efforts to subsidize it at the time of crisis
to protect their existing stake. This applied in particular to American investment, the overwhelming majority of it direct. Contrary to the general
pattern of net outflows between 1960 and 1964, U.S. capital provided a
net inflow for every year except 1960.[29] As the managing director of
Goodyear Tire Company (South Africa) told an interviewer, American
business in the Republic must inevitably be "counterrevolutionary" and
actively opposed to radical political change.[30]

A group of U.S. financiers obtained a vital $150 million loan for the
South African government from the International Monetary Fund, the
World Bank, Chase Manhattan Bank, First National City Bank, and a
group of American leaders not publicly identified. A key role in this loan

was played by Charles Engelhard of the United States, who was also instrumental in setting up the South Africa Foundation and the American South African Investment Corporation to attract American capital back into South Africa. He was the largest single investor in South Africa, with direct control of twenty-three major enterprises, and, through chairmanship of Rand Mines, control of many gold, uranium, and other companies. At this time, several American companies were running advertisements proclaiming their faith in South Africa's future.[31]

The total inflow of foreign capital started to revive, once it became clear that the country had substantial overseas financial backing as well as a government determined to maintain and strengthen its hold on the country at all costs. By 1970, ten years after Sharpeville, South Africa's foreign reserves had quadrupled, and American investment also quadrupled.[32] In 1970 the United States sent a record $98.4 million to South Africa. This revival of the foreign economic commitment to the Republic during the 1960s coincided with a wave of repression and elimination of dissent.

FOREIGN INVESTMENT AND SOUTH AFRICA'S MILITARY-INDUSTRIAL COMPLEX

According to the former chief of the combined combat forces:

Modern war is total: in the sense that it is carried on in all fields of endeavour, ideological, psychological, technological, economic, diplomatic as well as military. *Equally, therefore, must strategy be total and all-embracing;* it must take account of all the means available.

We are so to say 'at war'—or to put it in its widest connotation, we are 'at issue' all the time, be it in ideology, trade, diplomacy, military preparedness or in any other field.

The peace-time employment of economic strategy is fairly well understood, but it seems to me that more thought should be given to it as a method of exerting pressure. . . . According to Beaufre . . . "The decisions are obtained by creating and then exploiting a situation resulting in sufficient moral disintegration of the enemy to cause him to accept the conditions it is desirable to impose upon him."

Again, pressures in various commercial or industrial fields may help to produce the desired effect. The manipulation of international finance in order to undermine the enemy's fiscal system, to cause inflation or somehow else to create economic chaos are possibilities.[33] [Emphasis in the original]

Foreign investment is vital to the strength of South Africa's armed forces, which are used for internal repression as well as strike capability against independent African countries. In the first place, it provides essential technology, manpower, and licenses for the more sophisticated sectors of the economy related directly to defense requirements. Secondly every dollar invested in South Africa makes foreign exchange available for the purchase of weapons and equipment and also boosts the ability of the economy to support massive defense expenditure without strain.

A survey of South Africa's strategic position by Lewis H. Gann of the Hudson Institute concludes that the economic strength of the Republic is vital to the preservation of the regime from both internal and external opposition:

> South Africa is the only sub-saharan state with an industrial and logistical infrastructure strong enough to maintain an up-to-date system of land, air, and sea defense. . . .
>
> South Africa's industrial potential allows the republic to maintain a relatively strong force at relatively low cost. In 1968, South Africa's military expenditure amounted to no more than 2.5% of its GNP . . . (compared with 12.5% in Egypt and 6.3% in Algeria). . . .
>
> The Southern African bloc does not have to carry a weight of military sufficiently heavy to prevent economic progress, or to excite widespread discontent among the whites. South Africa's industrial potential has enabled the country to manufacture weapons as varied as the R.1 rifle . . . the Panhard armored vehicle, the Impala jet trainer, the Cactus air defense system (developed in cooperation with France), and computers. . . .
>
> The production of these machines simply reflects the general advances made by South Africa's manufacturing economy during the last ten years.[34]

South Africa's defense expenditure per capita is the highest in Africa. From an annual budget of $50 million in 1958, it reached $443 million in 1970 and $556 million in 1971.[35] By early 1975, government spending on defense had risen so rapidly that real outlays on infrastructure were on the decline.[36] Services for the Blacks are the most severely affected by the cuts.

The Republic, thanks to foreign companies' know-how and willing cooperation, is well on its way toward independence from foreign arms suppliers for some major items.[37] In other words, foreign investors have largely taken over the role of arms suppliers from their governments, which have imposed in various degrees an arms embargo since the early 1960s. Owing to the extreme secrecy covering all military and related issues, it is impossible to be precise about which companies are involved in supplying South Africa with arms and equipment, and which are not. However, it is known that prominent individuals in industry and finance are on the boards of subsidiaries of ARMSCOR, which manufactures defense supplies. Private industry is reported to have obtained contracts of about R70 million ($100 million) in 1972-1973 from the Department of Defense.[38] After interviews with the minister of Defense, the *Financial Mail* indicated that the electronics and engineering industries were of particular importance.[39] This field includes a number of U.S. subsidiaries.

Once operating inside South Africa, foreign companies are at liberty to perform any service for the South African government, including its defense forces, without details of the contracts necessarily being known. There is clearly no question of the U.S. government maintaining any check on U.S. subsidiaries' defense contracts in South Africa, and both the Republic's government and the U.S. company involved would have an interest in keeping the deals secret. Many of the American corporations operating in South Africa are major operators in the United States and have large defense contracts here; among them are IBM, Dow Chemical, Kaiser Aluminum; and the auto companies, GM, Ford, and Chrysler. The auto companies sell large quantities of military and other trucks and transport equipment to the South African government quite openly. In addition, their entire plants could easily be adapted to military production in any emergency, if necessary, by government requisition, in which case the companies' policies toward the government would be irrelevant; only their presence would count. According

to the *Financial Gazette:* "In times of emergency or war, each plant coul(
be turned over rapidly to the production of weapons and other strategic r
quirements for the defence of Southern Africa."[40]

Government takeover of foreign enterprises is clearly envisaged by Sou
Africa, even in times of peace. AECI, a huge company in which the Britis!
ICI has a 47.5 percent stake, guaranteeing the supply of international tec!
nical resources, has been building up munitions plants which are taken ov
at a certain point, by prior agreement, by the government.[41] This case illustrates the connections between apparent civilian operations and eventual military capacity. One observer has described the partnership betwee
foreign interests and government as

> one of the pillars on which the entire industrial structure of South Af-
> rica rests. . . . The immense resources of the world-famous British com
> pany [ICI], its technical skill and all the fruits of its research program
> have always been at the disposal of its partner [Anglo-American]. In a
> most all the new branches of the chemical industry now established in
> South Africa, ICI acted as pathfinder, so that when the time came to
> build a [munitions] factory here, most of the trials and errors insepar
> able from establishing new manufacturing techniques were over and t!
> blueprints were accurate. . . . [42]

AECI was alleged to be producing the defoliants used by the Portuguese
gainst civilians in Mozambique.[43]

Due to the refusal of U.S. companies faced with disclosure resolutions
to reveal any defense-related information, it is impossible to estimate the
American contribution that may follow this pattern. It would be rash to
assume that it does not exist, expecially in the case of ITT, GE, and the :
companies. Nor is it likely, in view of the complete censorship of any me
tion of defense operations in the South African press, that any evidence
become available to prove or to disprove the allegations of complicity th
are made from time to time. Any policy statements by the company are
little significance in the event of an emergency, in which the South Afric
government can be expected to expropriate U.S. operations in much the
same way as the illegal regime in Rhodesia has done. The minister of defense, Mr. P.W. Botha, announced in August 1973 that a register would !
compiled of all industries in South Africa that would be able to take par
in defense manufacture. In the event of an emergency, this register woul

enable the country to produce defense equipment with a minimum delay.[44]

South Africa's atomic capacity has been developed almost entirely by foreign assistance, both governmental and corporate. Through the U.S. government's commercially-oriented Atoms for Peace program, South Africa acquired a research reactor from Allis-Chalmers. It also obtained invaluable scientific and technological information, making possible the development of an enrichment process, with help from West Germany and elsewhere.[45] South African government spokesmen have repeatedly stated that they are technically capable of making an atomic weapon, and the probability that they have already done so is fairly high. Perhaps more disquieting is the prospect of very large-scale production of enriched uranium without adequate safeguards. South Africa has not signed the Nuclear Nonproliferation treaty. The construction of an enrichment plant, which is the stated intention of the government, would almost certainly require massive foreign financing, possibly by means of bank loans to state corporations.

FOREIGN INVESTMENT
AND WHITE IMMIGRATION

The program of encouraging large numbers of skilled immigrants to South Africa, largely from Britain, with a few from Europe, has been an important feature of government economic and social policy. It was originally thought that large-scale immigration, by providing the workers demanded by the expanding economy, would make it unnecessary to upgrade any black workers at all. As *Die Vaderland,* a semi-official mouthpiece for government policy, announced in 1967: "There is no question at all of skilled non-whites [sic] taking over the work of whites in white areas. . . . The government's policy of large-scale immigration has also resulted in a drastic diminution of the shortage of skilled workers."[46] A comprehensive study of the effects of the great immigration surge in 1962-1963 showed that this movement, occurring at a time of great economic revival, effectively restrained the rate of increase in money wage levels—which, as we have seen, worked largely to the disadvantage of the poorest elements of the population.[47]

In purely economic terms, these skilled immigrants were of enormous value to the South African regime. The British ambassador to South Africa estimated that each skilled person leaving Britain for South Africa

represented an initial British investment of nearly £6,000 (about $14,00
According to government spokesmen, South Africa has been receiving a-
bout R150 million worth ($210 million) of professional and technical
skills every year through its immigration drive,[49] and over the period of
Nationalist government's major effort in this field the estimated value
amounts to about R800 million ($1,120 million).[50]

There is a clear correlation between the inflow of foreign capital and
inflow of immigrants from Europe. High rates of growth, dependent on
fed by foreign capital, coincide with high levels of immigration, while lo
levels coincide with a reduced inflow. A large proportion of the advertis
and promotion of immigration is done by individual employers and som
times by white trade unions in South Africa. The American auto compa
in particular, advertise frequently for skilled workers in Europe. Chrysle
for example, recruits through its own offices in London and Switzerlan
Ford has also brought in large numbers of immigrants. American compa
also contribute to the supply of high-level management and top technol
ical expertise by transferring their own people from operations around
world to do a tour in South Africa as part of the regular career schedule

AFRICAN ATTITUDES
TOWARD FOREIGN INVESTMENT

The basic consideration relating to claims that Africans in South Africa do or do not favor foreign investment is that there is no freedom of
speech and, in particular, no free debate about the merits of foreign eco
omic intervention or withdrawal. Without open debate it is impossible t
assess clearly African attitudes toward investment. However, the general
tone has been described by the Institute of Race Relations: "It is clear t
there is much frustration and bitterness among Africans, particularly th
in urban areas, but through fear of informers and of political action, few
these people are willing to give open public expression to their feelings.'
The Terrorism Act clearly applies to any individual or organization advc
cating the withdrawal of foreign business from South Africa. Section 2(
(a) of this statute creates the offense of "participation in terroristic acti
vities" as comparable with treason. Two requirements are set forth: (a)
proof of the commission of "any act," and (b) proof of intent to endan
the maintenance of law and order. Advocating economic withdrawal cle

constitutes an "act." As far as proof of intent is concerned, this is established by presumptions under subsection (2), which provides as follows:

> If in any prosecution for an offence contemplated in subsection (1) (a) it is proved that the accused committed . . . the act alleged in the charge, and the act had or was likely to have had any of the following results in the Republic . . . namely:
>
> (d) . . . prejudice any industry or undertaking . . .
>
> (f) . . . further or encourage the achievement of any political aim . . .
>
> (1) . . . embarrass the administration of the affairs of the State. . . .
>
> the accused shall be presumed to have committed such act with intent to endanger the maintenance of law and order in the Republic unless it is proved beyond a reasonable doubt that he did not intend any of the results listed.

Clearly, advocating withdrawal could have any or all of these effects. Once the act of advocating withdrawal is proved, the presumption of the requisite intent follows, and the offense is established. Since the penalty for treason includes death, the offense under section 2 (1) (a) of the Terrorism Act is so punishable.[52]

The application of the act is at the discretion of the government and is by no means automatic. However, together with many other "security" measures, it is a powerful weapon against the free expression of opinion on foreign investment. Under conditions of surveillance and draconian penalties for careless talk, it is obviously unreasonable for company representatives fresh from the United States to conduct their own opinion surveys, especially among their own employees, as to whether they should remain in South Africa or leave.

In the light of the constant claims by interested parties that even "South African leaders" are voluntarily advocating increased investment, it is instructive to take note of a case where apartheid-based institutions opposed such investment. The South African Students' Organization (SASO) was originally hailed by the government as "separate development" in action, since black students had refused even to deal with their white counterparts. In 1971 SASO adopted a strong resolution opposing foreign investment in South Africa, saying that foreign investors made it possible for the regime to spurn world opinion while maintaining its racist policies; that they boost

South Africa's international image; and that they make it an ideal land for investment despite the social evil perpetrated by the regime.[53] The call was rapidly taken up by the Black People's Convention, a political party formed soon afterwards, which wrote to all overseas companies with interests in South Africa asking them to withdraw their business. The letters quoted a resolution passed unanimously at the first national congress in December 1972 which noted, *inter alia:*

The role played by foreign investors in maintaining and supporting the economic system of South Africa . . . ;

That foreign investors claim their presence in this country contributes towards the development of the black community;

That this claim is disputed by reality of the black experience in this country;

Therefore resolves:

To reject the involvement of foreign investors in this exploitative economic system;

To call upon foreign investors to disengage themselves from this white-controlled exploitative system.[54]

Other community-based organizations have taken similar stands. The Coloured Labour party, representing the majority of Coloured voters in local elections, has made the withdrawal of foreign investment a major priority. The party leader, Sonny Leon, has said:

A situation is developing that has become explosive. Very few of the American and British concerns are prepared to give our people responsible and meaningful positions as they have adopted the *baaskap* (white supremacy) attitude.[55]

Our call for disengagement of foreign investment is supported by a large number of organizations and movements who are against those who advocate violence as the only solution to gain political and social freedom for the millions of oppressed and underprivileged people in South Afric:

The most representative meeting of South African blacks was a three-da Black Renaissance Convention, held in Hammanskraal in December 1974 t der the sponsorship of the Christian Institute. Participants included members of all church denominations, trade unionists, professional people, and others; delegates from Coloured and Indian organizations attended. The meeting voted to appeal for a complete international boycott of the South African racist Government and racist institutions," including all economic, labor, military, educational, and cultural relations.[57]

These strong statements rejecting foreign investment by organizations that represent important communities by means of elected officials (unlike the Bantustan "leaders" approved by the government) have met with very strong reaction on the part of the government. Successive elected officials of SASO and the Black People's Convention have been jailed or banned, and both organizations have been largely destroyed by intimidation, arrests, bannings, police raids, and other punitive measures. A major trial under the Terrorism Act is in progress at the time of writing, involving officials of SASO, BPC, and other organizations. They have been detained for long periods without trial, and there have been reports of torture used on them.[58]

The pattern of action being taken specifically against those who advocate the withdrawal of foreign investment is unmistakable and extends even to white students critical of foreign investment. Given this enforced silence, the apparently uncontested appeals of government-approved officials in the "Bantustans" can be made to appear to be the voice of the people of South Africa. A concerned investigator could not accept such an illusion in good faith, given the background of punitive action against any who dare to voice public opposition to the Nationalist party line.

FOREIGN INVESTORS—SECOND THOUGHTS?

Until the recent elaboration of an "invest and reform" theory by interested public relations concerns, businessmen considering investment in South Africa in the light of social responsibility saw their choice as being either total involvement in apartheid or a refusal to participate at all. They dismissed as unrealistic sentimentality the idea of investing for the purpose of undermining the system. Neil Wates of Wates Construction (United Kingdom) created considerable controversy in business circles by his report to the board on the implications of investment—which he acknowledged could have been very profitable for Wates. Among the points he made are the following:

I will confess that I travelled to South Africa hoping that I would find good reasons for doing business there; privately I had always considered critics of South Africa to be shrill and emotional. Just as I think with hindsight it would have been totally wrong to do anything to connive with Nazism in those days (1930s), so also I think we should do nothing that would help to perpetuate *apartheid.*

. . . I must report that the idea of doing business in South Africa is totally unacceptable. We could not be true to the basic principles on which we run our business and we should lose our own integrity in the process. We should have to operate within a social climate where the colour of a man's skin is his most important attribute and where there is virtually no communication between the races; we should be locked into this system. We should have to operate within an economic climate which is designed deliberately to demoralize and to maintain an industrial helotry; we should, in turn, profit from much exploitation and ultimately end up with a vested interest in its maintenance.

We should have to operate within a legal climate where the rule of law has been abolished in favour of rule by decree, which bids fair to become a reign of terror.

The cumulative effect of all these factors in the long term must be self-defeating; within the short term it must make it impossible for ourselves individually, or as a company, to connive at anything which would serve to perpetuate a system which in the last analysis has no other justification than the preservation of white supremacy as an end in itself.[59]

It is worth noting that although Wates was not seeking publicity on this, it in fact attracted widespread attention resulting in many new contracts in Britain and a major deal in Zambia.

An attitude similar to Neil Wates' was expressed by a group of thirty-five American company presidents from the Young Presidents' Association who visited South Africa as part of an African tour. A report characterized the mood of several as "antiapartheid," and some who had considered investment in South Africa had decided against it. The leader of the mission, Mr. E. Cabell Brand of Virginia, said:

There are two reasons I have decided not to seek any business links with South Africa. First, production costs are too high. . . . Second,

and perhaps more important, I am not prepared to do business with
any company that does not pay equal pay for the job without color
prejudice.

Mr. Robert M. Ayres, an investment banker from Texas, added:

> And I would not recommend investment in South Africa on moral
> grounds. I see an affluence similar to our own—but I'm worried about
> apartheid. . . . 15 years ago things were similar in the States—and
> there's nothing worse than advice from a reformed prostitute. Still,
> I can't recommend investment here, It's a moral judgment.[60]

The motivation for second thoughts about South Africa is rarely entirely moral, of course. Social convention in the United States and elsewhere is becoming less tolerant of the more blatant kinds of racial discrimination. Questions of social acceptability, and eventual economic
pressures, would tend to reinforce the moral issue in the minds of investors. A well-known conservative columnist in the London *Financial
Times,* C. Gordon Tether, has said that the antiapartheid campaign in the
United States and Britain has been accompanied by a sharp falloff in the
inflow of foreign capital to South Africa, starting in 1970.[61] A South African business mission which at this time attempted to forge new economic
links abroad, was "politely but emphatically rejected," and a spokesman
said: "We were told in simple terms that there are easier places to do business than South Africa."[62]
     Calculations about the safety of investment are also subject to revision.
According to a survey in 1970, an increasing number of North American
businessmen consider South Africa "subject to serious jeopardy due to
racial and economic unrest," and those expecting continued expansion at
a healthy rate declined by almost half.[63] A spokesman for the U.S. Department of Commerce has commented: "I think, speaking as a businessman, that the average corporation has a real concern for the long term
political and social stability of the countries in which they operate and
there has been a degree of hesitancy to push forward with any major expansion program in South Africa, keeping that more on a holding basis."[64]
     Those making new commitments to South Africa have been increas-

ingly insisting on secrecy, particularly in the case of bank loans. Others
find the controversial nature of South Africa sufficient to deter involvement altogether. The South African *Financial Mail*'s assessment in 1975
was that "political factors do not help matters. South Africa's borrowing
potential must inevitably be smaller than that of countries which are
more widely acceptable politically."[65]

The "political risk" factor has traditionally been stated in terms of
"revolution," depicted as some kind of spontaneous combustion. While
such an explosion is considered distinctly possible—by almost unanimous
agreement among observers of South Africa—the probability is incalcu-
lable because no information is available on the extent of African resistance or its reaction to any particular events. What is not so often taken
into account in estimating the risk factor are the currently observable,
even measurable, social trends. These include: the increasing impoverishment of the African population as a whole and the increasing disparity of income between the favored minority and the majority; the
rising incidence of malnutrition, which makes people who are seemingly
apathetic unpredictable in moments of stress; the increasing numbers of
landless rural Africans; the resulting influx of "illegal" Africans into urban areas; increasing unemployment; social dislocation caused by migrant labor; the concentration of social "rejects" in camps, often with
former political prisoners and "banned" people; and the construction
of huge "barracks" or "hostels" for male workers separated from their
families, in the townships.

The analogy often used to describe risk in the South African context
is that of a lid of political repression being forced down onto a boiling
kettle of African resentment, the result being an unpredictable and inevitable explosion. This does not seem adequate as a description of the
social forces operating here, since trends toward increasing violence, especially in gang fights and individual crime, and desperation (through unemployment and impoverishment) are apparent, and a reasonable pro-
jection into the future indicates a high probability of continued deterioration. Taken together with the continuing regional tensions in which
South Africa is deeply involved—in Namibia, Southern Rhodesia and
Angola—the social and economic strains at the center of the region may
be seen as related to the direct challenge to South African rule at the
periphery. This could involve an increasing drain on the resources and
white manpower of the center. A withdrawal of some of South Africa's ex-

ternal subsidies would probably result from any economic dislocation and would also contribute to the weakening process. Recognition of this danger is probably an element in the South African government's pressure on the Rhodesian regime to come to terms with the liberation movement there. Just as economic growth, foreign capital inflows, and white immigration have tended to reinforce each other during the boom of the 1960s, a serious economic reversal would also be self-reinforcing. The Rhodesian case has already demonstrated the deterrent effect of increased conscription and the call-up of reserves on white immigration and the increase in emigration. This in turn posed serious problems for many employers faced with total or partial loss of their skilled labor force. South Africa has a long way to go before reaching Rhodesia's position, but also has more to lose and an economy already burdened with skilled labor shortages. The director of the Police Training College, Brigadier J.G. van Heerden, has said that the demand for forces on southern African frontiers is creating a national shortage of white police.[66] Intervention in the Angolan civil war clearly strained South African forces.

European immigrants to South Africa are attracted by its image as a white paradise with unlimited growth prospects. However, they are not committing themselves to the system as such and are easily deterred by economic adversity. As the former President of the Trade Union Council of South Africa (TUCSA), Mr. Tom Murray, has complained: "We want skills and know-how, but in the middle group—technicians, accountants, and so on—we can't compete any more, and the prospective immigrant decides he's better off where he is." He noted that only one-quarter or less of the total postwar immigration of 600,000 has become citizens (as compared with Australia, where over 60 percent of its immigrants have become citizens); and the ratio of citizens to temporary immigrants has fallen, from over one in three in the years 1961-1966 to barely one in seven in 1970.[67] Even those who take out citizenship retain their British nationality as well. The immigrants therefore, representing a highly skilled portion of the population, are willingly accepting the benefits of apartheid but are apparently ready to leave if their position deteriorated economically relative to that of immigrants in Australia, for example. Their departure from South Africa could represent a major problem for the maintenance of the high growth on which apartheid is structured.

Investors are taking a somewhat belated look at the exchange controls set up in June 1962. Regulations cover private and business travel by residents, emigration allowances, overseas investment, and the export of capital by nonresidents.[68] As with so much else in South Africa, applications are considered individually, and sympathetic treatment would depend on currying favor with the authorities. For this reason, any decision to disinvest would have to be carefully obscured under technical justifications to avoid antagonizing the authorities, as in the NASA case, where the decision to phase out operations was taken as a result of political pressure.

Although there are no restrictions on dividend payments abroad, nonresidents must pay a special dividend tax.[69] Foreign equity investment is automatically "blocked" once inside the country, by means of a bank endorsing shares as "nonresident." Repatriation assurances are no longer given in respect of direct, long-term investments as they were in certain instances in the early 1960s.[70] Repatriation of capital is possible through arbitrage, but this can become expensive when the discount gap widens, as it did in 1969 to 20 percent.[71] If anything happens to set off a new flight of capital, as in 1960-1961, it would become quite unrealistic to expect to withdraw anything worthwhile, both for lack of purchasers and because of the full enforcement of foreign exchange controls.

Loan funds introduced by foreign residents are also liable to be blocked at any time. If 25 percent or more of a South African company's voting securities, capital, or earnings is held or controlled by nonresidents, local borrowing requires specific Exchange Control approval.[72] American interests are particularly affected by this provision, since they are mainly in the form of wholly owned or majority-controlled subsidiaries of large corporations. As argued above, this provision aggravates the problem of U.S. concerns being unable easily to withdraw their financial commitments to South Africa once there, by obliging them to retain earnings for reinvestment there and to throw in new free funds to supplement what is blocked inside the country. The rules here are being applied with increasing stringency, as announced by the South African Reserve Bank:

> Exchange control measures also had an important influence on foreign investment, in particular the more effective application, since April 1968, of the rule limiting the local borrowing by South African subsidiaries of foreign companies to approximately 25% of the foreign capital invested

in the South African concern. This measure takes account of the fact that South Africa is still a capital importing country and that its own financial resources are not unlimited, and favours the financing of subsidiaries of foreign companies by means of new foreign investment or retained profits.[73]

The impact of controls in the short term was positive for South Africa, but in the long term is a disincentive to new investment because of the element of insecurity. The leader of a group of U.S., Canadian, and British security analysts visiting South Africa, Mr. Michael Lipper, recently commented: "If the Government does not let South Africans take money out of the country and imposes restrictions on foreign investors, how does it expect an increase in overseas investment in the economy?"[74]

Concern has also been expressed by a number of businessmen about the possibility of arbitrary action by the government against foreign capital and foreign-controlled companies, particularly in the strategic chemical, motor vehicle, and petroleum industries—all the focus of American participation. The minister of Economic Affairs, Mr. Louwrens Muller, felt obliged to offer reassurance at the opening of the AHI Congress in May 1973, stating that foreign capital was still needed and that foreign-controlled companies should not be taken over "too hastily" by South African interests.[75] However, the action taken against foreign-controlled banks has caused serious misgivings. The *Financial Mail* seems to be expressing the strong feelings of those involved about the policy decision to reduce foreign holdings in all the banks to 10 percent:

Having provided the Republic with capital, enterprise and expertise; having faithfully served the country's economic development—one for over a century; having shouldered the risks and backed their faith in our future with hard cash, they are now being kicked in the teeth. . . .

For sheer brutality, this unexpected and unnecessary sequel to the Franzsen Commission almost beggars description. . . . Indeed, to outside critics it will be seized on as much the same senseless discrimination that has come to be expected from General Amin. . . .

And if this extreme form of "expropriation" is regarded by the South African Government as necessary to protect the national interest in banking, what, overseas investors may wonder, is there to stop some less strictly controlled "strategic" industries—like vehicles and explosives, for example—from sooner or later getting the same treatment?[76]

The *Mail* sees troubled times ahead, citing labor unrest in South Africa and the strengthening of the liberation movements bringing the prospect of armed conflict in South Africa in the next decade or two. It points out that investment by foreign companies in branches and subsidiaries in South Africa has, in fact, tailed off since the boom of the late 1960s and fallen in the first four years of the 1970s.[77] In 1971 the net inflow of capital was R752 million; in 1972 it fell almost one-third to R510 million, and in 1973 it fell by over one-half to R235 million.[78] In 1973/74 there was a net outflow, particularly of short-term capital.[79] Immigration is also falling: in 1973 South Africa gained only 18,000 whites which was half the number for 1968.[80]

Certain realignments in international economic relations are having a negative impact on South Africa's overall position, and these are likely to become increasingly serious. The first is the termination of the Overseas Sterling Area in June 1972, meaning that British investors (holding almost two-thirds of foreign-owned assets in South Africa) now have to pay a premium for their investment in South Africa; this has already cut back the supply of new capital, depressed share prices in Johannesburg, and resulted in the first net outflow of capital in many years, in September 1972. The second is also related to the withdrawal of Britain from its international economic role: with accession to the European Economic Community, the Commonwealth Preferences on South African exports to Britain (one-third of total exports) are being phased out, with serious consequences for South African exports. Finally, worldwide recession and high interest rates are reducing South African exports and the availability of capital, compounding the various structural problems. The outflow of capital in 1973/74 was followed in mid-1975 by the beginning of a serious recession in South Africa, just as other industrialized countries were showing signs of recovery.[82]

The common argument that "if we don't invest, the Japanese will" is, in the light of these self-reinforcing trends toward more or less investment, not one which can be justified by empirical evidence. It is in fact more difficult for Japanese investors to acquire a stake in South Africa, since the government of Japan maintains an embargo on investment there. While Japanese businessmen are operating in South Africa, they frequently rely on American and other companies to provide essential services: Mitsubishi cars, for example, are marketed, guaranteed, and serviced by Chrysler. To see investment opportunities as invariable factors is economically unrealistic; clearly the growth of an economy, boosted by large-scale investment, provides expanding opportunities for further investment. A serious reduction in new investment would affect the expansion of the whole economy and therefore the possible return on any other operations. Investors tend to look over their shoulder to see what competitors and other businesses are doing. Success breeds success, and doubt obviously creates further doubt. If foreign investors ever seriously decided, for whatever reason, to withdraw from South Africa, it would become virtually impossible for an American business to recover any substantial portion of its original stake. In light of questions that are being raised about the economic prospects and political risks inherent in involvement in South Africa, a farsighted investor may well decide to look into his options before everybody starts to have second thoughts about his commitments in South Africa.

NOTES

1. Figures from S.H. Frankel, *Capital Investment in South Africa* (1938), quoted in Martin Legassik, "South Africa: Capital Accumulation and Violence," in E. Laclau, ed., *Capital Accumulation and Violence* (forthcoming).

2. T. Gregory, *Ernest Oppenheimer and the Economic Development of South Africa* (Oxford: Oxford University Press, 1962); *Financial Mail* Supplement, 4 July 1969.

3. Legassik, *South Africa.*

4. For documentation of the process *see* Ibid.

5. Ruth First, *Foreign Investment in Apartheid South Africa* (New York: U.N. Unit on Apartheid Notes and Documents, No. 21/72, October 1972), p. 1.

6. *Foreign Investment in the Republic of South Africa* (New York: U.N. Unit on Apartheid, ST/PSCA/SER. A/11, 1970), p. 13.

7. South African Reserve Bank, *Quarterly Bulletin* (September 1971) : 13-30; also, Mr. de Necker, in presidential address to the AHI Congress; *The Star* (Johannesburg) week of 5 May 1973.

8. Sean Gervasi, *Industrialization, Foreign Capital, and Forced Labour in South Africa* (New York: U.N. Unit on Apartheid, ST/PSCA/SER. A/10, 1970): 58.

9. *Financial Times* (London), "South Africa Survey," 17 July 1972.

10. South African Reserve Bank, *Quarterly Bulletin* September 1971): 29.

11. E.J.van der Merwe and G. van Niewkerk, "Changes in Foreign Liabilities and Assets of South Africa, 1968 to 1970," S.A. Reserve Bank, *Quarterly Bulletin* (December 1971): 17.

12. *Financial Times,* "South Africa Survey," 14 June 1971.

13. President of the AHI, quoted in *The Guardian* (London) 13 March 1973.

14. Chris van Wyk, "Foreign Capital or Bust?" *Management* (August 1971): 15.

15. Julian R. Friedman, *Basic Facts on the Republic of South Africa and the Policy of Apartheid* (New York: U.N. Unit on Apartheid Notes and Documents, No. 5/72, February 1972): 1-2.

16. Van der Merwe and van Nieuwkerk in *Quarterly Bulletin* (December 1971), p. 19.

17. Gervasi, *Industrialization* (supra.), p. 60.

18. *Financial Times,* "South Africa Survey," 17 July 1972.

19. *Financial Mail* (Johannesburg), 18 April 1975.

20. *Financial Times,* "South Africa Survey," 17 July 1972.

21. Michael Chester, financial editor, in *The Star* (Johannesburg), week of 21 October 1972.

22. Gervasi, *Industrialization,* pp. 58-63.

23. Standard Bank Group, *Annual Economic Review, South and South West Africa* (July 1971): 3.

24. *Financial Mail* (Johannesburg), 1 October. 1971.

25. Ibid., 9 June 1970.

26. *New York Times,* 7 May 1960.

27. First, *Foreign Investment,* p. 1.

28. Merton Dagut, "The South African Economy through the 60s," *Optima* (Johannesburg: Anglo-American Corporation, September 1969).

29. First, *Foreign Investment,* p. 1.

30. Tim Smith, *The American Corporation in South Africa: An Analysis* (New York: Center for Christian Social Action, United Church of Christ, 1971), p. 13.

31. Ibid., pp. 112-13.

32. First, *Foreign Investment,* p. 8.

33. C.A. Fraser, "Strategy and Strategic Action,"*Kommando* (January 1970): 7.

34. Lewis H. Gann, "The Military Outlook: Southern Africa," *Military Review* (July 1972) : 70-76.

35. Institute of Strategic Studies, *Annual Survey* (London) 1969 and 1972.

36. *Financial Mail,* 20 June 1975, quoting Reserve Bank figures.
37. P.W. Botha, minister of Defence, at Potchefstroom, quoted in *The Star,* week of 14 October 1972.
38. *Financial Mail,* December 1972.
39. Ibid.
40. *Financial Gazette,* 17 June 1967.
41. *The Times* (London) 12 February 1970.
42. A.P. Cartwright, *The Dynamite Company,* quoted in First, *Foreign Investment.*
43. *Sunday Times* (Johannesburg) 9 July 1972.
44. Johannesburg International Service in English, 1600 GMT, August 25, 1973 *(Foreign Broadcast Information Service,* Washington, D.C.).
45. Testimony by John J. Flaherty, U.S. Atomic Energy Commission, November 12, 1971, in U.S. Congress, House of Representatives, Foreign Affairs Committee, Subcommittee on Africa, (Washington, D.C.: Government Printing Office, 1972).
46. *Die Vaderland* (Johannesburg) 19 January 1967.
47. L.E. Gallaway, R.K, Koshal, and G.L. Chapin, "The Relationship Between the Rate of Change in Money Wage Rates and Unemployment Levels in South Africa," *South African Journal of Economics* 38, 4, (December 1970): 367-73.
48. Sir Arthur Snelling, British ambassador to South Africa, speech at Port Elizabeth, October 21, 1971, reported by *Agence France Press,* October 22, 1971.
49. Peter Weidman, deputy secretary for Immigration, quoted in *South African Digest,* (Pretoria: Department of Information, October 10, 1969).
50. P.G. Koornhof, deputy minister for Immigration, in *House of Assembly Debates (Hansard),* June 9, 1969, col. 7584.
51. *Survey of Race Relations in South Africa 1969* (Johannesburg: Institute of Race Relations, 1970), p. 9.
52. U.S. Congress, House of Representatives, Foreign Affairs Committee, Subcommittee on Africa, "Memorandum on the Application of Terrorism Act to Advocacy of Business Withdrawal from South Africa," *The Faces of Africa* (Washington, D.C.: Government Printing Office, 1972), appendix 24, p. 408.
53. *Rand Daily Mail* (Johannesburg) 11 April 1972.
54. Ibid., 17 January 1973.
55. *The Star,* week of 2 December 1972.
56. Ibid., week of 9 December 1972.

57. *The Times* (London), 11 January 1975.

58. *Arrests, Detentions and Trials of Members and Supporters of:SASO, BPC, BAWU, TECON* (Johannesburg: Program for Social Change, 1975), mimeographed.

59. Neil Wates, report to the Board of Directors of Wates Construction Co., reprinted as special pamphlet, *A Businessman Looks at Apartheid* (New York: U.N. Unit on Apartheid, October 1970

60. *The Star,* week of 7 August 1971.

61. *Financial Times,* (London), 29 May 1970.

62. *Rand Daily Mail,* 20 April 1970.

63. Fourth Annual Study of Attitudes of North American businessmen operating in South Africa by Market Research Africa and Business Intelligence Services; *Financial Mail,* 25 September 1970.

64. Hon. Harold B. Scott, Director of the Bureau of International Commerce, U.S. Department of Commerce, testimony to Africa Subcommittee June 15, 1971; *U.S. Business Involvement in Southern Africa*, Part I, p. 238.

65. *Financial Mail,* 18 April 1975.

66. *Rand Daily Mail,* 24 May 1973.

67. Tom Murray, past president of TUCSA, quoted in *The Guardian,* week of 4 November 1972.

68. *Quarterly Economic Review: Southern Africa* (London) Annual Supplement 1971, pp. 21-2.

69. *The Guardian,* 13 March 1973.

70. *Financial Mail,* 4 February 1972.

71. *Financial Times,* "South Africa Survey," 17 July 1972.

72. Standard Bank Group, *A Guide to Business Expansion in South Africa.*

73. Van der Merwe and van Nieuwkerk in *Quarterly Bulletin* (December 1971): 18.

74. *The Star,* week of 2 March 1975.

75. *The Star,* week of 5 May 1973.

76. *Financial Mail,* 19 October 1973.

77. Ibid.

78. *The Star,* week of 25 August 1973.

79. South African Reserve Bank, *Annual Report, 1974* (Pretoria: Government Printer, 1974), p. 21.

80. Republic of South Africa, *South African Statistics* (Pretoria: Government Printer, 1974).

81. South African Reserve Bank, *Quarterly Bulletin,* (June 1972);

82. *Financial Mail,* 25 July 1975.

chapter 4 _____

THE ROLE OF UNITED STATES INVESTMENT IN SOUTH AFRICA

THE SCOPE AND CHARACTER OF
UNITED STATES INVESTMENT

According to the U.S. Department of Commerce, "The United States government neither encourages nor discourages investments in South Africa."[1] The rapidly growing commitment of U.S. companies to South Africa, then, may be considered their own responsibility. The U.S. stake was the fastest growing of all foreign investment in South Africa during the 1960s, and its profitability was above average. It was estimated at the end of 1970 that 17 percent of all foreign assets were from the dollar area, and that the United States alone accounted for 15.8 percent.[2] This probably understates the U.S. commitment, for there is substantial investment from Canadian, British, and West European companies that are wholly or partly owned by American corporations.

The direct U.S. involvement makes it the second largest investor, after the United Kingdom, and these two represented around 70 percent of foreign investment in South Africa at the end of 1968. The U.S. stake, unlike. the British, has been largely in the new and rapidly expanding manufacturing and related sectors of the economy, which are highly profitable. Although U.S. investment was about 21 percent of the British stake in 1968, American profits were 66 percent of British profits, making the American operations over three times as profitable as British operations. In addition, the United States and Canada accounted for 27 percent of overseas investment by South Africa.[3]

There are well over three hundred U.S. corporations with direct interests in South Africa, and their investment exceeds $1 billion at current value.[4] There is very little indirect investment; the United States differs from other nations in that its companies invest directly by establishing and running their own subsidiaries.

U.S. investment has been growing rapidly over the past decade, largely through reinvestment of unusually high earnings. Between 1960 and 1971, U.S. direct involvement in South Africa increased by almost 340 percent —from $286 million to $964 million.[5] In 1973 it reached $1,240 million.[6]

While this investment increase is of exceptional importance to South Africa, the rate is not above the worldwide U.S. average. It represents only about 1.1 percent of the total foreign direct investment of the United States—a proportion that has remained more or less unchanged since 1959.[7] Investment in independent Africa is almost double that in South Africa, standing at $2,830 million in 1973.[8] The stake of independent Africa is also considerably more valuable in terms of rates of return to the United States: earnings as a proportion of total investment in 1973 were 21.8 percent for independent Africa as compared to 18.9 percent for South Africa.[9] The implications of American investment in independent Africa being double that in South Africa, and providing higher earnings, has been pointed out by President Kaunda of Zambia, who questioned which nations in Africa should be considered the friends and allies of the Western powers: "Is it independent Africa, or the minority with their dwindling market? Both from the material angle as well as from the moral angle, the West has got a case to answer there."[10]

SCOPE AND CHARACTER OF U.S. INVESTMENT

Apart from its quantitative importance, U.S. investment has a qualitative impact on South Africa far out of proportion to its financial value. Since the U.S. commitment is dominated by the giant multinational corporations, which are richer and more influential than most nation-states, their decisions about investment climates tend to have great effect in attracting other foreign investment and loan capital. The timing of the major American commitment has also been crucial. This has included the support given to South Africa in the lean years following Sharpeville, and the continued commitment of new resources at a time when black opposition parties, press, and leadership were jailed, banned, or exiled and "security" laws passed permitting virtually complete police powers of detention and interrogation without trial. During this period, urban Africans lost their residential rights, and many were deported to barren rural areas or camps. The whole apartheid system was consolidated. Expressions of abhorrence and opposition to apartheid from almost every government in the world, including the United States, seemed to be quite unrelated to the growing involvement of U.S. corporations. The apparent contradiction of government and corporate policy is reminiscent of the massive private U.S. investment in Nazi Germany in the 1930s, while the governments of the world protested the Hitler regime.

U.S. investment has been going into the most dynamic sectors of the South African economy, often providing critical technology and managerial expertise to promote industrial expansion in key areas, especially in manufacturing. By 1970, U.S. investment in this sector had grown four times since 1959, to 50 percent of the U.S. total, while mining interests, historically important, dwindled in relative terms to 10 percent. Petroleum accounted for 20 percent.[11] Specific industries, where U.S. participation is strong, are the automobile industry (where U.S. firms control nearly 50 percent of the market), petroleum (44 percent), mining, banking, chemicals, rubber, and computers. All these are strategically significant to the South African economic and political structure and, to a large extent, determine its military capability. U.S. and Canadian involvement in mining, especially in what the U.S. government calls "strategic commodities," is often in consortia involving South African mining houses, the state, and local capital. For example, the Africa Triangle Company, which operates in Namibia as well as South Africa, involves U.S. Steel with South Africa companies; Impala Platinum involves International Nickel of Canada, and Englehard; Palabora Mining involves the Newmont Mining Company and the Industrial Development Corporation (IDC); Alusaf (smelting aluminum at Richards Bay) involves Alcan Aluminum and the state-controlled Union Steel Corporation with IDC.[12]

Although U.S. investment covers over 300 firms, a major proportion of this commitment is in fact controlled by only 12 major corporations. Mobil Oil accounts for 13.6 percent of all investments, while the three auto companies, Ford, GM, and Chrysler, account for over 25 percent. It will, therefore, be relevant to consider briefly the twelve top companies operating in South Africa. These are delineated in table I.

TABLE 1

NAME OF FIRM	U.S. Owner(s)	Approximate Investments (U.S. $m.)	Approximate Percent of U.S. Total
General Motors South Africa	GM	125	14.1
Mobil Oil Southern Africa, Mobil Refining Co. S.A.	Mobil	122.5	13.5
Caltex Oil S.A.	Texaco, Standard of California	103	11.4
Ford South Africa	Ford	80-100	11.0 approx.
Standard Telephone and Cable (and other companies)	ITT	50-70	7.8 approx.
South African General Electric	GE	55	6.1
Chrysler South Africa	Chrysler	45.0	5.0
Firestone South Africa	Firestone	25-30	3.0 approx.
Goodyear Tire & Rubber Co. South Africa	Goodyear	15	1.7
Minnesota Mining and Manufacturing Co. South Africa	3M	12	1.3
IBM South Africa	IBM	8.4	1.0
Caterpillar (Africa) and Barlow Caterpillar	Caterpillar	6.4	0.7
TOTAL		648-692	72-77

Source: Compiled from data in Corporate Information Center, National Council of Churches, *Church Investments, Corporations, and Southern Africa* (New York: Friendship Press, 1973).

The concentration of half of the investment in the first four corporations, and approximately three-quarters in the first twelve, illustrates the concentration of decision-making power in a small number of very powerful boardrooms. The top companies in South Africa are among the largest multi-national corporations in the world, with no lack of alternatives for investment or socially responsible improvements. All are involved in strategically significant industries: automobiles and trucks, oil, tires, computers, electrical and communications equipment, and construction equipment. These top companies, together with others that have a significant investment in South Africa will be examined by industry category.

The Auto Industry

The three U.S. auto companies in South Africa—General Motors, Ford, and Chrysler—control among them nearly 50 percent of the automobile market in the Republic. Their presence is of major importance to the whole economy, since the motor vehicle manufacturers and assembly sector has been described by a leading South African economist as " . . . the government's chosen instrument for achieving the crucial sophistication of industrialization over the next decade, when gold mining is expected to decline in significance."[13] A Standard Bank publication elaborated in 1968:

> The motor industry is one of the most dynamic forces in the expanding South African economy. From a core of vehicle manufacture and assembly its influence extends to most manufacturing industries, to the distributive trades and to service industries. Investment in the motor industry exceeds R150 million, two-thirds of which has been made in the 1960's. . . . Its future pattern of growth will affect the whole economy.[14]

More recently, however, the motor industry has suffered severe cutbacks in sales. Although this is common to many of the industrialized countries, it is particularly serious in South Africa because of the extreme fragmentation of the already limited market. Volvo of Sweden decided in 1974 to terminate plans for new investment in South Africa, stating that "this matter is purely economical, not political."[15] Vehicle sales remained depressed in 1975.[16]

The "local content" program has been a major policy objective of the
South African government over the last few years, aiming toward an increasingly localized motor industry that would affect a significant saving
in foreign exchange, provide a stimulus to the whole economy, promote
a strong and specialized engineering sector to fill a major gap in the national industrial structure, promote a strong and specialized engineering
sector to fill a major gap in the national industrial structure, promote
military self-sufficiency, and provide the basis of an export industry.
Within days after the first regulations were issued, Ford and General
Motors announced plans involving $11.2 million and $29.4 million respectively to start building engine assembly and machining plants.[17]
The estimated increase in investment in the components industry alone,
resulting from the companies' adherence to the local content program,
was from $18.6 million in 1960 to $210 million in 1970—an increase of
over eleven times in ten years. Total capital investment in the auto industry was estimated at $430 million, of which two-thirds has taken place
since 1960, and of this, over 60 percent was American capital.[18] At
the opening of the new GM plant in 1965, Dr. Diederichs, the minister
of Economic Affairs, commented that the local content percentage reached
by General Motors had "far exceeded anything anybody ever expected or
even thought possible."[19] By 1970, the motor industry was contributing
7 percent of South Africa's gross national product (GNP), and providing
some 14 percent of the total investment in the South African economy.[20]
General Motors alone is currently buying local components and services
worth $35 million a year from 500 local suppliers.[21] Dollar sales in 1971
amounted to $1,140 million, and GM produced its millionth vehicle.[22]
Its operations are very capital-intensive; the eleventh largest company in
South Africa, GM is only forty-first in number of employees, and of
these, only 11 percent are Africans.[23]

Ford recently opened a plant in Port Elizabeth, for which it is recruiting white staff in Britain at a cost of $14 million. The plant con-
tains some of the most modern assembly equipment in the world.[24]
Such facilities are, of course, very capital-intensive, offering in this case
only 1,000 jobs. The same move was undertaken earlier by Chrysler,
which explained the rationale in an advertisement:

At Chrysler Park near Pretoria, Chrysler has built the most modern

plant in Africa and, indeed, in the whole of the Southern Hemisphere.
Why?

Because this is the fulfillment of Chrysler's faith in South Africa.
Faith so strong that it is backed by every resource that Chrysler
can bring to bear.[25]

The resources available from Chrysler, as well as from Ford and GM,
are immense by any standards. Of the "Fortune 500" top companies in
the United States which dominate those of the world, GM was the largest, Ford third, and Chrysler seventh in 1971. Their capability to provide major military services is also impressive: in 1972, GM received $225.7
million in U.S. government contracts. Its military business has amounted
to $3.3 billion since 1966, producing such strategic weapons and compon-
ents as tanks, engines and transmissions for armored personnel carriers
and howitzer artillery; the M-16 rifle, jet engines for military aircraft,
jungle warfare helicopters; and other such items.[26] Chrysler received
$94.4 million in military contracts from the U.S. government in 1972
and has produced combat vehicles (M-60 series tanks, M-615 trucks),
fire control components, projectiles, and military trucks.[27]

Ford is perhaps the most obviously useful to the South African government from the military point of view. It is one of the largest military contractors in the United States, with nearly $197 billion in contracts
in 1972. Its military products include jeeps, grenade launchers, missiles,
and communications systems for antiguerrilla warfare in Southeast Asia.[28]
One of its major customers in South Africa is the government, and an episode in the mid-1960s serves to illustrate the importance attached to cul-
tivating that relationship.[29] Ford Motor Company of South Africa is actually a wholly owned subsidiary of Ford Motor Company of Canada,
which in turn is 81 percent owned by the U.S. parent company. In 1965,
Ford South Africa bid on a contract to supply four-wheel-drive vehicles
to the South African government. The Canadian government decided the
items might violate the United Nations arms embargo and refused to issue
an export permit to Ford Canada. In retaliation, the South African government refused to allow Ford to bid on contracts for the next two years.
Since then, Ford has regained its position as a major supplier and makes
every effort to avoid conflict with the government.[30] Although the com-

pany refuses to disclose the nature of its dealings with the government
of South Africa, it is known that the Defense Force has bought seventeen
transport buses, among other things, from Ford.[31]

Historically, the automobile companies are at least consistent. A Senate
antitrust subcommittee has reported that foreign subsidiaries of GM and
Ford were principal suppliers of armored half-tracks and other war material to the Nazis during World War II.[32] A GM spokesman countered that
the Nazi government took over responsibility after the outbreak of the
war. However, the most serious allegations relate to the prewar period:
evidence was given that the auto industry was "uniquely convertible" to
war, and that GM in particular was the "essential ingredient" of both the
Allied and Nazi war efforts. The study stated that subsidiaries of General
Motors, and also of Esso (Exxon), at "the urgent request of Nazi officials"
in 1935 and 1936, joined German chemists in erecting plants to supply
the mechanized German forces with scarce synthetic leaded fuel. In 1938,
GM's chief for overseas operations was "awarded the Order of the German
Eagle (first class) by Chancellor Adolph Hitler," largely for having agreed
to build a heavy truck facility in a position invulnerable to air attack. Further, in 1938, the same award went to a Ford executive for opening a
truck plant with the "real purpose" of making "troop transport-type vehicles" for the German Army, according to U.S. Army intelligence. After
the war broke out, the various auto plants were rapidly and expertly con-
verted to manufacture bomber propulsion systems, military transports,
and armored vehicles.[33]

Heavy Engineering

The Caterpillar Tractor Company of Illinois has a total of $6.4 million
invested in South Africa, with a total employment of ninety-three people.
It imports construction and earth-moving machinery, and also has a parts-
processing and warehousing operation, and facilitates local procurement
of replacement parts for Caterpillar equipment, as well as providing essential backup service to local dealers with imported parts.[34] The local
operation does 50 percent of its business with the South African government.[35] The company's resources and experience are unique, since Caterpillar is the major manufacturer in the United States of earth-moving
and related equipment for construction, agriculture, petroleum, and other

industries and also produces diesel engines for land and marine applications. It is a true multinational corporation, with 49 percent of its sales abroad and operations and ownership around the world. It has provided construction and land-clearing equipment for the war in Southeast Asia, among other areas.[36]

General Electric is another giant with massive resources whose investment in South Africa is an estimated $55 million. Its work force is 1,500 people, of whom only 120, or 8 percent, are Africans. GE is the largest manufacturer of electrical and electronic equipment in the United States and ranks as the fourth largest company on the "Fortune 500" list for 1971. It is also the fourth largest military contractor, with over $12 billion in contracts in 1972 for products that included machine guns. jet engines, radar, missiles, and a host of others. GE views its international orientation as building the "GE World System." It has a sophisticated method for penetrating foreign markets and production processes in its line of business. It has, for example, licensing agreements with many Japanese firms, providing technological expertise in production of military and other equipment. General Electric has defended its position in South Africa, despite strong competition and a "less than satisfactory" profit picture, by saying that "the Company has recognized that broad geographical representation in the marketplaces of the world is essential to GE's long-term success."[39]

South African GE imports and manufactures a wide range of GE products, including industrial controls, locomotives, magnet wire, mobile radios, and automated drives for steel mills. Its friendly relations with the government are demonstrated by the awarding of permission to manufacture television sets to the GE consortium in the face of fierce competition and influence-mongering. In cooperation with Plessey, General Electric also has a major electronics deal with the South African government along the lines of ITT's agreement. GE is also a major supplier of locomotives for the government railroad: following the delivery of 115 locomotives for $30 million in 1970, GE was awarded a $24 million contract for another 75 locomotives. For the first order, the Export Import Bank granted South African Railways a $11.7 million loan guarantee. In this way, GE is instrumental in U.S. government financing of South African railroads, and further, its links with General Motors are apparently to be mobilized in the production of the locomotives for the second contract. GE is in a strong position to bid on such projects as the proposed nuclear power station and the uranium enrichment facility in light of its experience in the United States. In this, as in many other ways, the giant multinational U.S. corporations are irreplaceable, and the claim that any other company of any nation could replace them is misleading. One of the valuable, politically sensitive services rendered by GE was the construction of 130 control relay panels for the South African terminal of the power grid for the Cabora Bassa Dam in Mozambique. GE had tried previously to sell direct current conversion equipment for the dam, but the Export Import Bank finally declined to provide guarantees for the sale, which failed as a result.[38]

The tendency to expand U.S. commitments in South Africa is demonstrated by the Armco Steel Corporation of Ohio, which manufactures and markets steel products in a factory opened in 1961; it is the country's only producer of galvanized steel piping. Armco's total investment and number of employees in South Africa are not known, but in 1971, the company announced a $3-$4 million expansion of its plant there, as well as taking on new involvements in mining ventures, purchasing agreements, and partnerships.[39]

Industrial and farm equipment is manufactured and assembled by Deere and Co. in South Africa, which has $14 million invested for a total employment of only 360 persons. Deere has achieved a substantial increase in exports to neighboring African countries, Britain, and the United States. In 1970, exports were about $2 million.[40] Agricultural and construction equipment is also made in South Africa by the J.I. Case subsidiary of Tenneco, Inc. of Delaware, but very little is known about the extent of its involvement.[41] Case is the thirteenth largest military contractor in the United States. Similar operations are carried out by International Harvester, which in 1971 began constructing a new $2.8 million factory in Pietermaritzburg, a designated border area.[42] Ingersoll-Rand also markets industrial equipment in South Africa, and one of its tunnel machines is involved in the Orange-Fish River project, a major political priority for the South African government.[43]

Electronics and Computers

The managing director of Burroughs South Africa has commented:

"We're entirely dependent on the U.S. The economy would grind to a halt without access to the computer technology of the West. No bank could function; the government couldn't collect its money and couldn't account for it; business couldn't operate; payrolls could not be paid. Retail and wholesale marketing and related services would be disrupted.[44] During the mid-1960s, the value of the country's installed computer equipment grew by 35 percent annually. Although the rate has slackened to around 30 percent, this is still well above the European growth average of 20 percent, and it raised South Africa's per capita investment in computers from nineteenth place in 1969 to fifteenth in 1970.[45] A 1971 survey found 530 units in South Africa, and probably some government computers were uncounted in this figure. Annual sales totalled about $45-$55 million.[46] An above average rate of growth is expected during the 1970s.[47]

One of the major functions of computers is the automation of industry, which reduces the number of semiskilled and unskilled workers required in relation to investment. Computers have been officially promoted as a means of alleviating some of industry's labor problems without removing racial barriers.[48] One means by which this is facilitated is by access to international computer networks, so that shortages of computer technicians and programmers need not necessarily be a problem. In 1971, a joint U.S.-South Africa venture was initiated between the Computer Sciences Corporation and Anglo-American of South Africa to give firms access to a worldwide time-sharing network, so that they could get maximum computer usage at a lower cost than by installing their own machines.[49]

There are no South African computer firms; U.S. companies control over 70 percent of the market, with Britain's ICL taking the rest. IBM has about 50 percent of the total market, with additional involvement of National Cash Register, Burroughs, Control Data, Univac-Sperry Rand, Honeywell, Singer, and 3M. Computers are widely used by the South African government, including, of course, the defense forces. Electronic aids are vital to the South African military structure, and to its attempts to forge an alliance with the United States and other Western governments. The new surveillance center at Silvermine, a key installation in the effort to increase cooperation with the U.S. Navy, is a very advanced, computerized nerve-center for monitoring naval movements. The crucial importance of computers to the South African military has been described by the Johannesburg *Sunday Times:*

> Computers have been built into the South African Air Force early-warning systems to make it far more sophisticated and effective. . . .
>
> The computers have been incorporated in the underground nerve-center of the Northern Air Defence Sector at Devon, in the satellite radar station at Ellisras, near the Botswana border, as well as at Marieskop on the edge of the Transvaal Drakensberg escarpment commanding the Lowveld and the Portuguese border.
>
> A computer also functions in the latest equipment of the Mobile Radar Unit—a branch of the Strike Command. . . .[50]

Since only American and British computers are used in South Africa, and since all concerned have denied that their products are used by the South African military, obviously at least one company is lying.

An interesting controversy that arose recently in Britain serves to underline the way computer companies may undermine the policies of Western governments, whether their own or others. ICL, a British government-backed computer firm, sold a large computer to the Department of Bantu Affairs for the computerization of the pass law system for the Africans, and two other computers to local authorities for "Bantu administration" and "repatriation" in South Africa. Strong protests were made that British companies should not supply the means of repressing and controlling Africans and that ICL computer sales were in violation of the U.N. arms embargo against South Africa. However, IBM is supplying computers for the pass law operation in relation to Coloureds, Asians, and whites, and in reply to the suggestion that IBM had refused to tender for the "Bantu" contract because the political risks were too serious, IBM spokesmen protested vigorously that they would supply computers without restrictions to the South African government. In fact, IBM machines will be used for "Bantu control" in the future, taking over the functions of the ICL computers in many cases.[51]

The role of IBM in South Africa is a revealing case study: for an investment of $8.5 million, IBM employs just over 1,000 people, of whom 933, or 92 percent, are white. There are 84 Africans, Asians, and Coloureds employed by IBM. Since all menial work such as cleaning is done by outside contractors (a rarity in South Africa), IBM is able to point to its handful of Africans in relatively skilled positions (and therefore with an impressive-sounding average wage) as justification for its presence. However, in South African terms, the impact of IBM's activities is immense, and the status of its few African employees can be made to seem the vital issue only by a concerted public relations presentation that plays down the role of the company in strategic South African affairs. "Keeping up with our South African businessmen isn't easy. . . . We do our best to help the South African businessman grow."[52] This is the IBM image in South Africa. The full range of IBM computers and other equipment, with backup technical assistance, is available in South Africa. All sectors of the economy benefit from this invaluable service, including many of the U.S. giants' subsidiaries; customers include Anglo-American, Mobil, Caltex, Firestone, the Chamber of Mines, ITT, and many government departments, which together account for 25 percent of IBM's market. A major new installation was set up for South African Airways; computers have gone to the Department of Prisons, for keeping track of pass law offenders, among other things; to the Council for Scientific and Industrial Research (the government body that oversees all civilian as well as military research in South Africa); and to the Department of Defence. At least one IBM computer is used in Namibia, at Consolidated Diamond Mines. Volkskas, an Afrikaans bank, chose IBM to set up a national information network that "is likely to be the embryo of an international data bank system."[53] IBM has also initiated a time-sharing service with special features in Johannesburg, CALL 360, which is already used by the government. The special capabilities of the system are reported to be of assistance in financial planning and extremely useful to government planners in guiding the economy through labor shortages, job reservation, and the mass of legislative and administrative restrictions.[54] This unique "software" is matched by IBM's worldwide organization and services relating to top-flight hardware offered to South Africa. The extraordinary military capacity of IBM is, if nothing else, an illustration of its strategic position in the international economy, where it controls 70 percent of the computer business. IBM is the twentieth largest U.S. military contractor, with over $259 million in contracts in 1972. The quality of IBM's contribution, of course, is much more vital than its quantity. The company holds major contracts for data processing and handling systems for the Defense Communications Agency's National Military Command Center, and for Air Force and Army missile systems. Many IBM computers and related equipment systems are provided in the areas of navigation and aircraft guidance, which were of direct application in the war in Southeast Asia. IBM is a crucial part of the "automated battlefield" described by General Westmoreland in 1969: "I see battlefields on which we can destroy anything we locate through instant communications and the almost instantaneous application of highly lethal firepower."[55] This concept is highly relevant to antiguerrilla warfare in southern Africa, as was demonstrated in Southeast Asia, where aircraft dropped countless electronic censors, which detect movement on the ground; these sent coded signals to relay aircraft, which, in turn, signaled the information to two IBM computers, which designated targets and communicated coordinates to artillery units or aircraft for destruction. An important characteristic of the system is that it does not distinguish between civilians and military personnel.[56]

Burroughs Corporation, whose investment in South Africa is not known, employs 530 people, of whom around 92 percent are white, with 40 to 50 Asian, African, and Coloured workers. The South African operation is managed through Burroughs of Britain and accounts for 8 or 9 percent of the computers in South Africa. White skilled labor is recruited in Britain, and officials stated in an interview that most black employees perform menial tasks. The company is proud of its contribution of technical expertise to the development of South Africa.[57] Another source of computers and other electronic equipment, including automatic controls for industrial processes—an obvious African labor substitute— is Honeywell, whose total sales in South Africa during 1971 were $3.4 million. The company apparently feels that it will accomplish something for Africans by remaining in South Africa and expanding operations there. Of its 169 employees, however, 144 or 85 percent, are white.[58] Control Data Corporation, with $5 million invested, has 100 employees and over 90 percent of them are white. The South African operation markets the full range of computer systems, products, and services, and provides customer support with a variety of services to government agencies and state corporations. Control Data, like Honeywell and Burroughs, is a major military contractor in the United States.

National Cash Register (NCR, Inc.) of Dayton, Ohio, has its sixth largest subsidiary in South Africa, with an annual sales volume of $14 million on cash registers and adding machines, and at least $3-$4 million in computer revenue, providing about 14 percent of the computers in South Africa. NCR contributes major specialized training facilities to South Africa, including the construction of a $15 million complex that will house a computer center and a computer training facility; it has sent a number of employees—probably all white—abroad for highly specialized training in great demand in the South African context.[60] Sperry-Rand Corporation of New York is following the same pattern, with $5.8 million invested in South Africa. In mid-1970, a Univac division was established for the computer business, which had sold or leased over $15 million worth of equipment by the end of 1971, in addition, of course, to the sales of Vickers industrial equipment, Remington Rand business machines, and Remington personal and household equipment. The company plans to expand greatly over the next five years by reinvesting earnings and adding $20 million in outside funds. The vice-president of the U.S. company has stated that Sperry-Rand's policy is to continue and expand operations "as a good member of the community" and to increase training programs.[61]

Several other U.S. companies provide electronic instruments and services of various kinds. Motorola, Inc. owns 40 percent of Motorola South Africa, producing mobile two-way radio sets for which the major customer is the South African Police. Other products include a range of electronic measuring, recording, and control instruments. In 1971 Motorola launched a $1.3 million expansion program.[62] Addressograph-Multigraph markets a wide range of products, including typesetting equipment and tape-preparation devices.[63] Xerox controls 35 percent of the copying industry in South Africa, with assets there of about $14 million.[64] Singer produces radios and high-fidelity equipment, office and data-processing equipment, and other sensitive items.[65] Minnesota Mining and Manufacturing Company (3M) manufactures a wide range of products, including chemicals, tapes, copiers, tape recordings, photo recording and surveillance equipment, and many other things. 3M investment is estimated at $12 million. As stated in its annual report, 3M sees its international operations as potentially "the strongest bond between nations that man has ever known."[66] This presumably applies to the United States-South Africa bond.

One of the major electronics organizations, almost in a class of its own, is ITT, operating in South African through Standard Telephone and Cables, Ltd. (STC) and other subsidiaries. ITT is the ninth largest company in the world, with major military contracts in the United States totaling $257 million in 1972. Supplies include components and services for the "automated battlefield," as well as essential communications systems in innumerable military operations. This military expertise is clearly applied in South Africa. The *Financial Mail* in 1968 underlined the vital importance of the electronics industry as "a key to an up-to-date defence force." To boost the industry, the Post Office signed a ten-year "telecommunications agreement" with STC and two other firms:

> In return for guaranteed minimum purchases . . . they were asked to launch crash local manufacturing programmes, each getting the right to supply its own "specialty lines." The companies had to establish factories and increase local content yearly. . . .

> Recently all the companies have branched into manufacture of electronic components . . . and, of course, some make equipment for the SA Defence Force—about which little is known and less can be said.[67]

STC is leading the field, according to its former managing director, quoted in the same article:

> Most important of all, we're completely self-sufficient as far as trained personnel and know-how are concerned. For example, there's no local demand yet for the latest, most sophisticated electronic components like the minute integrated circuits used in computers. But we have the facilities and signers to make them or any other equipment required.[68]

ITT's affiliates have contracts with a number of government agencies, accounting for a large portion of the company's South African business. In 1970, an STC symposium on conductors was attended by representatives of the Defence Force. Because STC's role in supplying communications equipment is concerned with the police, many employees must have security clearance for their jobs. At the Simonstown Naval Base, STC provides telecommunications equipment and also recruits and employs engineers and maintenance supervisory personnel to operate it. In connection with the proposed construction of French Mirage jets in South Africa—undermining the U.S. government's arms embargo policy—ITT's French subsidiary makes flight simulators for this aircraft and the company could well get involved in direct manufacture of Mirage jets.

STC's business with the Post Office is a direct contribution to reducing the use of African labor; the relationship accounts for about half of STC's business and includes construction of postal automation machinery. When fully installed, the automation equipment is expected to reduce the unskilled staff required for sorting mail by 88 percent. ITT's South Atlantic Cable Company has played a major role in designing and constructing the Cape Town-Luanda cable link. Other subsidiary operations include two commercial colleges that are open to whites only. The company's stake in South Africa has grown rapidly in the last few years; STC alone increased its assets from $16 million to $23 million in 1970 and announced further $4 million expansion plans. ITT's total investment in South Africa is estimated at $50-$70 million.[69] The Managing Director of STC has stated that the tremendous range of products produced by it in South Africa is entirely due to ITT divisions elsewhere around the world, together with recruitment of technical personnel from England to provide skills completely lacking in South Africa.[70]

A recent study of ITT's subsidiaries in South Africa by a church organization, Spro-cas, stressed that the company's dependence on the government as a purchaser must inevitably make it very sensitive to the government's demands. It is estimated that about seventy percent of STC's products were sold to government departments. Many skilled white workers are recruited in Britain, and STC's white workers have imposed a closed shop rule excluding blacks from jobs and training. Meanwhile, ITT Supersonic has moved to a "border area" and undoubtedly is helping to bolster the government's program there, which involves the enforced deportation of an African township and a nearby African-owned area. A technical school has been set up as compensation, but basic trades, such as welding, cannot be used by Africans in the border area where the school operates. STC's alleged concern for its African workers is apparently not very deep, since negotiations with the church researchers broke down when management refused to allow a survey of its employees.[71]

STC advertisements give an indication of where its concern is concentrated:

STC manufactures in Boksburg for export to the African Continent and the rest of the Southern Hemisphere—Good for South Africa.[72]

This partnership is important to South Africa, because it enables us

to share in the tremendous progress being made in world-wide telecommunications and electronics. It enables STC (SA) to make a significant
contribution to South Africa's economy by . . . contributing substantially to our telecommunications and electronics industry . . . exporting
. . . employing 1500 people . . . saving foreign exchange.[73]

In 1970, STC announced its intention of selling a portion of its stock to
the South African public, stating that this was an indication of ITT's close
identification with South Africa.[74]

The Oil Industry

South Africa has no domestic source of oil, apart from an oil-from-coal
plant that produces only about 8 percent of its needs. The importance of
the six international oil companies operating there is of self-evident mag-
nitude, particularly in light of the Arab nations' total embargo of southern
Africa. Three of the six companies are American—Mobil, Caltex, and Esso
(Exxon); two are British—Shell and BP; and one is French—Total. The
services they supply are indispensable, including the supply of crude oil
in their own tankers, often by evading the Arab embargo; the hiring of
government-company Safmarine's tankers with the provision that they can
be requisitioned at any time; huge inputs of capital and expertise in exploration, refinery construction, and other aspects of the complex oil business; and public relations work in Western countries in behalf of South
Africa. As the *Financial Mail* said: "Without the massive resources of the
big international oil companies, applied through their South African subsidiaries, the oil industry in the Republic would not have built into a
R700 million [$900 million] business."[75] Another business observer state
"Five years ago SOEKOR [the government-established exploration cor-
poration] had practically no personnel trained in these very specialized
technical and technological fields and was largely dependent upon imported skill and experience. Today the corporation, almost completely independent of overseas consultants, maintains a high standard of work."[76]

Because of its strategic importance, the South African government has
taken special steps to bring the petroleum industry under its direct control. In 1967 it announced that all foreign-controlled oil companies, as a
condition of remaining in South Africa, would be required to: (1) make
their refineries available for processing crude products from any source,
when excess capacity was available; (2) give South Africans the oppor-

tunity to buy shares in the company; (3) ensure that the major proportion of their earnings remain in South Africa to finance the future expansion of the industry; and (4) be prepared to produce specialized petroleum and oil products required for strategic and other logistical reasons irrespective of the commercial potential. The objective of these measures was said to be the achievement of a closer identification of the international oil companies with South Africa and her interests, which would include resistance to any restriction of supplies and neutralization of the controlling influence of parent companies.[77]

As the managing director of the Industrial Development Corporation stressed, "dependence on imported fuel is one of South Africa's most vulnerable points."[78] Oil consumption is increasing by around 9 percent a year, well above the world average. The search for domestic sources is therefore seen as an economic as well as strategic necessity. In 1970, American companies were operating seventeen oil-prospecting concessions in South Africa and Namibia.[79] South African observers claim that the declining enthusiasm of foreign companies as a whole and the consequently heavier burden on the government in its search for oil was partly due to the unwillingness of American companies to participate in exploration in South Africa because of pressure at home—an indication that if the U.S. companies hold back, all the others do so as well.[80] It is also considered unlikely that oil will in fact be found in South Africa in commercial quantities, and the technical problems of off-shore drilling are formidable. It is probable, then, that some of the exploration activity is dictated not by the expectation of finding oil, but rather by the need to curry favor with the government to obtain marketing consessions. Distribution can be very lucrative indeed, for as the *Financial Mail* points out, "In South Africa, all you need are a few Africans under White supervision."[81]

Mobil, Esso, and Caltex between them control about 44% of the petroleum products market in South Africa.[82] Mobil's sales account for 20 percent of the market and more than 50 percent of U.S. investment in the petroleum industry. In early 1972, the company announced a $35 million expansion plan for its Durban refinery, which the South African government reported will save about $16 million a year in foreign exchange.[83] The new investment brings Mobil's total stake in South Africa to around $122.5 million for a total employment of only 2,852 in 1972, of which 63 percent were white. As the company's operation became increasingly automated, with massive capital investment and the computerization of its activities (through IBM), employment of African, Asian, and Coloured labor declined by 18 percent in the decade between 1962 and 1972, and the trend is continuing. It is estimated that 84 percent of the African workers receive wages below the Minimum Effective Level and half of the Coloured employees are also below this level.

Mobil has huge resources, ranking sixth on the "Fortune 500" list and producing a wide and diversified range of products, including petroleum and chemical products in which plastics and herbicides are prominent. Mobil is also a major military contractor, with over $110 million in U.S. defense contracts in 1972. It is therefore uniquely capable of supplying the specialized petroleum and oil products that may be required at any time, under the 196 regulations, by the South African government for strategic and other logistical purposes. Its identification with government policy is stressed in its advertising. A major advertisement headed "The Power Seekers" reads: "Every one is conscious of South Africa's need for its own supply of crude oil—and Mobil is doing something about it!"[84]

Caltex (owned 50 percent each by Texaco and Standard Oil of California) has a similar approach: "Ahead of Caltex lies lonely years of search and perhaps disappointment—or the discovery which will free South Africa, for all time, from dependence on outside oil supplies."[85] Caltex now has an investment in South Africa totalling $103 million at the end of 1971 and claims 20 to 21 percent of the local market as a result of a vigorous refining program. Prospecting activities cover both South Africa and Namibia on an unusually large scale. Of its 2,000 employees, 65 percent are white. No wage data has been disclosed. The potential as well as actual value of Caltex to South Africa is similar to that of Mobil: both Texaco and Socal produce a huge range of petroleum and other products; they rank eighth and twelfth respectively on the "Fortune 500" list; and they are both major military contractors in the United States, with $24.7 million and $57.5 million respectively in 1972 contracts.[86] In 1975 Caltex announced plans to invest a further $134 million in its South African refinery.

The other U.S. company involved in marketing in South Africa is Exxon, a relatively late arrival in 1963-1964. Esso SA's investment is about $16 million, and its sixty-five service and filling stations are few compared to over a 1,000 each for Mobil and Caltex. Of its 224 employees, only sixty-seven are African, representing 34 percent of the total. The company's biggest market has been the agricultural sector, where the mechanization of white farming has enabled the government to remove large numbers of African rural dwellers from productive land to the camps or "closer settlements"—landless villages in the Bantustans. Explaining the decision to invest in South Africa, Exxon's local managing director, E.R. Hartman, explained: "We did it because the Republic is a most attractive and stable country."[87] The company is exploring for viable uranium occurrences, and while reluctant to give details it has stated that "in concert with government attitudes on multinationals operating in South Africa, development of any project will either come through funds arising out of a local equity proposition or by operating in partnership with one of South Africa's mining houses."[88]

Mining and Smelting

"We've been in South Africa a long time. . . . We like it here!" may be taken as Union Carbide's motto.[89] The company is investing heavily in chromium mining and vanadium mining and smelting, as well as in marketing the variety of Union Carbide products in South Africa. The production of a new vanadium alloy for the first time outside the United States has been hailed by the press as a "big boost" to mineral exports and "should earn considerable foreign exchange" for South Africa.[90] Operations are very extensive in southern Rhodesia, also, and the company maintains strict secrecy about the size of its investments in both areas. Ranking twenty-fifth on the "Fortune 500" list, Union Carbide is also a major contractor in the United States for the Atomic Energy Commission and operates Oak Ridge, the nuclear energy facility where many South Africans have been trained.[91]

Newmont Mining is another major investor in Namibia and two South African mining operations: the O'okiep Copper Company, the second largest copper producer in South Africa, where Newmont owns 57.5 percent; and the Palabora Mining Company, the largest copper operation, in which it owns 28.6 percent. Palabora took over lands formerly designated as "native reserves" as soon as minerals were discovered there. Newmont also owns 14.5 percent of Highveld Steel and Vanadium Corporation and has a wholly owned subsidiary, Newmont South Africa, Ltd., involved in mineral exploration throughout South Africa and Namibia.[92]

United States Steel has numerous and increasing investments in South African mining and is involved in developing the ferro-chrome industry, using Rhodesian chromium ore, through Ferroalloys. U.S. Steel has been among the companies lobbying in the U.S. Congress for the continued importation of chrome and ferrochrome originating in southern Rhodesia in violation of international commitments.

Phelps Dodge, another U.S. mining company, is just beginning to invest in South Africa. In August 1972 it announced the discovery of a copper and zinc body in its concession area, purchased the land, and opened full-scale operations.[93] In 1974 the South African minister of mines stated that the projects could produce metals worth more than R1,000 million ($1.4 billion) a year.[94]

Chemicals

Phillips Petroleum owns 50 percent of Phillips Carbon Black, South Africa's only producer of the commodity used as a binding agent in the manufacture of rubber—an essential product for the automobile industry. It is exported to other areas of southern Africa.[95] Another chemical concern is Monsanto Company, which imports and markets a range of products, primarily plastic fibers and agricultural chemicals. Like many smaller distributor operations, Monsanto's effect on employment is negligible: it employs only two black workers.[96] A similar operation, run by the Dow Chemical Company, was set up in 1959 to sell mining and general industrial chemicals and plastic raw materials; its products are sold in many African countries through Dow Chemical Africa, which is based in South Africa.[97]

Rubber and Tires

Obviously of great strategic importance, like the auto industry and like it dominated by American companies, the rubber industry in South Africa is controlled by Firestone and Goodyear. Firestone is South Africa's leading tire and rubber manufacturer, and its investment, though undisclosed, is probably in the $25-30 million range. In 1969, the company began construction of a new $10 million plant at Brits, a designated "border area," which allowed reduced wages for Africans. On the *Fortune* survey of fifteen companies in South Africa, Firestone's wages were the lowest. A major multinational corporation ranking thirty-fourth on the "Fortune 500" list, Firestone is also a major producer of military products and components.[98]

Goodyear is the leading tire manufacturer in the United States and, like Firestone, makes a range of other chemicals. In 1972 it received $86 million in defense contract sales. In South Africa, where its investment totals $15 million, Goodyear produces tires and tubes as well as repair materials and other rubber products. It has refused to make any disclosures about its operations in South Africa on the ground that such revelations might jeopardize its position with customers and the South African government.[99]

Pharmaceuticals

There are numerous large U.S. investments in cosmetics and pharmaceuticals in South Africa. One of these, Colgate-Palmolive, was affected in early 1973 by the withdrawal of their labor by ten African laboratory technicians who had recently replaced white workers—at much lower rates of pay. The ten protested in a petition to the management:

We, the undersigned technical staff, having been promised rises that turned out to be unattainable, and taking cognizance of the fact that our pay ratings differ (with reference to equal pay for equal work— especially with the Lab Staff) . . . therefore resolve:

(1) That the pay rise which is rightfully ours be forthwith implemented.

. . . This resolution is a result of many futile attempts by some of us to negotiate individually but to no avail.

The employees were immediately dismissed from the company. They had been employed for up to four years each and faced immediate deportation to one of the camps or Bantustans as soon as they were unemployed.[100]

Other pharmaceutical and cosmetics companies include Johnson and Johnson, Gillette, and Pfizer and Company. Pfizer had some $6 million invested in South Africa as of 1970 and plans construction of manufacturing facilities, based largely on the success—over $5 million in profits—of its Coty cosmetic division. The company has actively participated in the border industry policy.[101] Eli Lilly, which recent acquired Elizabeth Arden cosmetics in addition to its other interests, has a $2 million investment and employs 103 people, 78 percent of them white.[102]

Photography

The photographic industry in South Africa is dominated by Kodak, which also exports to other regions of southern Africa. Its investment is around $6.5 million, and the company has built a new $1.4 million headquarters in Cape Town. Kodak is an important military contractor in the United States. Some business is done by Polaroid, through a local distributor, Frank and Hirsch. It has been accused of selling Polaroid equipment to the South African government for its Defence Force and for use in prisons and in the production of African "passes." Frank and Hirsch has also spent $100,000 on a major public relations campaign to announce a South African "experiment," following demands of U.S. employees that it withdraw from South Africa. The company's wages are still below even the Minimum Effective Level. The "experiment" has served to distract attention from the many more important aspects of the financial involvement of the United States in South Africa.

Miscellaneous Manufacturing

Weyerhauser has a $1.8 million investment in South Africa in four plants, one of them in a border area, for the manufacture and sale of corrugated shipping containers. These, of course, are a substitute for African longshoremen at the ports. Burlington Industries has a minority shareholding in Burlington Hosiery Mills. Bristol-Myers has $5-10 million invested, employing 185 whites (55 percent) out of a total of 335 workers. Owens-Illinois owns 16 percent of Consolidated Glass Works, with which it is also reported to have a technical assistance agreement. Owens trains South African personnel in the United States—almost certainly whites only—and has also helped Consolidated to obtain two unsecured loans in Euro-dollars from Barclay's Bank of the United Kingdom and Owens-Illinois Overseas Capital Corporation. General Foods has contracts with a subsidiary of the locally owned South African Breweries to operate certain pieces of manufacturing equipment for the production of General Foods products.[103]

Banking

Chase Manhattan, the third largest U.S. bank, has a 13.77 percent interest in the British-based Standard and Chartered Banking Group, which controls Standard Bank of South Africa, one of the major South African financial institutions with branches in southern Rhodesia and Namibia. The First National City Bank, second largest in the United States, now has eight branches in South Africa. Of its 230 employees, 202 are white.[104]

ATTITUDES AND BEHAVIOR OF AMERICAN BUSINESSMEN IN SOUTH AFRICA

From this survey of the major fields of U.S. investment and practices in South Africa, it is evident that the major investment is in strategically important industries; that American business plays a significant role in the reduced employment of African labor—through increased automation of industry and agriculture, as well as in its own employment policies; and that it is extremely capital-intensive—in some cases actually replacing labor with capital and in many cases employing an almost exclusively white work force. Although no attempt has been made here to analyze the detailed information on wage scales that some companies have made available, it is generally accepted that no U.S. employer in South Africa is paying all its workers above the Effective Minimum Level, with the exception of IBM, which avoids responsibility by having its menial work contracted out.[105] In reading some of the companies' statements, however, one would be given precisely the opposite impression—that they are offering major employment opportunities to Africans, paying a living wage to all their workers, are in the forefront of social progress, and have no dealings with the government.

This disparity between the public relations image and the reality, as well as the absolute refusal of many companies to disclose any substantive information, can be seen as a defensive response to the increasing momentum of criticism of their involvement in South Africa. Some illusions about the nature of U.S. business in South Africa have become current, though they have no place in objective analysis. In particular, the U.S. companies have been portrayed as social revolutionaries, martyrs to the cause of African employment and betterment, charitable institutions unconcerned with profit. We would do well to consider briefly the fact that the U.S. investor in South Africa, especially the dominant interests of the giant multinational corporations, behave there precisely as they do in any other country—that is, they act primarily, if not entirely, for the good of the company. It would be rash indeed to assume that the interests of a major multinational corporation, whose objective is to maximize profits, are the same as those of the majority population of South Africa who have no protection against the exploitation of their labor.

The U.S. State Department has described the situation as follows:

> South African society, and thus the South African economy, is built on discrimination in favor of whites, and against blacks. In this situation, U.S. subsidiaries and affiliates have generally blended into the woodwork. Many have treated their non-white workers better than man South African firms, but as a group their record has not been outstanding. They have been less progressive than the most progressive South African firms, and not rocking the boat has been an important guide to action.[106]

A South African researcher commented that U.S. businessmen "adapt very easily to the South African situation and become conditioned to South African norms with facility."[107] Even *Fortune* magazine, which was enthus astic about what it saw as "a climate ripe for change," complained: "What strikes an observer forcibly, however, is that few American subsidiaries in South Africa seem to know it—or want it."[108] In this context, the public relations industry promoting investment in South Africa seems carried away by its own rhetoric in describing U.S. companies as anything but loyal to their own profit motives and acquiescent to the apartheid system in which they operate. Indeed, a public relations leader, Mr. William Cotter of the African-American Institute, appealed, "I believe we should try to convert U.S. business into a force to break down apartheid."[109] The wishful thinking suggested here, however, was rejected by another member of the proinvestment lobby, Mr. John Chettle of the South Africa Foundation, which takes a public stance similar to that of Mr. Cotter. In his report to member companies and his South Africa executive, Mr. Chettle stated:

> The basic responsibility of a corporation is to its shareholders. The shareholders of the corporation have invested their money in the belief that the management of the corporation, within the bounds of the corporation, will attempt to ensure that these shareholders receive the best return on their investment. An international corporation is justified in concentrating on this basic tenet of capitalistic enterprise, while leaving the morality of its activities to the decisions of the government, whose foreign policy affords guidelines as to where a corporation can do business.[110]

Publicly, the South Africa Foundation vigorously promotes the idea that greater investment in South Africa will automatically destroy apartheid and, as a refinement, that foreign investors are, or are about to be, in the forefront of paternalistic labor relations. This idea of "converting" U.S. and other foreign businesses into charitable institutions and reforming forces has even been advanced by a representative of the U.S. Department of Commerce: "U.S. investors already in South Africa, or opting for a new investment there, are encouraged to adopt the maximum progressive practices possible for their non-white labor."[111] Even South African businessmen lay claim to good intentions—for others to implement. According to the findings of a business survey, 85 percent of leading businessmen declared that a major national effort should be made to raise the average wage of the African worker.[112] Evidence that they intend to translate their pious intentions into company policy is not forthcoming, however.

A study of British, North American, and South American firms showed that, without exception, the respondents still paid wages below the minimum level, and this was considered representative of the whole economy.[113] The leader of the Coloured Labour party, Sonny Leon, expressed the bitter-

ness felt among South African blacks toward the hypocrisy of foreign investors: " . . . their double standard attitudes and pious utterances are meaningless if on the one hand they, in their own countries, practice integration,
and in their activities in South Africa, do the opposite and shield behind the
apartheid system . . . because their involvement endorses the system."[114]
There is no doubt of the operation of the "double standard" in South Africa. Many U.S. investors excuse their operations there by laying great
stress on their equal pay programs *at home,* and they tend to give large
grants to civil rights organizations in the United States to dampen criticism
of their operations in South Africa. Gulf Oil and Union Carbide, perhaps
the most blatant supporters of minority regimes in Angola, South Africa,
and Rhodesia, are particularly assiduous in benevolent activities in the
United States.

It is frequently argued that while corporations will not initiate any
reform on their own volition, they can be made to do so by pressure
from groups in the United States. According to this line of thinking,
moves that are initially unacceptable to the companies—demanding withdrawal from South Africa, for instance—will eventually result in compro-
mise and reform, acceptable standards of behavior willingly adopted by
U.S. subsidiaries. This would indeed be a welcome option, if it showed
any sign whatever of being effective, in view of the time, money, and effort that has been devoted to making U.S. operations in South Africa a-
gents of reform. All the evidence, unfortunately, refutes such hopeful
claims.

The "experiment" with which Polaroid declared itself fully satisfied
was a response to demands for withdrawal—a response manifested not in
making a human standard of living the minimum for all employees, but
rather in token charitable contributions and a continuing public relations
campaign that includes setting up press conferences for Chief Buthelezi
to urge Americans to invest more. A much more honest attempt to adopt
the standards of employment one would expect of a U.S. investor has in
fact been made by an agency of the U.S. government, the National Aero-
nautics and Space Administration (NASA). Pressure came originally from
Congressman Charles C. Diggs, Jr., chairman of the House Subcommittee
on Africa, who visited the NASA tracking station in South Africa, reported
fully on its segregated facilities and employment practices, and summoned

NASA to three separate hearings on its direct responsibility for the discrimination. For each hearing, great effort was required to persuade NASA officials to appear, and long question periods about the details of NASA involvement slowly brought to light the basic facts of the situation. NASA officials finally admitted to being ashamed of the conditions at the station and decided on some reforms designed to provide primary schooling for African employees' children, to build housing for *all* workers (housing for whites already existed), and otherwise to ameliorate conditions with similarly simple measures.

During the third hearing, however, when they proudly presented their record of outstanding achievement—relative to private U.S. employers in South Africa—NASA officials were confronted with their own evidence that training programs, recruitment, hiring, promotion, wages, fringe benefits, and other aspects of the tracking station's operation remained discriminatory. A representative of the Equal Employment Opportunities Commission (EEOC) testified that practices at the tracking station would certainly not satisfy minimum U.S. employment guidelines. NASA finally stated that it was unable to meet such guidelines in the South African operation, largely because of the veto power of its partner, the government's Council for Scientific and Industrial Research (CSIR). Following a strong challenge of the South African element of NASA's budget on the floors of the House and Senate, with the threat of further hearings in the Senate, NASA suddenly announced that it would phase out its operations in South Africa over the next two years.[115] Although public justification was given in technical terms, sources close to the agency confirm that the decision to withdraw resulted from the failure of the attempt to introduce U.S. standards and the mounting political pressure focusing on the South Africa operation. This case is the most clear-cut to date of an effort to achieve meaningful "reform," an effort that merely threw into sharper relief the discrimination inherent in U.S. operations in South Africa.

The question arose in the NASA case of whether the agency was bound by U.S. legislation against discrimination in employment in its operations outside the United States. An EEOC memorandum stated that, as a matter of principle, courts have held that actions taken in foreign jurisdictions by foreign subsidiaries of domestic corporations are reachable under U.S. law. In the case of Title VII of the Civil Rights Act, under which EEOC operates, the provision is specifically excluded from application to the employment of aliens outside the United States.[116] However, American employees of companies operating in South Africa are covered by Title VII, and it is quite possible that the statute could be invoked in the case of multinational corporations sending their own executives and technicians to subsidiaries in South Africa. It has been argued elsewhere that U.S. law on nondiscrimination in employment is, in fact, applicable to all the activities of multinational corporations abroad.[117]

The general principle, in law and in ethics, is clear: South African subsidiaries of U.S. corporations are not justified in their practice of applying employment policies at variance with standards applicable to them in the United States. It should be obvious, but seems to require repetition, that this does not necessarily mean paying U.S. wage levels where these are very different from local wage standards. It does mean the application of such standards as nondiscrimination on grounds of race or other such criteria in wages, fringe benefits, and other employment policies and practices.

The corporations have specifically rejected this nondiscrimination principle and have even practiced nonmandatory discrimination, often through ignorance of what South African law actually says, as well as observing discriminatory laws with particular scrupulousness. The director of the South African Productivity and Wage Association, J. Ferreira, speaking specifically about subsidiaries of U.S. corporations, has complained: "I doubt if some of them know, or care, that there's no law in South Africa that says you can't pay a black man any amount you wish."[118] An article in *Fortune* magazine quoted a senior American diplomat with long experience in South Africa to the effect that ignorance of the law and unwillingness to explore legal possibilities are especially prevalent in subsidiaries headed by American nationals

They believe the myths. They think everything is illegal, and they don't care. South Africa may be just another step in their corporate careers, and their stay is likely to be a short one. Their success is measured in the short-run terms of this year's profits, and many of them are simply not interested in anything else. They come and they go, and what happens after they leave South Africa does not concern them. "They're semi-skilled barbarians," concludes the American diplomat. "They have little minds. . . ."[119]

A Chrysler official in Detroit has explained, "We try to play it even straighter than the local citizens will with their government in order to get certain privileges."[120] A spokesman for 3M has written: "We tend to follow local customs and refrain, as foreigners, from attempting to impose our own views and policies—which, in our case as an American company, involve the active promotion of the equal-opportunity-employer concept."[121]

Some proponents of the theory that investment in South Africa will automatically break down apartheid have argued that it is in the interest of the U.S. companies to raise their African wages to promote greater productivity and competitiveness. However, a detailed study by the Economics Commission of Spro-cas, which contained many eminent academic and business economists, indicated that foreign firms would not have a natural interest in black advancement. They would not find it useful to train blacks to perform jobs from which they are, or might be, excluded through white union protectionism. They would arouse the hostility of the local white groups, especially white workers on whose goodwill they are most dependent. It is also not true, according to this report, to suggest that providing "satisfactory" wages and conditions would be profitable to them in reducing the high labor turnover from which they all suffer, since this can be done at a fraction of the cost by providing marginally better conditions than those offered by other firms. Indeed, many U.S. companies claim to pay "above average" rates, but they are still below the Minimum Effective Level.

The study further points out that businessmen often complain about restrictions on the use of black labor—which are imposed by white labor in alliance with the government—but are silent on the question of higher wages and the establishment of negotiating machinery for blacks.[122] The attitude toward "job fragmentation"—using blacks in white-designated jobs—is favorable, since this is obviously in the interests of the company. One American heavy equipment plant, where welding jobs are reserved for members of the white union, apparently has the welding actually done by black "assistants" who work twice as fast for one-third the pay, according to the *Fortune* survey. It quotes the managing director as saying:

> I get six times the production per dollar out of my Bantu. The blacks cannot afford to be prima donnas, for there is a vast pool of unemployed

African labor. Once an African lands a job, he does his best to keep it. If he quits or gets fired, he runs the very serious risk of being shipped back to his "homeland".[123]

Given the African workers' position of total subjection to the employer, the U.S. manager will obviously have an interest in exploiting the situation as much as possible. In this, he will repeatedly clash with his white employees and their powerful unions, which he cannot afford to antagonize. An arrangement will be made to suit both parties at the expense of the Africans: either a formal "job fragmentation" agreement, with major benefits accruing to the whites, will be reached, or, more often, whites and management will connive in an informal situation where work officially reserved for whites is done by Africans, since given a guaranteed income almost without regard for performance, white workers need not insist on actually doing the work for which they are paid. Some refuse to show up at all unless there are Africans to perform their jobs for them.[124] While this is extremely wasteful and inefficient, it is part of the "social contract" in which U.S. concerns operate: what they lose by overpaying unproductive whites, they regain by underpaying and exploiting blacks. Their complaints about the white workers, and their silence about the work done by the blacks, is part of the game they play with the white unions. Many of them claim back in the United States that this trade-off procedure, and the use of blacks to do the work for which whites are paid, is breaking down, rather than perpetuating, apartheid, that basic confluence of white interests. The argument seems to rest more on the proponent's interests in preserving the system than on an objective analysis of it.

The alleged interest of U.S. concerns in raising the political and economic status of blacks in South Africa is belied by their attitude toward black trade unions, the most logical means of achieving their betterment. The companies, in response to pressure at home, are sometimes prepared to give raises that, in percentage terms, sound impressive, but that contain no cost-of-living guarantees and so are eroded within a year or two—by which time the social reformers back home can be counted upon to have turned their attention elsewhere. Interviews with American businessmen in South Africa, however, found them unanimously opposed to the concept of trade unions for Africans. They sometimes advance the existence of a "works committee" for their company as an adequate substitute, although recent strikes have revealed these as totally unrepresentative of black workers' feelings and useless as a bargaining mechanism. Some U.S. companies have been openly hostile to the enrollment in unions of Coloureds working in their own enterprise, though this is perfectly legal; the outstanding example of this is Chrysler Corporation.[125]

Perhaps the major problem in the whole controversy is the lack of complete and accurate information about what the companies are actually doing, as opposed to the aspects they wish to disclose to illustrate their claims of "progressiveness." Many U.S. companies with multimillion dollar investments —notably Union Carbide, but including many others—have simply refused to discuss their operations in South Africa on a substantive level. U.S. law provides no compulsion for them to even disclose the value of their holdings there. Of those companies that have disclosed some aspects of their operations in response to stockholder resolutions in 1973, most—nine of eleven—refused to reveal the value of their investment in South Africa, and only one stated the profit from its investment there.[126]

This illuminates one of the major difficulties of efforts to "reform" apartheid by pressure on U.S. companies with investments in South Africa. The universal experience of researchers with widely varying political objectives has been the impossibility of extracting the relevant data from the companies concerned by which the possibilities for improvement could be assessed and the correlative potential for reform evaluated. There is no obligation on U.S. companies to disclose information about the operations of their subsidiaries abroad. They have no interest in continuing to provide information if disclosures result in effective pressures to adopt higher standards of employment for Africans than purely profit requirements would suggest.

It is therefore instructive to consider the major investigation made by a parliamentary subcommittee in Britain, armed with subpoena power and a determination to use it. After months of detailed hearings, including lengthy arguments with companies unwilling to accept responsibility for their South African operations, the subcommittee produced a comprehensive report supported by voluminous evidence with detailed information on company practices that far surpassed anything attempted—or likely to be attempted—in the United States. The report concluded that companies had conspicuously failed to exercise their responsibility for their South African subsidiaries; that even after hurried wage increases following adverse publicity, almost half the companies, including the biggest in the country, were still paying minimum wages below the Poverty Datum Line for their area; and that only new legislation and procedures for compulsory monitoring of company practices in South Africa would have any impact on them.[127] Although declining to comment on the merits of the companies' presence in South Africa, on the ground that this was outside its terms of reference, the subcommittee stated:

> If their subsidiaries or associates argue that they cannot afford to pay wages above the PDL to all adult male employees, British companies should seriously consider whether to retain their business interests in South Africa.[128] The ability to pay basic wages above the relevant Poverty Datum Line now at least to all adult male employees should be regarded as one of the minimum conditions for maintaining or establishing a business interest in South Africa.[129]

The report adds that, in some cases, it expects the new-found interest of companies in South African operations to subside, and that the higher real wages of African employees will be short-lived unless further publicity is anticipated.[130]

British companies, like their U.S. counterparts, had long been claiming to be exemplary employers in South Africa. Until the facts were revealed, first by a major press campaign, with damning evidence brought to light by the London *Guardian*,[131] and then by exhaustive inquiries in Parliament,[132] their claims were tacitly accepted. On being compelled to disclose their operations, many company representatives expressed horror and disbelief at what had been going on in South Africa. This may not be entirely due to bad faith on the part of the headquarters spokesmen: it seems to be commc practice for the South African subsidiary to keep its home office in blissful ignorance until it is forced to make a serious effort to determine conditions abroad. Where details of wages and conditions are concerned, the *Fortune* survey found that local managers, to protect themselves from awkward questions from headquarters, were quite prepared to falsify information. A U.S. auto company executive in South Africa is quoted as saying:

> Corporate decisions are made from tiny slips of paper with maybe just the figures written on them. The slips are distillations of reports from the field. But no subsidiary tells its home office the truth. We all lie as much as we can get away with. We even lie about figures, so you can

imagine how much we lie about everything else. If anybody back there really knows what we're doing, it's certainly not our fault.[133]

The team of church representatives that visited South Africa in 1971 complained about misrepresentation:

> Management in the U.S. does not necessarily get clear reporting of their "non-financial" South Africa operations.

> At General Motors we were told that South African management had reported to their Detroit headquarters that they had 30 employees in a minority training program. According to a report given us by black employees, there are only 8 trainees in fact. . . .

> Again at GM, management reported there were 60 "non-whites" receiving technical training at a technical school. In actuality, GM workers reported they were getting very little technical training. Rather, they were being taught elementary drawing, arithmetic, and communications skills, even though the people there have had this instruction already. There were no blacks in this program, only Coloreds.

> At Ford, we were told that black and white employees receive the same food, even though in separate dining rooms. Our own observation was that they received distinctly different menus. The white workers received meat and the black workers received rice and eggs. . . .

> Most companies do not pay "equal pay for equal work" despite their assertions that they do. It was our observation that many workers doing the same or comparable work were not receiving comparable pay. In addition, the question of equal pay for equal work must be seen in the light of whether or not there are the same jobs open for black and white employees. . . .

> Goodyear management in South Africa said clearly they gave equal pay for equal work, then noted a differential between the starting pay of black and white workers . . . our understanding of Goodyear policies do not indicate equal pay for equal work. . . .

> Mobil management contended that they did not keep records of their wage levels, but further research showed that Mobil paid a monthly starting wage of between $52 and $76 to "non-white" employees.[134]

The problem of misrepresentation extends not only to the details of companies' operations in South Africa, but also applies to the organizations that are directly financed by the companies and whose objective is to depict "separate development" in the most favorable light possible. Anyone working in the context of southern Africa is quickly aware of the many myths that gain wide circulation and acceptance with no justification or shred of evidence to back them up, but that by dint of constant repetition through the South Africa public relations network are taken as conventional truths. Among these, for example, are the notions that Africans are better off in South Africa than elsewhere in Africa; that Europeans reached South Africa before any other people; and (as even the State Department has accepted as fact) that, in the words of former Assistant Secretary of State Newsom, South Africa "is one of the richest countries in the world in natural resources. Not only in gold and copper and nickel, chrome—these same resources are found in central Africa but not probably in as concentrated a form."[135] In point of fact, South Africa's minerals, though plentiful, are in a form of unusually low concentration and their profitability is dependent on abundant, cheap labor to extract them, as well as large inputs of foreign capital to support the operations. The whole gold mining industry would be crippled if Africans were paid a wage comparable to those prevalent in independent Africa: average wages in mining and quarrying in Ghana were 270 percent above those of Africans in South Africa in 1967, for example, and in gold mines in Gabon, average wages were 440 percent higher than those of Africans working in South African mines; the Gabon wages had more than tripled in four years of independence, compared to a rise in South Africa of only 22 percent in the same period.[136] As the South African gold mining industry has evolved, the proportion of total costs allocated to African wages has fallen substantially—from 13.7 percent in 1936 to 8.9 percent in 1969.[137] The decrease has helped to subsidize production, which is by no means assured in view of rising costs for extracting low grade ore. The situation is similar for other major minerals, particularly coal. As Dr. Van Eck, chairman of ISCOR and the IDC, has himself pointed out, the relative poverty of the supposedly wealthy mineral resources of which the country boasts means that, "We must glorify not the metals of the earth but our remarkable human material."[138]

The misinformation and biased presentation of the situation in South

Africa in the effort to win American and other foreign support for the white minority there is so prevalent, in forms more or less subtle, that it is hard to know where to start in putting the record straight. It is important to be aware of the role played by the South African Department of Information and other agencies in spreading a favorable picture of South Africa. Working along similar lines, and in close collusion with the department, is the South Africa Foundation, a coalition of domestic and foreign business interests that was originally formed along the lines of a German organization created by business interests to promote a favorable image of the Nazi regime in the 1930s. The approach is sophisticated, acknowledging the problems of "petty apartheid" and urging fairly minor reforms by investors, but insisting that South Africa be given time to work out its own "solutions." The considerable achievements of the foundation, to which most large U.S. investors contribute as one means of gaining government favor, have been outlined by its president, Sir Francis de Guingand:

> There is no doubt that the South African Foundation has done much to help this country during the last decade by spreading information correcting the wrong impressions and making known the tremendous achievements that have taken place. Our policy of inviting to this country opinion makers of high stature has proved most successful and has paid valuable dividends.[139]

The foundation played a crucial role in the decision by President Nixon to change American policy to one more favorable to South Africa's interests, under the slogan of "communication." It is known that both Nixon and Kissinger read Norman Macrae's version of the O'Dowd thesis, "The Green Bay Tree." Following this up, Sir Francis met with both of them, at a time when, as he later described it, "the Administration was re-evaluating the U.S. policy toward South Africa, and the occasion was taken to bring to the President's notice some points which have received too little attention in the past. It would be hard to overestimate the importance to South Africa of that discussion."[140]

Public relations work and lobbying, of course, are not confined to the South Africa Foundation. The major investors have large lobbying operations of their own in Washington and have no difficulty in conveying their interests to the appropriate quarters of the State, Commerce, Treasury, Defense, and other departments, and, of course, to the White House and the Congress. Well-organized and financed, and with top-level contacts and "clout" arising from the power of their giant headquarters, they are way ahead of the embryo "Africa lobby" in effectiveness, and much of their work is done out of the public eye. The most clear-cut case known so far was the lobbying effort by companies with economic and political interests in the white regime to legalize imports from Southern Rhodesia in violation of international sanctions. They included Union Carbide and Foote Mineral, with direct interests in mining in Rhodesia, backed strongly by Allegheny Ludlum, U.S. Steel (which manufactures ferrochrome, probably from Rhodesian ore, in South Africa), other steel companies, and the Ford Motor Company, all in close collaboration with the Rhodesian Information Office, the Liberty Lobby, and other interests.

An indication of the dominant position that business is assuming in foreign policy-making on South Africa is the recent restructuring of the State Department's Advisory Council on African Affairs, which has been reduced from fifty to seventeen members, all but one of them inexperienced in this field, but with major business interests in the region. As one of the business advocates for South Africa in Britain has said, "We are heavily involved in South Africa, and we shall continue to prosper there only if South Africa itself prospers."[141]

The argument is therefore reduced to its basic essentials: not the merits or demerits of the respective arguments about investment, but the resources and influence of those interested in promoting it, together with the powerlessness of those with no vested interest but a desire to eliminate support for racism, whether within or outside the United States.

A NOTE ON U.S. BANK LOANS TO SOUTH AFRICA

In recent years, South Africa has relied increasingly on direct loans, often to the government, state corporations, or local municipalities, to supplement foreign investment as a source of capital inflow. Switzerland, West Germany, and other European nations have been the major sources of these loans, but certain moves have been made to involve U.S. banks in large consortia for the same ends. This trend, however, more readily than direct investment, may be affected by the growing debate on the ethics of financing South Africa.

The first major consortium loan to come to light was, in fact, the cause of the original church involvement in South African issues. The church groups mobilized strong opposition to the ten U.S. banks involved in a consortium supplying revolving credit arrangements of $40 million for the South African government. In the wake of a campaign that was fairly brief but that threatened to gather momentum, the banks announced that the loan would be terminated immediately, but on the alleged ground that South Africa no longer needed it. This campaign was important because it prompted the churches to investigate their own involvement through investment portfolios in South Africa, and also because it illustrates the greater sensitivity of banks than other businesses to adverse publicity, as well as the relative weakness of the justifications they can produce. Whereas a company investing directly may claim to be capable of challenging official policy and changing apartheid by subversion, this cannot be credibly said of making loans to the government responsible for the system in the first place. The argument that investment creates employment is also much weaker in this case, since the government is just as likely to use the foreign exchange made available for purchases of strategic or essential commodities abroad—including any arms it may wish to buy from, say, France—as for social welfare. Once the bank loan is made, the lender can claim no control over its use.

These factors have reemerged with the appearance of new loan consortia involving a quite different set of banks, not of the first rank. The European-American Banking Corporation (EABC) has organized loans totalling over $210 million to the South African government and its agencies since 1970 and involves forty banks in the United States, Europe and Canada. Participants in two of the six loans, representing $70 million of the total, include eleven U.S. banks. Those involved in credits to the Finance Ministry for general balance of payments purposes are: Wells Fargo Bank ($2 million); the Central Bank in Chicago ($1 million); Merchants National Bank and Trust Company of Indianapolis ($1 million); City National Bank of Detroit ($0.5 million); Republic National Bank of Dallas ($3 million); First Israel Bank and Trust Company of New York ($2 million); First National Bank of Louisville ($2 million); Maryland National Bank ($2 million); and the United Virginia Bank ($2 million). The Wachovia Bank and Trust Company, Winston-Salem, North Carolina, also contributed $2 million to an ISCOR loan.[142] Following exposure, and pressure—including the withdrawal of accounts—from a number of communities, some of these banks have given up their participation in the loans, or at least agreed to undertake no new ones.

The EABC appears to have a particular commitment to the minority regimes of southern Africa, however. It has been planning a secret loan to the illegal regime in Southern Rhodesia.[143] It is also reported to have offered to finance ISCOR's proposed Sishen-Saldanha rail and harbor project for the bulk export of iron ore to Japan.[144] Much of this financing may well be solicited from U.S. banks. However, banks considering committing their assets to such a scheme might do well to contemplate the reaction of the Montgomery County Council to the information that the Maryland National Bank, where the council keeps $0.5 million of its funds, was participating in a loan to South Africa. The county executive, Mr. James Gleason, summed up the reaction in simple but straightforward terms: "This government does not support a policy of putting its money in banks if they are going to make loans to South Africa or to other countries with discriminatory policies." Following debate on the importance of withholding financial support from governments or organizations involved in institutionalized racism at home or abroad, the council members announced their intention of examining all the investments, direct or indirect, personal or corporate, they might have in South Africa.[145] Meanwhile, the Maryland National Bank disposed of its South African loans and announced a policy of not making any more, "in order not to convey the impression that we support South Africa's policy of apartheid."[146]

NOTES

1. U.S. Department of Commerce, Overseas Business Reports, *Establishing a Business in South Africa* (OBR 70 -50, September 1970).

2. F.J. van der Merwe and G. van Nieuwkerk, "Changes in Foreign Liabilities and Assets of South Africa, 1968 to 1970," South Africa Reserve Bank, *Quarterly Bulletin* (December 1971): 19-20.

3. *Foreign Investment in the Republic of South Africa* (New York: U.N. Unit of Apartheid, ST/PSCA/SER. A/11, New York, 1970) p. 61, with additional calculations by the author.

4. U.S. Department of Commerce statistics; also *see* "Apartheid and Imperialism: A Study of U.S. Corporate Involvement in South Africa," *Africa Today*, 19, 2 (Spring 1972), pp. 1-39.

5. Calculated from U.S. Department of Commerce statistics for 1960 and 1971.

6. J.N. Friedlin and L.A. Lupo, "U.S. Direct Investment Abroad in 1973," U.S. Bureau of Foreign and Domestic Commerce (Department of Commerce), *Survey of Current Business*, 54, 8, Part II (August 1974): 18-19.

7. E.L. Nelson and F. Cutler, "The International Investment Position of the United States in 1967," *Survey of Current Business*, 48, 10 (October 1968): 19-32; also D.T. Devlin and F. Cutler, "The International Investment Position of the United States: Developments in 1968," *Survey of Current Business*, 49, 10 (October 1969): 23-36.

8. Friedlin and Lupo, *Survey* (August 1974): 18-19.

9. Calculated from ibid.

10. *Zambia Mail* (Lusaka), 20 December 1969.

11. *Current Business* (October 1969): p. 23-36; also *Foreign Investment in the Republic of South Africa*, pp. 62-3.

12. Martin Legassik, "South Africa: Capital Accumulation and Violence" in E. Laclau, ed., *Capital Accumulation and Violence* (forthcoming).

13. Ralph Horwitz, *The Political Economy of South Africa* (London: Weidenfeld and Nicolson, 1967), p. 328.

14. Ieuan L. Griffiths, "The South African Motor Industry," Supplement to *The Standard Bank Review* (June 1968), p. 1.

15. *The Star* (Johannesburg), week of 23 March 1974.

16. *Financial Mail* (Johannesburg), 20 June 1975.

17. Griffiths, "Motor Industry," pp. 7-10.

18. "Special Survey on the Motor Industry," *Financial Mail*, 13 March July 1970.)

19. Ibid., 9 April 1965.

20. *South African Digest*, (Pretoria: Department of Information, 1 July 1970.)

21. Ibid., 8 December 1972.

22. *General Motors and South Africa*, presentation by Mr. E.N. Estes of General Motors, 16 October 1972, to the Council of Religion and International Affairs Seminar (reprinted and distributed by GM).

23. General Motors, "Report on Progress in Areas of Public Concern" (10 February 1972).

24. *The Star*, week of 28 July 1973.

25. Chrysler advertisement in the *Financial Mail,* "Special Survey on the Motor Industry," 13 March 1970.

26. Corporate Information Center, National Council of Churches, *Church Investments, Corporations, and Southern Africa* (New York: Friendship Press, 1973), p. 75.

27. Ibid., p. 56.

28. Ibid., p. 63.

29. Letter and materials sent to Ronald L. Phillips, research director, Corporate Information Center, National Council of Churches, from John A. Banning, Executive Director, International Government Affairs Staff, Ford Motor Company, 5 October 1972, quoted in ibid., p. 64.

30. R.J. Scott, managing director of Ford South Africa, in an interview (30 July 1970) quoted in ibid., p. 65.

31. *Financial Gazette* (Johannesburg), 30 November 1973.

32. *Washington Post,* 27 February 1974.

33. Ibid.

34. Caterpillar's reply to the Corporate Investment Center quoted in *Church Investments,* pp. 53 and 55.

35. Ian Leach and Steve Green, managing director and personnel director of Caterpillar (Africa) respectively, in an interview with Tim Smith, 13 August 1970, in Johannesburg; quoted in Ibid., pp. 53-55.

36. Ibid., pp. 51, 144.

37. General Electric, *The General Electric Investor* (Summer 1972).

38. Ibid., pp. 51, 144.

39. Ibid., p. 142.

40. Ibid., p. 146.

41. Ibid., p. 162.

42. Ibid., p. 154.

43. Ibid., p. 153.

44. C. Cotton, Managing Director of Burroughs South Africa, interviewed by Tami Hultman and Reed Kramer in Johannesburg, 3 March 1971: in *IBM in South Africa* (New York: National Council of Churches, Corporate Information Center, 1972) p. 3.

45. *Sunday Times* (Johannesburg), 6 December 1970.

46. *Management,* November 1971, p. 37.

47. Research project commissioned by Sperry-Rand; in ibid., p. 27.

48. See for example D.J.M. Vorster, Director, National Institute of Personnel Research, "Labour Requirements for the 1970's: how can they be met?" mimeographed (Address to the 9th Annual Business Outlook Conference) p. 12.

49. Ruth First, *Foreign Investments in Apartheid South Africa* (New York: U.N. Unit on Apartheid Notes and Documents, No. 21/72, October 1972), p. 12.

50. *Sunday Times*, 26 September 1971.

51. *Financial Mail* 14 September 1973; *Die Vaderland* (Johannesburg) editorial, 6 September 1973; *The Guardian* (London) 6 September 1973; *Financial Times* (London), 6 September 1973.

52. Advertisement in the *Financial Mail*, 28 January 1972.

53. *The Star*, 24 July 1971.

54. *Financial Mail*, 31 August 1973; *Sunday Times*, 2 September 1973.

55. Gen. Westmoreland, chairman, Joint Chiefs of Staff, speaking at the Annual Luncheon of the U.S. Army, 1969, quoted in Kramer and Hultman, *IBM*, p. 15.

56. Information digested from Kramer and Hultman, *IBM*, p. 15, and *Church Investments*, pp. 100-7.

57. *Church Investments*, p. 144.

58. Ibid., p. 152.

59. Ibid., p. 146.

60. Ibid., p. 158.

61. Ibid., p. 161.

62. Ibid., p. 157.

63. Ibid., p. 142.

64. Ibid., p. 164.

65. Ibid., p. 161.

66. Ibid., p. 118.

67. *Financial Mail*, 27 September 1968.

68. Ibid.

69. Information digested from *Church Investments*, pp. 108-117.

70. *ITT and South Africa: A Presentation to Representatives of the United Presbyterian Church and the National Council of Churches by Peter Loveday, Managing Director, Standard Telephones and Cables (SA) Ltd., New York, January 18, 1973* (New York: ITT, 1973), p. 38.

71. *". . . a people company": Report on an Investigation into STC (South Africa) Ltd.* (Johannesburg: Spro-cas, on behalf of the United Presbyterian Church in the U.S.A., December 1973).

72. Advertisement in the *Financial Mail*, 20 September 1968.

73. Ibid., 17 October 1969.

74. *The Star*, 7 March 1970.

75. "Oil: the Great Gamble," Special Survey of the *Financial Mail*, 5 March 1971.

76. "What About South Africa?", *Auge* (Mexico: offprint in English distributed by South African advertisers), April 1971, p. 302.

77. *Southern Africa* (London: published by companies with an interest in South Africa), 6 February 1967.

78. Dr. Kuschke, managing Director of the Industrial Development Corporations, quoted in the *Sunday Times,* 1 November 1970.

79. Ruth First, *Foreign Investment,* p. 11.

80. "Oil: the Great Gamble, *Financial Mail,* 5 March 1971.

81. Ibid.

82. First, *Foreign Investment,* p. 11.

83. *South Africa Digest,* 5 January 1972.

84. "Oil: the Great Gamble, information on Mobil mainly digested from *Church Investments,* pp. 122-31.

85. Caltex advertisement in "Oil, the Great Gamble."

86. Digested from *Church Investments,* pp. 46-50.

87. "Oil: the Great Gamble."

88. *Financial Mail,* 20 June 1975.

89. Union Carbide advertisement, *Financial Mail,* 2 August 1968.

90. *Sunday Times,* 1 March 1970; *Financial Gazette,* 11 June 1971.

91. *Church Investments,* pp. 132-41.

92. Ibid., pp. 38-9.

93. Ibid., p. 160.

94. *The Star,* week of 14 September, 1974.

95. *Church Investments,* p. 160.

96. Ibid., p. 147.

97. Ibid., p. 147.

98. Ibid., pp. 61-2.

99. Ibid., pp. 84-6.

100. Report and Recommendations of the Colgate-Palmolive representatives on Investigation in South Africa, 23 March 1973; reprinted in *U.S. Business Involvement in Southern Africa,* Part III, appendix 22, pp. 506-511; see also the Africa Subcommittee hearings on the incident, also in Part III, pp. 152-3.

101. *Church Investments,* pp. 150, 158-9, 163-4.

102. Ibid., p. 155.

103. Ibid., pp. 143, 144, 150, 158-9, 163-4.

104. Ibid., pp. 145, 149.

105. As stated by Mr. Newsom in testimony before the House Subcommittee on Africa, 27 March 1973; *U.S. Business Involvement in Southern Africa,* Part III, p. 30.

106. U.S. State Department, *Employment Practices of U.S. Firms in South Africa* (February, 1973).

107. Dudley Horner, research officer of the Institute of Race Relations, quoted in the *New York Times,* 19 August 1972.

108. John Blashill, "The Proper Role of Corporations in South Africa," *Fortune* (July 1972): 50. This article is widely promoted to justify U.S. investment in South Africa.

109. William R. Cotter, testimony to the House Subcommittee on Africa, in United States, *Congressional Record,* 1 June 1971, p. 17434.

110. John H. Chettle, director of the U.S. Office of the South Africa Foundation, "U.S. Corporations and South Africa," *South Africa International* (July 1971), p. 54.

111. The Hon. Harold B. Scott in *U.S. Business Involvement in Southern Africa,* Part I, p. 236.

112. Market Research Africa, cited in "Barometer of Business Opinion," *Sunday Times,* 1 September 1968.

113. *Report on the Polaroid Experiment* (Johannesburg: Institute of Race Relations, 1971).

114. Sonny Leon, quoted in *The Star,* week of 9 December 1972.

115. For records of the debate in Congress, see *Congressional Record,* 20 April 1973, p. H3377-80 and 22 May 1973, pp. H3948-50; U.S. Congress, House of Representatives, Foreign Affairs Committee, Subcommittee on Africa, *U.S. Business Involvement in Southern Africa* (Washington, D.C.: Government Printing Office, 1972) Part II, pp. 15-37 and appendices 1-4; Part III, pp. 1830208 and appendices 70-75; and *The Faces of Africa: Diversity and Progress: Repression and Struggle,* U.S. Congress, House of Representatives, Foreign Affairs Committee, Subcommittee on Africa (Washington, D.C.: Government Printing Office, 1972), pp. 159-60.

116. George P. Sape, Special Assistant to the General Counsel, EEOC, in testimony to the House Subcommittee on Africa, 6 April 1973; *U.S. Business Involvement in Southern Africa,* Part III, p. 194.

117. W. Joseph Dehner, Jr., "Multinational Enterprise and Racial Non-Discrimination: U.S. Enforcement of an International Human Right," (Winter 1974), pp. 71-125.

118. Quoted in "Few U.S. Concerns Aid Africa Blacks," *New York Times,* 19 August 1972.

119. *Fortune* (July, 1972), p. 53 and 89.

120. Chrysler official in Detroit, quoted by Harold Chesnin and William Lane, Jr., *The Silent Citizen: The Role of the American Corporate Presence in South Africa, 1957-1967* (mimeographed) p. 149.

121. Tim Smith, *The American Corporation in South Africa: An Analysis* (New York: Council for Christian Social Action, United Church of Christ, 1971), p. 14.

122. Spro-cas, *Power, Privilege, and Poverty* (Johannesburg: Report of the Economics Commission of the Study Project on Christianity in Apartheid South Africa, 1972), pp. 63-4.

123. *Fortune* (July 1972), p. 53.

124. Ibid.

125. Smith, *American Corporation in South Africa*, p. 36.

126. *Update* (New York), September, 1973, pp. 1-6.

127. *Wages and Conditions of African Workers Employed by British Firms in South Africa*, 5th Report from the Expenditure Committee, House of Commons, Session 1973-74 (London: HMSO, 1974) and *Minutes of Evidence*, Vols. I-III, Trade and Industry Subcommittee (London: HMSO, 1973).

128. Ibid., p. 70.

129. Ibid., p. 102.

130. Ibid., pp. 97-98.

131. *The Guardian* (London), 12 March 1973, and subsequent articles.

132. *Wages and Conditions*.

133. *Fortune* (July 1972), p. 91.

134. *U.S. Investment in Southern Africa—A Focus for Church Concern and Action*. (Report of an ecumenical church team that visited South Africa in November 1971 to research and report on the involvement of U.S. corporations there); reprinted in *U.S. Business Involvement*, Part III, pp. 605-17.

135. David Newsom, testimony to the House Subcommittee on Africa, reprinted in *Issue, Journal of the African Studies Association* 1 (Fall 1971)

136. Mohamed Awad, *Apartheid—A Form of Slavery* (New York: U.N. U on Apartheid Notes and Documents, No. 37/71, August 1971).

137. Francis Wilson, *Labour in the South African Gold Mines, 1911-1969* Africa Studies Series (Cambridge: Cambridge University Press, 1972), p. 40

138. M.J. van Eck, speech at Vereeniging, quoted in *Rand Daily Mail*, Johannesburg, 22 April 1967.

139. Sir Francis de Guingand, Presidential Address to the South Africa Foundation Annual General Meeting, Durban, 24 March 1971.

140. South Africa Foundation, *10th Annual Report* (Johannesburg, 197C

141. W.E. Luke, chairman of the United Kingdom-South Africa Trade As sociation, quoted in *The Star* (Johannesburg) week of 23 November 1971.

142. *The Frankfurt Documents: Secret Bank Loans to the South African Government,* brief of the Corporate Information Center, insert in the *Corporate Examiner,* New York, July 1973.

143. *Sunday Times, 14 April 1974.*

144. *Financial Mail,* 30 May 1973.

145. *Washington Post,* 30 March 1974.

146. Letter from the Maryland National Bank to the Montgomery County Executive, quoted in the *Washington Star-News,* 9 April 1974.

chapter 5 _____

NAMIBIA

The situation in Namibia, formerly known by the colonial name of South West Africa, is very little known internationally; however, it consti tutes one of the major issues in international law and the territory is also a crucial part of the southern Africa region. It is impossible here to des- cribe the full ramifications of the Namibian situation, which involves a major test for the United Nations and International Court of Justice, que tions of Western countries' willingness to implement their almost unani- mous support for the United Nations' legal stand, and a variety of other political, legal and economic issues. However, since the case of Namibia i of major interest to investors in the southern African complex, it is rele- vant to point out some of the consequences of American involvement there. It must always be borne in mind that American companies operat- ing in South Africa tend to operate to some extent in Namibia, since the two are administered largely as one territory. Many of the companies operating in South Africa have indicated that they have at least minimal operations in Namibia as a result.[1]

At the turn of the century, South West Africa was a German colony, and during World War I was invaded and occupied by South Africa. Its occupation was legitimized by a League of Nations Class "C" Mandate in 1920, the international mandate system having been created at the insistence of South Africa's General Smuts, backed strongly by President Woodrow Wilson, as "a sacred trust of civilization." Smuts was originally, however, very reluctant to apply the mandate system to South West Africa, which he wanted to annex. After World War II South Africa refused to change its mandate to the trusteeship system worked out by the United Nations (the only mandate-holder to refuse) and argued that with the demise of the League of Nations, it was no longer accountable to the international community. This view was overruled by the International Court of Justice (ICJ) in 1950, which stated that although South Africa was not obliged to accept the U.N. trusteeship system, the mandate was still in existence; the United Nations had taken over the supervisory functions of the League; and South Africa could alter the status of the international territory only with the consent of the United Nations.

THE LEGAL SITUATION OF NAMIBIA

There has been constant conflict in the United Nations over Namibia since then, as well as periodic referrals to the International Court of Justice. One of the best-known of these was the move by Ethiopia and Liberia in 1961 to request the ICJ for a contentious opinion that South Africa had violated the terms of the mandate and should withdraw its administration. In a highly controversial reversal of its original acceptance of the case, the ICJ ruled in 1966, after years of hearing substantive evidence, that it could make no ruling on the case. This was hailed by South Africa as a victory for its side and widely promoted as a vindication of its administration in Namibia—although in fact, the court had not pronounced on the merits of the case. The 1966 General Assembly, immediately following the court's "nonverdict," in passing Resolution No. 2145, for which the United States voted, decided that South Africa's mandate for Namibia having been terminated, the United Nations therefore took over direct responsibility for the territory. This resolution was confirmed by the Security Council in Resolution No. 269 of 1969.

The final step was the decision of the Security Council to refer to the International Court of Justice the question, "What are the legal

consequences for States of the continued presence of South Africa in
Namibia, notwithstanding Security Council Resolution 276 (1970)?"
This latter resolution had called for South Africa to withdraw its administration from the territory by a date which had passed with no
move by South Africa to comply. The ICJ's advisory opinion leads as
follows:

> The Court is of Opinion . . .
>
> (1) That, the continued presence of South Africa in Namibia being il-
> legal, South Africa is under obligation to withdraw its administration
> from Namibia immediately and thus put an end to its occupation of the
> Territory;
>
> (2) That States Members of the United Nations are under obligation to
> recognize the illegality of South Africa's presence in Namibia and the
> invalidity of its acts on behalf of or concerning Namibia, and to refrain
> from any acts and in particular any dealings with the Government of
> South Africa implying recognition of the legality of, or lending support
> or assistance to, such presence and administration.

The United States participated in the court's proceedings, and the final
opinion was in many ways similar to the arguments put forward by the
United States. On October 4, 1971, U.S. Secretary of State William P.
Rogers told the General Assembly:

> In Africa, where the right to a freer existence is still denied to many,
> we are constant in our support of practical and peaceful means to
> achieve self-determination and end racial confrontation. . . . Consis-
> tent with that objective we have decided to accept the advisory opin-
> ion of the International Court of Justice on the legal consequences
> for states of South Africa's continuing occupation of Namibia.[2]

The full consequences of the advisory opinion have not as yet been
fully calculated, although the legal implications are complex and may
have a very practical impact on the economic relations of other states with
South Africa, "implying recognition of the legality of, or lending support
or assistance to, such presence and administration." One major reason why

implementation of the advisory opinion has been held up has been the initiative, launched by the governments of France and Argentina, for the U.N. secretary-general to enter into "contacts with all parties concerned" with the question of Namibia; this initiative led to an attempt at "dialogue" with South Africa, which lasted from February 1972 to December 1973, when the Security Council—in a rare unanimous vote—decided to terminate the attempt on the grounds of South Africa's bad faith in the negotiations. Almost simultaneous with this move came the appointment of a strong U.N. commissioner for Namibia, Mr. Sean MacBride.

More determined attempts to translate the court's opinion into enforcement action may be expected. At the very least the question of Namibia is likely to continue as a major item on the U.N. agenda, and hence a source of embarrassment to states such as the United States, which support the position of the United Nations, but whose companies are committed to various economic activities under the illegal South African occupation regime. Current debate focuses on the implementation of the U.N. Council for Namibia's decree no. 1, adopted by the General Assembly in 1974, which makes all exports of Namibian goods subject to seizure.

The United States government has announced its intention of discouraging investment by its citizens in Namibia; of denying credit guarantees and other assistance for trade with that territory; and of withholding protection against the claims of a future lawful government of Namibia. In supporting Security Council Resolution No. 283, the U.S. representative made a point of singling out paragraphs 4-7 as being consistent with and, in fact, reflecting, the policy already enunciated and being implemented by the U.S. government. The relevant paragraphs are as follows:

The Security Council . . .

4. *Calls upon* all States to ensure that companies and other commercial and industrial enterprises owned by, or under direct control of, the State cease all dealings with respect to commercial or industrial enterprises or concessions in Namibia;

5. *Calls upon* all States to withhold from their nationals or companies of their nationality not under direct governmental control, government loans, credit guarantees and other forms of financial support that would be used to facilitate trade or commerce with Namibia;

6. *Calls upon* all States to ensure that companies and other commercial enterprises owned by, or under direct control of, the State cease all further investment activities, including concessions in Namibia;

7. *Calls upon* all States to discourage their nationals or companies of their nationality not under direct governmental control from investing or obtaining concessions in Namibia, and to this end withhold protection of such investment against claims of a future lawful government of Namibia.

The former assistant secretary of state for Africa, Mr. David Newsom, has been at pains to distinguish U.S. investment in Namibia from that in South Africa, which the U.S. government "neither encourages nor discourages":

We adopt a much more restrictive policy with respect to Namibia, particularly because of our position that South Africa's presence in the Territory is illegal since the termination of its Mandate in 1966. (The legal soundness of this position has subsequently been established authoritatively by the ICJ advisory opinion of June 21, 1971.) Since May, 1970, we have followed a policy of discouraging further American investment in the Territory and have advised potential investors that we will not intercede to protect their investment against claims of a future legitimate Government in the Territory. The Export-import Bank and OPIC provide no facilities for activities in Namibia. Any American firm which have decided to invest there since 1970 can be presumed to have done so in spite of their awareness of U.S. policy.[3]

Newsom's deputy, Mr. Robert Smith, elaborated on this statement:

I might add that since the International Court's conclusions in 1971, we, the U.S. Government, have not entered into any new treaty relationships with South Africa in which the South African Government purports to act on behalf of or concerning Namibia, nor have we invoked or applied any existing treaties concluded by South Africa on behalf of or concerning Namibia which involve active intergovernmental cooperation. Furthermore, we have not included the territory of Namibia within the jurisdiction of diplomatic or special missions sent to South Africa, nor have any U.S. consular agents been sent to Namibia . . . we have informed all such firms which are there of the U.S. Government's refusal to protect investments, rights, franchises, titles, or contracts against future lawful governments of Namibia.[4]

One of the many complex issues arising out of the U.S. decision not to recognize South Africa's right to legislate or enter into agreements on behalf of the territory of Namibia is the question of representation in a variety of international organizations, both within the United Nations family and outside, some of them of substantive importance to the economy. South Africa purports to represent Namibia in such organizations as the International Atomic Energy Authority, the International Civil Aviation Organization, Universal Postal Union, International Telecommunications Union, General Agreement on Tariffs and Trade, International Monetary Fund, International Bureau for Weights and Measures, International Bureau for Protection of Industrial Property, South East Atlantic Fisheries Organization, and many more specialized organizations. When asked whether the U.S. government considered that South Africa should be allowed to represent Namibia in such forums, Mr. Smith stated: "We do not think that, Mr. Chairman. We have made clear that we do not recognize South Africa's administration of the territory or its legal right to occupy the territory. It seems to me it follows from that that we do not think that South Africa should speak for Namibia."[5] In addition, there are five bilateral treaties that, according to the State Department, "might raise questions with respect to application to Namibia." They are: visa agreements, as amended, March 31, 1958 (TIAS 4076 and 3544); agreement relating to Air Transport Services of May 23, 1947, as amended (TIAS 1639 and 6512); Convention for the Avoidance of Double Taxation of December 13, 1946, as amended (TIAS 2510); Extradition Treaty of December 18, 1947 (TIAS 2243); and Parcel Post Convention signed April 17 and June 20, 1919 (41 Stat. 1956). Although no question has arisen with regard to arrangements such as visas, air transport services, or the other issues covered, any difficulty encountered in these areas by American investors in Namibia may not be capable of resolution by reference to and invocation of these treaties.

One small move that is indicative of possibly more far-reaching measures at some time in the future is the decision to collect statistics for U.S.

economic relations with Namibia separately from those with South Afric.
A State Department directive on this reads: "The Bureau of the Census
(CESA) has not heretofore maintained statistics on which to base such
figures. In the future, separate statistical bases will be maintained and sep
arate figures published."[6]

A logical consequence of the legal position, as accepted by the U.S.
government, is that the invalidity of all "laws" of the unlawful occupying power since 1966 includes "laws" that purport to confer any right,
title, claim (prospecting claims, etc.), interest, or franchise. The invalidity of such "laws," would presumably mean that they could not be
accepted by U.S. government agencies as a basis for business activities,
including the raising of capital for Namibian operations in the United
States. The agency most immediately affected by this situation is the
Securities Exchange Commission (SEC), which was asked by Congressman Charles Diggs, chairman of the House Subcommittee on Africa, to
look into the question of "whether the SEC would approve an issue of
shares based wholly or in part on licenses, franchises, titles, and interests granted by the illegal administering authority of South Africa, for
activities inside, or related to, Namibia."[7] In a hearing April 4, 1974,
an SEC official stated that such share issues would not be approved and
that there had already been a case in 1972, involving Gemstone Mining,
where a proposal to raise capital in the United States for a Namibian
venture had been abandoned following discussion with the SEC and
State Department.

American companies that are prospecting for or exploiting minerals
in Namibia, in terms of purported rights bestowed on them by the illegal occupying power, would clearly be affected by decisions of the
SEC on share issues or the provision of loans in the United States that
are based wholly or in part on their Namibian "rights." Most of the
U.S. companies currently in Namibia are in fact involved in mineral,
including oil, prospecting. These with prospecting "concessions" purportedly granted by the illegal occupying power could be affected also by
controversies with regard to offshore waters, including the question of
rights to fishing and to minerals on the seabed.

For those investors already in Namibia, or those who created a
stake recently despite the uncertainties involved, the major issue arising
out of Namibia's unique legal character is the question of Security Coun-

cil Resolution No. 310 of 1972 and the Universal Declaration of Human
Rights. Operative paragraph 5 of Resolution No. 310, which the United
States supported, reads as follows:

The Security Council . . .

5. *Calls upon* all States whose nationals and corporations are operating in Namibia notwithstanding the relevant provisions of Security Council resolution 283 (1970), to use all available means to ensure
that such nationals and corporations conform in their policies of hiring Namibian workers to the basic provisions of the Universal Declaration of Human Rights.

The full text of the Universal Declaration of Human Rights is given
in Appendix IV. Of particular relevance to the Namibian situation and
resolution No. 310 is Article 23 of the declaration, which reads:

Article 23. (1) Everyone has the right to work, to free choice of employment, to just and favorable conditions of work and to protection against unemployment.

(2) Everyone, without any discrimination, has the right to equal pay
for equal work.

(3) Everyone who works has the right to just and favorable remuneration ensuring for himself and his family an existence worthy of human
dignity, and supplemented, if necessary, by other means of social protection.

(4) Everyone has the right to form and to join trade unions for the protection of his interests.

Article 25 (1) is also relevant:

Article 25. (1) Everyone has the right to a standard of living adequate
for the health and well-being of himself and his family, including food,
clothing, housing and medical care and necessary social services, and the
right to security in the event of unemployment, sickness, disability,
widowhood, old age or other lack of livelihood in circumstances beyond
his control.

These and other provisions of the declaration are of course not observed by the government, white workers, or employers in South Africa, and the situation in Namibia is analogous or, if anything, more oppressive of African workers. American companies, being very large-scale employers of contract labor in Namibia, in fact operate a system under their own volition that deprives workers of all security, the right to free choice of employment, equal pay without discrimination, trade unions, and the rest. The labor system in Namibia is described in more detail below.

The State Department has implemented Resolution No. 310 to the extent of establishing a list of all U.S. companies involved in Namibia and informing them of the human rights issues raised in the resolution. The letter sent read, in part:

> I am sure you share our concern with regard to the human rights of the people of the international territory of South West Africa (Namibia), and I hope we can count on your cooperation in taking such steps as may be necessary to ensure that any operations in the territory in which your corporation has an interest are fully consonant with the Declaration. While Articles 23, 24, and 25, dealing with rights respecting employment and adequate standards of living are especially pertinent, many others, such as Articles 1, 2, 4, 13, 16, 18, 19, and 20, are also relevant to the situation in the territory.

> In the United States the employee enjoys such rights under the Constitution and federal and state laws. To protect these rights, he has open to him such avenues of recourse as labor organizations, freely elected representatives in legislative bodies, and the courts. In the international territory, under South African administration, many of these rights are routinely denied. The employer there thus incurs a special and heavy burden of responsibility, for frequently he will be the only party with the knowledge, bargaining power, and independence effectively to support his employees' rights.

> We realize, of course, that it is not within the power of foreign business enterprises in the territory of South West Africa to cause the provisions of the Declaration of Human Rights to be implemented fully with respect to their employees. The United States nonetheless gives its support to paragraph 5 of SC Res. 310 (1972) in the belief that what foreign businesses do in this respect makes a significant difference to their employees.[8]

This thoughtful statement is, of course, readily applicable to the question of U.S. investment in any of the minority regimes of southern Africa. The State Department has indicated that it would probably intervene on behalf of U.S. companies if the South African regime were interfering with their attempts to implement the Declaration of Human Rights.

As long as U.S. investors are there under the present illegal government we are able to provide assistance to the American firms in connection with telling them how we think they ought to deal with the welfare of their workers, and if this led them to difficulties with the local authorities, we would want to be in a position to help them vis-a-vis the local authorities.[9]

Notwithstanding the invalidity of any act of the part of South Africa purporting to be on behalf of Namibia, South Africa must be held responsible in the Territory for obligations under international law. As noted by the World Court, the fact that South Africa has no legal right to administer Namibia does not relieve it of international obligations. The United States would therefore continue to exercise its discretion in protecting U.S. firms in Namibia in relation to the present illegal administration.[10]

AFRICAN RESISTANCE TO THE OCCUPATION OF NAMIBIA

The major African opposition party in Namibia is the South West African People's Organization (SWAPO) which operates as a legal party and also conducts an armed resistance struggle against the South African armed forces, the military activity being concentrated mainly around the northern border area and the strategic Caprivi Strip. Although South African communiques naturally minimize the extent of the operations involved, an indication of their impact is that, for the first time in its history, South Africa has recently started to recruit Africans and Coloureds into the army for operations in Namibia, where they are alleged by SWAPO to be used for patrolling mined areas. The armed resistance began in 1966, following the ICJ's failure to pronounce on the merits of the case brought by Ethiopia and Liberia; it was at this point that SWAPO, which had until

then been involved in peaceful domestic and international opposition to
the occupation regime, decided that the Namibians were now confronted
with a failure of international diplomacy and law and could rely only on
themselves to confront seriously South Africa's continued occupation.
Since then, South Africa has made great efforts to wipe out the resistance,
but there is no evidence that guerrilla operations have been reduced; on
the contrary, both sides report periodic clashes, mine explosions, and even,
at the end of 1971, a level of conflict sufficiently serious for South African
troops to invade Zambia in retaliation for SWAPO's external headquarters
being based there. Namibia therefore represents a continuous challenge for
South Africa in what it claims as its own territory. There are probably abou
as many South African troops in the Caprivi Strip as in the whole of Southe
Rhodesia. In 1975 South African troops started crossing the border into
Angola to attack SWAPO camps there.

The Namibians' refusal to accept South African occupation is expressed
in the statement of Toivo ja Toivo, SWAPO's regional secretary for Ovamboland (where much of the fighting has taken place) on being sentenced by
a South African court under the retroactively applied Terrorism Act:

> My Lord, we find ourselves here in a foreign country, convicted under
> laws made by people whom we have always considered as foreigners. . .
> It is the deep feeling of all of us that we should not be tried here in
> Pretoria. . . .

> We are Namibians and not South Africans. We do not now, and will
> not in the future recognize your right to govern us, to make laws for
> us in which we had no say; to treat our country as if it were your prop-
> erty and us as if you were our masters. We have always regarded South
> Africa as an intruder in our country. . . .

> A man does not have to be formally educated to know that he wants
> to live with his family where he wants to live, and not where an official
> chooses to tell him to live; to move about freely and not require a pass;
> to earn a decent wage; to be free to work for the person of his choice
> for as long as he wants; and finally, to be ruled by the people that he
> wants to be ruled by, and not those who rule him because they have m
> guns than he has. . . . We do not believe South Africa is in South West
> Africa in order to provide facilities and work for "non-whites." It is
> there for its own selfish reasons. . . .

Your Government, my Lord, undertook a very special responsibility when it was awarded the Mandate over us after the First World War. It assumed a sacred trust to guide us towards independence and to prepare us to take our place among the nations of the world. We believe that South Africa has abused that trust because of its belief in racial supremacy (that white people have been chosen by God to rule the world) and Apartheid.

We believe that for fifty years South Africa has failed to promote the development of our people. Where are our trained men? The wealth of our country has been used to train your people for leadership and the sacred duty of preparing the indigenous people to take their place among the nations of the world has been ignored. . . .

We feel that the world as a whole has a special responsibility towards us. This is because the land of our fathers was handed over to South Africa by a world body. It is a divided world, but it is a matter of hope for us that it at least agrees about one thing—that we are entitled to freedom and justice. . . .

I am a loyal Namibian and I could not betray my people to their enemies. I admit that I decided to assist those who had taken up arms. I know that the struggle will be long and bitter. I also know that my people will wage that struggle, whatever the cost.

Only when we are granted our independence will the struggle stop. Only when our human dignity is restored to us, as equals of the whites, will there be peace between us.[11]

During a visit to Namibia immediately after the announcement of the advisory opinion of the ICJ declaring South Africa's occupation to be unlawful, we found a very high level of awareness of the legal situation involved and a virtually unanimous opposition to South Africa's occupation. This was expressed by a series of school demonstrations, deputations to the local "Bantustan" authorities, an open letter to the South African prime minister from the two largest churches in Namibia, and numerous other episodes of opposition that met with repression by the occupation authorities. There was an overwhelming atmosphere of impatience and frustration at the continued occupation after it had been condemned in international law.

It was therefore not surprising that at the end of 1971, six months after the court's advisory opinion, a general strike broke out among the contract workers in the mines, local government, industry, and even the isolated white farms. Thirteen thousand five hundred contract workers were involved in a strike that lasted for two months and showed a solidarity of purpose, without any open organization, which took the South African occupation and many other observers by surprise.[12] The strike was followed by severe unrest in Ovamboland, where the frontier fences with Angola were cut down for a large part of their length and there was substantial resistance to the attempt to impose a "Bantustan" administration, including the formation of a new political party, the Democratic Cooperative party, by the leader of the strikers, Mr. Johannes Nangutuuala. As a result of the wave of unrest against the unlawful occupation, a state of emergency was imposed on Ovamboland on February 4, 1972, which allowed the armed forces unlimited discretion; several incidents involving the shooting of unarmed people have been reported by various sources, as has the detention of hundreds of people without trial, and the widespread use of torture.

Resistance on a variety of levels, including the increasingly militant demands, rallies, and protests of the SWAPO Youth League, has been continuing, as have the increasingly repressive measures by the South African occupation regime to crush the opposition. Demonstrations have been broken up by violence; more than 100 people have been publicly flogged in Ovamboland by the "Bantustan" appointees for political opposition (despite a prior restraining order obtained by church ministers in South Africa's Namibian courts); and many of the most outspoken opponents of the occupation, including the leading figures in the SWAPO and SWAPO Youth movements, have been arrested and detained without trial. Many of the outspoken, possibly as many as 2,000, were forced to leave the country in the middle of 1974, and the exodus is continuing.

This followed perhaps the most decisive indication of grass-roots opposition to South African occupation and in particular its reinforcement of the apartheid system in Namibia by the forced pace of "Bantustan" creation: this was the popular boycott of the Ovambo "Bantustan" elections. When polling took place on August 1 and 2, 1973, fifty-two of the fifty-six seats were uncontested by any except the proapartheid "Bantustan" party, since it had refused to register either SWAPO or Demkop, the Democratic Cooperative party. The boycott's significance lay in the fact

that Ovamboland contains about 46 percent of the Namibian population.
Of these, only 2.4 percent participated in the "Bantustan election," according to press reports.[13]

AFRICAN CONTRACT LABOR IN NAMIBIA

In 1967 the International Commission of Jurists found that the system
of recruitment of African workers operating in Namibia was unique in
its organized and efficient application of conditions that were "akin to
slavery." To the Anglican (Episcopal) bishop of Damaraland, whose di-
ocese covers the whole of Namibia, it may have been even worse:

> To be with these men is to feel, or have a feeling of total remorse
> and to have a man stripped of his family and from those he loves is one
> of the cruelest things that you can do to a person. It destroys . . . family
> life. It destroys human decency, and it is spreading alcoholism, venereal
> diseases, and tuberculosis, which are rife in Namibia.[14]

The bishop pointed to the consequences of American involvement in
the contract labor system:

> Now you cannot allow firms to take advantage of that. . . . [In Britain]
> a question was asked, "Is there any other country worse to live in than
> South Africa?" A peeress of the realm said, "Yes, Siberia." I would have
> liked to ask her this question, "Would you then invest in slave labor in
> Siberia which gave you a 30 percent return on investment?"

> The answer is that no right thinking person would. Slave labor exists
> in Namibia, and America cannot afford to allow this to be done in her
> name.

> See 50 and 60 men sleeping on a bunk. See 1,000 men naked in the way
> you treat cattle, and realize this cannot go on. The very name "America"
> stinks in Namibia.[15]

Prior to the strike at the end of 1961, which was aimed directly at the contract labor system, the recruitment and distribution of African workers through a central allocation system was simple and, from the administration's point of view, efficient, leaving no choice whatever to the recruit as to length of service, pay and conditions, location, employer, type of work or anything else. The system was operated by the South West African Native Labor Association (SWANLA) in which employers and the administration had interests. Workers would be classified by SWANLA as they applied for work (this being a monopoly, so that no other means of leaving the "reserve" to find work was permitted, and "passes" are issued only to SWANLA recruits). The categories were (A) class, completely fit physically; (B) class, less so; and (C) class, either under sixteen years of age or an adult suffering from some injury or deformity. The wages of SWANLA recruits were fixed according to age, experience, and category.

Employers could "order" a certain number of workers of specified categories—(A), (B), (C) or "picannin" (child labor being very common, in fact preferred because of the low rates charged by SWANLA). They would then receive that number of workers of the specified categories.[16] The general practice was for SWANLA to put labels around the necks of recruits and dispatch them in trains, for collection by the employer marked on the ticket at the other end of the line. As in South Africa, it was a criminal offense for the worker to break the contract in any way by, for example, trying to change jobs or return home. Africans found in a "white area" without the permission of an employer or other authorization could be assigned compulsorily to public works as a laborer or to another private employer. There were of course no trade unions, and strikes were a criminal offense.

The migrant labor system is more prevalent in Namibia than so far in South Africa, although there it is increasing in importance. At the end of 1971 there were 50,000 African workers in Namibia, of which 43,000, or 86 percent, were contract workers. Forty thousand of them were Ovambos, from the major Northern reserve which contains over half the African population in a relatively small land area.[17]

The impact of this system on the Africans was indeed, as the International Commission of Jurists has described it, "akin to slavery." The methods used to extract sufficient work-seekers from the reserves were based on compulsion and the confinement of large numbers of people to a small reserve, resulting in extreme poverty. (Before the colonial conquest, well under a century ago, Namibians had practiced a traditional economy based on much larger areas of land, and free movement beyond it for trading and other purposes.) The contract labor system has been described in the following words by an Ovambo victim:

> If a Reserve does not supply enough labour, it is looked upon as a bad Reserve. A message comes from the Commissioner to the welfare officer. The welfare officer reads the letter to the board members, and tells them that they want a certain number of labourers to work on the farms or on the roads, and this number must be supplied. . . . Then the Ovambo is sent off with a ticket. He does not know where he is going. The name of the master and the place are written on the label, and the people at the railway station send him where he has to go. After the station master has read the label, he rings up the police station to come and fetch this "parcel," and he is taken to the police station, from where he is fetched by the farmer or taken by the police to the farmer. Sometimes men have to walk for fifty to sixty miles. They may just be shown the road and told to go.[18]

The treatment given to many of the contract workers, particularly on the isolated farms, is without any restraints. Several farmers have been tried, protesting loudly their rights to do what they like with "their" workers, and fined about R20 (about $28) for the murder of African employees. The cases that have been brought to court and reported probably represent the tip of an iceberg; we have heard a number of stories of beatings, violent attacks, and murder by white employers for trivial reasons—if the Africans speak English, for example, instead of Afrikaans.[19]

The general strike of 1971-1972, involving about three-quarters of the contract labor force in Namibia, showed up some very explicit grievances against the whole system. In a pamphlet outlining the strikers' demands, the following points were made:

1. Improvement of employment agreements to include: liberty for Ovambos to do the work they want to and of which they have experience and knowledge; freedom to change jobs without "fear of landing in jail"; freedom to have their families with them.

2. The rate for the job irrespective of colour, and equal treatment for all.

3. Employment bureaux in all regions and towns.

4. Mutual respect between employer and employee.

5. Sufficient pay for workers to buy their own food and provide for transport needs.

6. An identification card instead of a pass-book, which would comprise: name, tribal area, male or female, identity number, and photograph of holder.

7. The removal of the "barricade": the police-post at the Ovambo border.

The demands were very similar to the minimum standards set out in the Universal Declaration of Human Rights, which the Namibians have managed to circulate very widely inside the territory and which serves as an ideal to which many of them aspire. The pamphlet also made it quite clear that it was not a question of modifying the contract system, but eliminating it; it said the strikers did not wish "the contract labour system to be improved, or that it be given another name."[21]

The contract labor system in fact was revised and is substantially the same in its effect on African labor. The new regulations are the result of negotiations between the South African occupation regime, the major employers, including American companies—a representative of the Newmont Mining Corporation, for example, is a signatory to the agreement—and the new "Bantustan authorities" appointed by the administration, who now play a more prominent role in the recruitment and distribution of labor. This is very useful from the occupation's point of view, since it diverts som of the hostility felt by the workers toward the local appointees. The regulations were published on April 4, 1972 by the South African Proclamatior No. R. 83/72.[22]

Underlying the regulatory scheme is a network of labor bureaus, which, as in South Africa, are to be established in each district of Namibia outside the "Bantustan" areas. They will receive batches of workers from parallel bureaus, nominally set up under the "Bantustan authorities." Africans are forbidden to leave the reserve areas unless they have been granted an "Extra-Territorial or Northern Natives Identification Pass." This document wa central to the old labor system, and its use is undiminished in the present scheme. Policing the system will be "employment officers," who are white "government" or municipal officials (Regulation 2), but who are granted the same powers of arrest as "peace officers" appointed under the Criminal Code (Regulation 2 (20)). The definition under the new regulations of "employees" and "work-seekers" is the basis of the discriminatory system, being related to Africans only.

Employment officers have full control over the commencement of new employment of Africans in their areas and also the continuation of their existing employment. Where an employer and the employment officer are in agreement, the African worker can be used against his will, either terminating his work or continuing it, under conditions of the employer's choosing not subject to negotiation (Regulation 3 (3) (i)). In particular, the employment officer can intervene when a worker has taken up new employment without having previously been released by his former employer. In this way the central aspect of the earlier contract system, the tying of workers to their employers for a predetermined period, is retained. "Release" can only be secured (a) if voluntarily given by the employer, or (b) if ordered by the native commissioner (who controls the employment officers). The workers' only complaint procedure is via the operators of the system, in the first place the employer, and thereafter to the native commissioner—who is directed to consult with the accused employer about any complaint by his workers. This is the only form of recognized mediation of labor disputes, recourse through the courts or labor unions being withheld.

The regulations also deal with "work-seekers," who are Africans classified as workers who do not have or who have left employment. If the employment officer cannot offer suitable employment to the "work-seeker," or if the latter refuses such employment, the native commissioner having jurisdiction can order such a person removed to the "reserve," or to "any other place indicated in the order" (Regulation 4 (3)). The worker can then be forcibly removed. Any employee who unilaterally breaks his predetermined contract is deemed to be unlawfully within the work area, and the native commissioner can order the police to remove him to any place he may choose (Regulation 4 (6)). In addition to this the native commissioner can have the cost of deporting the employee in question, or of his accommodation pending removal, met from any money found in his possession, or otherwise belonging to him or accruing to him from any source. In other words, in leaving an employer the worker may forfeit part of the wage he has earned up to that time (Regulation 4 (7)).

In the work areas, any African who loses employment, or who is unemployed, must report to the employment bureau within seventy-two hours of becoming unemployed, or within fourteen days of attaining the age of sixteen years, or ceasing to be a full-time student (Regulation 6 (1)). Thus there is compulsion on workers to take up employment, which they cannot refuse under penalty of deportation to a reserve—even though they may have been born in an urban area. It may not even be a question of the "work-seeker" accepting the contract offered; if there is no "suitable employment" for him, he is still subject to forcible removal.

There is no alternative to the predetermined contracts, even outside the work areas, or "proclaimed areas." In nonproclaimed areas, such as farms or other nonurban areas, "work-seekers" must report after fourteen days, and the regulations specifically state that "a work seeker shall not seek work in a non-proclaimed area unless he has written proof that he has been released from the obligation of rendering service under an agreement of employment" (Regulation 6 (2)). Further, a "work-seeker" is restricted to seeking employment in the area of jurisdiction of the employment officer who originally registered his employment. This further reduces mobility of African workers, in addition to the complex of "pass laws" which include the Native Labour Proclamation of 1919, the Vagrancy Proclamation of 1920, the Native Administration Proclamation of 1922, the Native Passes (Rehoboth Gebiet) Proclamation of 1930, the Extra-Territorial and Northern Natives Proclamation of 1935, the Natives (Urban Areas) Proclamation of 1951, the Aliens Control Act of 1963, and various regulations issued under these laws.

The regulations prevail over any law or prior regulation inconsistent with their provisions. Heavy and escalating penalties—including heavy fines and imprisonment—are provided for any of the people covered by them who commit any act or omission in violation of them. In effect, an African worker has no choice of employer or of location or kind of work; cannot change jobs without his original employer's permission; and cannot bargain in any way by labor organization or appeal to any independent authority, even if the employer violates the terms of the contract. He is, in effect, owned by the employer and forcibly separated from his family for the duration of the contract. Although he has the nominal right to visit his family, he in fact cannot do so without the permission of his employer and cannot claim the expenses involved in such visits. Thus, in addition to the fact that the regulations and all the network of pass and other discriminatory laws are in fact illegal and invalid in light of the illegality of South Africa's occupation, the regulations in themselves are, by American or other Western standards, unconscionable, and the labor contracts that lie at the heart of the system are unconscionable contracts. They provide no legal redress for an employee who is dissatisfied with his employer's observation of the understanding, and rely entirely on controls, backed by penal sanctions, to force workers into work without any free choice.

The entire African population is, in effect, forced into these unconscionable contracts, whatever part of Namibia may be involved. In the "Bantustans," the pattern is for all employable Africans to be obliged to enter the contract system. The Labor Enactment for the "Owambo Bantustan" (No. 6 or 1972) reads in part: "Every Owambo resident in the area of a tribal labour bureau, who is unemployed but who is dependent upon work for his livelihood, shall . . . register himself as a workseeker at the tribal labour bureau of the area in which he resides.[23]

The "work-seekers" are then placed in employment in accordance with labor requisitions received by the bureaus, just as in the original contract system. No "work-seekers" are permitted to leave without having been registered at the labor bureaus and their employment contracts attested in terms of the enactment. If the employee then deserts,[24] the "Owambo government" takes responsibility for either refunding the various fees paid by the employer for the delivery service, or else replacing the employee for the unexpired period of the contract free of charge. It may recover from a deserting employee any payments that have been refunded to an employer.[25] The system offers an effective guarantee of a set number of man-hours to the employers, with provision for refund of payment or replacement of the goods in the best commercial tradition.

One of the worse aspects of contract labor in Namibia—which is beginning to be applied now in South Africa—is the compound system. Even a former director of SWANLA, now secretary of the Windhoek Chamber of Commerce and of the Association of Mining Companies, has said that conditions in the Windhoek compound were "disgusting." Visiting researchers reported that beds consisted of concrete boxes where personal possessions were kept, with a hinged wooden lid on top of which one slept.[26] The South African *Financial Mail* comments, "High brick walls crowned with broken glass, barbed wire and heavily guarded gates suggest a concentration camp rather than a compound."[27] One of the contract workers there, asked to describe the system, complained:

> Why must Ovambos stay in the compound? The cross above the gate is like a graveyard. Why must we sleep on concrete beds? They freeze our blood at night and we get sick. The food is pig food—a small piece of fish at supper. There has been no change in the contract. They broadcast for boys. We go there and find ourselves rounded up. They force the people to be recruited. . . . We don't see any change in the system. . . . This evil system still remains.[28]

A senior government official admitted the element of compulsion in the compound system, saying simply, "The Ovambo people do not want to stay in the compound."[29]

A detailed study of the contract labor system's effects on Ovambo workers has been drawn up by Rauhia Voipio, a Finnish missionary with twenty-six years' service in Namibia. It concludes, after analyzing replies to a questionnaire from more than 1,000 workers, that many of them lose touch with their families, form adulterous associations in their work area, and contract venereal diseases. Divorce and illegitimacy used to be unknown but are now very common events in Ovambo society. Even those who by great effort remain attached to the concept of family life in absentia find that their children no longer recognize them when they come home from long contracts and their adjustment problems are similar to those of returning prisoners of war. Heavy drinking is also a major problem and is regarded as a result of the contract labor system. Miss Voipio explains that "contract labour, although undertaken in the majority of cases on a voluntary basis, is the result of a choice between hunger and migrant labour."[30] That hunger is the motive force behind the whole labor system was emphasized by one employer, a member of the Master Builders Association, who commented on the attempt to bargain for improved conditions: "There are many thousands of Ovambo to choose from, and when they are hungry they will return to work." The association met after the strike to consider a minimum hourly wage for unskilled Africans; this turned out to be exactly one-third of that in the Transvaal area of South Africa.[31]

In a later report, Miss Voipio commented on the revised contract scheme: "The Ovambos got the impression after the strike that big changes in their favour were on the way. Disappointment is stronger and more conscious now than before the big strike."

Among the causes for dissatisfaction listed by Miss Voipio are meager wages and the fact that Ovambos do not always receive the money to which they are entitled under the contract; the arbitrary stopping of food privileges in some areas; the length of the working day (in one quoted case, sixteen hours a day, seven days a week); problems at the labor bureaus and problems of accommodation; and harsh treatment by employers. "All the above complaints are about details. The main complaint is that the system has, in reality, remained the same."[32]

The failure to revise or substantially improve the system is largely the result of action and pressures by the employers of contract labor, of whom the most important are the American companies involved in the Tsumeb Corporation. The president of the Association of Mining Companies of South West Africa, Mr. W. H. Bailey, said after the first settlement moves (before the regulations were issued) that the closing of SWANLA had deprived employers of an organization that had protected their interests and that the industry would have to form an employers' association to protect its interests in the labor market.[33] There have in fact been a series of "wage maintenance" agreements by groups of employers. John Kane-Berman summarizes these activities: "To stop wage rates from going up, different groups of employers have entered into agreements not to compete against one another by offering higher wages. Government officials are encouraging them to do this."[34] Even the voice of South African employers, the *Financial Mail*, comments: "Clearly exploitation of unorganized, voiceless workers continues."[35]

The *Financial Mail* further records that the revised contract labor system is still the old system existing before the strike,

which the Owambos now call *odalate,* a corruption of the Afrikaans word *draad,* meaning "wire"—the wire shackle that symbolically binds them to the contract. . . . Because the procedure of boss-worker disengagement is so complex an employer can hold a worker "captive," for unless a contract is terminated strictly in accordance with prescribed procedure, a worker leaving his job unilaterally, automatically becomes a fugitive because his papers are not in order. This *odalate* is hardly less restrictive than before. . . .

The contract system is repugnant because it can only be made to work by coercion and the denial of basic human rights.[36]

THE OPERATION OF U.S.
COMPANIES IN NAMIBIA

U.S. investment in Namibia has been valued at approximately $45 million to $50 million by the U.S. government.[37] Most of this—probably over 90 percent—is accounted for by the Tsumeb Corporation in which Newmont Mining Corporation and American Metal Climax jointly own a controlling interest.[38] The American stake may well be the largest foreign interest in Namibia, apart from South Africa's; the only other countries with an investment of any size are Britain, West Germany, and France. West Germany, despite the many cultural and commercial links with Namibia, does not have the kind of large-scale enterprises that would begin to approach the size of Tsumeb. Britain too, although it is by far the largest investor in South Africa itself, had a negligible stake in Namibia until Rio Tinto-Zinc started to open up the open-cast uranium mine at Rossing, where production has not yet started. Together with the Namibian agencies of British companies in South Africa, a Metal Box factory and the oil-exploration concessions of Shell Oil Company and BP, this British stake may not be even as much as one-half that of the United States. France has less than this—the major item being a recent interest taken by a French company in the Rossing mine.

The following is a short description of the American interests in Namibia as far as this is known at present. Because of South Africa's failure to release separate information on the territory, identification is not easy, and there are probably more companies involved than are indicated here. Much of the American investment dates from after 1966, the date after which the U.S. government considered South Africa's continued occupation of Namibia to be unlawful; and many companies have entered the field after the announcement in May 1970 of government policy to discourage investment in Namibia and not to protect any company investing after that date against the actions of a future lawful government. Companies investing after 1966 are marked * and those investing after May 1970 are marked**.

Tsumeb Corporation, Ltd.

Newmont Mining Corporation, which manages Tsumeb, holds 29.2 percent of its stock. Newmont also has a 57.5 percent interest in O'okiep Copper Company of South Africa, which has a 9.5 percent interest in the Tsumeb Corporation, giving Newmont a total interest of 34.6 percent.[39]

American Metal Climax (Amax) holds 29.2 percent of Tsumeb. Amax also has an 18 percent interest in O'okiep, giving it a total interest in Tsumeb of 30.4 percent.[40] The Tsumeb Corporation is therefore managed, and 65 percent controlled, by U.S. corporations.

The Tsumeb Corporation is the major item of U.S. investment in Namibia, and dominates the economy of the territory with the size of its output. The Tsumeb mine alone accounts for over 80 percent of base mineral production in Namibia, and for over 20 percent of all Namibia's exports; it is also the largest single employer of contract labor.[41] In addition, the corporation's participation in various established and new mining ventures means that it is represented in most of the major mining operations in the territory.

The Tsumeb Corporation has a 20 percent interest in the Africa Triangle Company, and a 75 percent interest in a joint venture with the South West Africa Company prospecting for copper. Substantial progress was reported for this venture in 1971, and the partners were reported to be applying for a mineral grant to cover this ore body.[42]

The corporation itself operates, in addition to the original Tsumeb mine, the nearby Kombat mine, and the new Matchless mine which was closed down soon after the commencement of the copper mining operation there, during the general strike.[43] However, the Matchless mine was recently reopened after long delays, which may have been linked to the claim by Newmont that it was starting no new investment ventures in Namibia since the 1970 decision by the U.S. government.

The Tsumeb mine is the most lucrative in Namibia and said to be one of the world's richest in terms of the grade of ore produced over the years.[44] It is also by far the most profitable of all the projects of the Newmont Mining Corporation, which manages it; it has commented that Tsumeb, together with O'okiep in South Africa, "enabled the company to consider projects much larger in scale than was previously possible."[45] As a result, Newmont is now a multinational corporation. A local historian comments: "No mine . . . ever returned so large a cash flow for such a relatively small investment as Tsumeb."[46] There was relatively little risk involved in this American investment, since as early as 1922 the administrator of South West Africa had reported, "Both from its richness and the size of its ore bodies, Tsumeb rates as one of the greatest base metal propositions in the world."[47]

The above-average profit generated by the mine does not result from the efficiency of the operation as conducted by Newmont, in terms of output per employee, but is a factor to some extent of the low tax payments, and to a much greater extent of the natural wealth of the ore body, and the fact that this fixed resource has by now been largely depleted without payment of compensation to the Namibian people.[48] In 1947, when Newmont started output at the mine, one ton of ore contained 9.5 percent copper, falling to 2.44 percent in 1971; 19.3 percent lead, falling to 12.22 percent; and 3.91 percent zinc.[49] It is estimated that present known resources will last only another fifteen years at present rates of production. Two further deep-level shafts are being sunk to speed up recovery of the ore.[50] A completely new mine is to be opened by Tsumeb at Aziz Ost, within its existing concession area.

The exploitation of the mine has given Newmont an annual average rate of return on its original investment over the past twenty years of 347.79 percent.[51] The return was the same for Amax. Their total assets grew sixteen times after 1947, and profits also increased about sixteen times.[52] This was due partly to the very high dividend payout, subject to no restrictions on the repatriation of dividends; in 1970, for example, 89 percent of Tsumeb's net income was paid out in the form of dividends to foreign corporate interests.[53] Reinvestment was therefore a small proportion of the gross income; even so, the corporation has financed an investment that now amounts to about $80 million, from an original input by the consortium formed in 1946 of just over $4 million.[54] The gross value of metals produced by the mine amounted to $824,518,865 by June 30, 1969.[55]

The Tsumeb Corporation is not only the major and most conspicuous item of U.S. investment in the occupied territory of Namibia; it is also of central importance to the illegal administration there. Taxes paid to the South West Africa administration up to June 30, 1969, amounted to $125,304,620.[56] In 1970, the tax bill of $14 million came to nearly 23 percent of the mining sector's contribution to public revenue and 8.6 percent of the occupied territory's annual budget.[57] The operation of the mine clearly has strategic implications for the continued occupation of Namibia by South Africa; the manager of the Tsumeb mine, Mr. J.A. Ratledge, said in one interview that Tsumeb's tax payments, together with its location (between the center of the territory and the northern frontier), justified the construction of the strategically important road between Cape Town and Luanda, Angola.[58] It is also the best potential customer for power from the Kunene Dam scheme on the Namibia-Angola border, which is itself of major strategic importance in building up centers of minority-controlled economic activity where the threat of guerrilla resistance is particularly strong.

Employing no less than 40 percent of all contract laborers involved in the mining industry, the Tsumeb Corporation is the largest single employer of migratory "contract" labor "and hence could alter the whole spectrum of black wages in the territory ," according to a South African researcher.[59] To make such a contribution would be a relatively simple matter for the corporation, since doubling the wages of all African employees would reduce the net profits of the corporation by only 13 percent.[60] If there were to be a serious attempt to apply the principles of the Universal Declaration of Human Rights, or at least the standards of employment practices in the United States, profits may well fall to something approaching a normal rate of return on the current value of the mine. It is estimated that if African wages were increased six times (which would probably not bring them up to the level of white wages, but would be a substantial contribution, bringing African unskilled workers to the ratio with white skilled workers that would be reasonable in the United States), then return on current equity would fall to about the average level earned by Newmont worldwide.[61] However, there has been no move to approach international standards, and in fact Tsumeb lags well behind the South African-controlled Consolidated Diamond Mines (CDM), the other major user of contract labor in Namibia; Tsumeb's minimum wage for contract laborers is about R17 ($24) per month, after the raise prompted by the strike (about one-fifth of the South African Poverty Datum line). CDM's, on the other hand, is R31.20 ($43.70), and a large proportion of its workers earns above the minimum. The lowest paid white worker at Tsumeb was paid $444 per month in 1971, plus bonuses and fringe benefits on a very lavish scale, which may have exceeded those provided to the Africans by a similar proportion to the cash wages.[62]

It appears that under these conditions no African will work at Tsumeb unless under compulsion. As Mr. Ratledge has admitted, "When Ovamboland has a good rainy season, Tsumeb has more difficulty recruiting employees. If it's a good year and they don't have to work, they stay at home." Despite the raise, almost the entire Tsumeb work force, which was among the first to come out on strike in December 1971, refused to return afterwards. Newmont reported in 1972 that it had to recruit a completely new labor force: "Most of the workers are new and must be trained."[64]

The labor policy of Newmont, tacitly backed by Amax, is shown up as largely the responsibility of management rather than an automatic consequence of operating in the territory. This is demonstrated by the attitude of another major foreign investor, Rio Tinto-Zinc (RTZ) of the United Kingdom, with which Newmont is closely associated through joint participation in the South African Palabora mine. In its new uranium mine in Namibia, RTZ is refusing on principle to use migratory labor. Its chairman stated at the 1972 annual meeting in London, "I am totally opposed to the contract labor system and will have nothing whatever to do with it. . . . We are going to employ our labour without the contract system."[65] While it is true that, given the capital-intensive nature of the uranium mine at Rossing, it is easier for RTZ to take this position, the statement of principle is nevertheless applicable to Tsumeb, which has never attempted to use anything other than African "contract" labor on any scale. Tsumeb has 5,385 African employees, and with the exception of less than 100 clerical workers (1.86 percent), all of them are one-year contract laborers living in the company's compound, separated from their families.

The reputation of the "American mine" is very bad among work-seekers from the North.[66] Bishop Winter, who has close links with the Ovambos

through the extensive missionary work going on in that area, has summed
up the impact of its presence and labor policies:

> In my own contact with the people there [in Ovamboland], even in
> the most remote areas, I am convinced that the overwhelming ma-
> jority of the people of Namibia are hostile toward the continuing U.S.
> economic presence in that land. Take, for example, the Tsumeb Corpor-
> ation copper mine. May I place on record that this company is really be-
> traying the name of America in my land. Its whole labor practices, the
> employment of near slave labor, is discrediting the whole image of the
> United States in Namibia. . . .
> I believe, sir, that it stands under our judgment most severely when its
> managerial employer states that they have an understanding with the
> Government of South Africa.[67]

Navarro Exploration Company*

Navarro is a wholly owned subsidiary of Zapata Norness, Inc., of
Houston, Texas. Zapata acquired Navarro in 1968. It has operated a
copper mine at Onganja, Namibia, since 1967, and reported in 1969 that
the profit contribution from Navarro, although negligible that year, "should
become substantial in 1970 and the years beyond."[68] Output from Onganja
had been considerably expended toward the end of 1969, reaching about
200 tons of copper per day. The ore reserves were reported to be limited.[69]

Navarro is also engaged in mineral exploration, and has over 750,000
acres of prospecting properties under "lease" from the occupying power,
on which a wide range of minerals, including silver, zinc, lead, and molyb-
denum, have already been discovered.

United States Steel*

This company entered Namibia after 1966; in 1969 it took an interest
—originally reported as 30 percent, but later as 1.8 percent—in the Africa
Triangle Company's prospecting ventures in Namibia.[70] The other share-

holders in African Triangle are South African companies and the Tsumeb
Corporation. In March 1971 African Triangle decided to move out its laboratory, vehicles, and plant, leaving only a skeleton staff to continue in-
vestigations, although previously it had announced that results justified
systematic drilling of the copper-bearing bands.[71] The decision is therefore likely to have been based on the legal and political situation.

Bethlehem Steel**

The company has been prospecting in Namibia since 1952, but abandoned all its original areas. In 1970 it was reported that Bethlehem had
entered into a new prospecting agreement with the Tsumeb Corporation
to explore for fluorspar near Grootfontein. The Johannesburg *Star* commented: "The decision is considered of particular interest in respect of
South West Africa as it runs contrary to publicly expressed United States
Government policy on investment there."[72]

Nord Resources**

Nord Mining, a subsidiary of Nord Resources of New Mexico, holds
huge concessions in the Omaruru area. Late in 1970 it announced its intention of developing a wolfram mine, at a capital cost of $7 million. It
increased its holdings to three further concession areas of 1971.[73] Nord
has also announced the discovery, in partnership with a French firm, of
a large deposit of copper.[74]

O'okiep Copper Company**

In 1972, minerals were discovered in the proposed "Damara Bantustan"
to which the Damara people, the second largest ethnic group in Namibia
after the Ovambos, were to have been confined despite strenuous resistance.
At the discovery of minerals, the South African occupation regime immediately granted prospecting rights to several corporations, including O'okiep
(in which Newmont and Amax jointly own 75.5 percent). Meanwhile, steps

were taken, without any consultation with the Damaras, to redraw the "Bantustan" boundaries to exclude the mineral-rich areas from it.[75]

Continental Ore Corporation**

Continental Ore is the joint owner with South Africa's Federale Volksbeleggings group of Minerts, with 47.5 percent of the equity of the Otjihase copper mine, about 16 km. from Windhoek. The other 52.5 percent of this mine is controlled by South Africa's Joint Consolidated Investments. Production is to start there at the end of 1975 after an initial capital outlay of R23 million ($30 million). The reserves of about 16 million tons of ore are expected to be processed at the planned mill rate of 100,000 tons per month.[76] This would presumably mean that the ore would be exhausted in just over thirteen years.

Hanna Mining and Marcona Company**

Recent reports indicate that these two companies are engaged in a mineral search.[77]

Falconbridge Nickel Mines, Ltd. (Superior Oil)**

Although registered in Canada, Falconbridge is controlled by U.S. interests, with 37 percent interest held by McIntyre Porcupine Mines, a company controlled by Superior Oil. It was announced in December 1972 that Superior Oil will earn 50 percent of all Falconbridge's activities in South Africa and Namibia. Falconbridge's net profit rose from $5.5 million in 1972 to $47.9 million in 1973. One of its board members, apart from directors of Superior Oil and other U.S. interests, is former Treasury Secretary John Connally.

Falconbridge's Oamites mine was opened on November 21, 1971, by the South African "administrator" of Namibia, Dirk Mudge. Oamites is 75 percent owned by Falconbridge and 25 percent by the South African

Industrial Development Corporation. The investment involved was $7 million, and 4.7 million tons of copper ore are expected to produce $6.6 million per year over the next five years; it is known that Falconbridge hopes to get as much as possible out of Namibia by the end of 1977. Falconbridge uses contract labor; Mudge in his opening speech praised the opening of the new mine, but added, "Unfortunately the mining officials found very little interest among the [Namibian] people." Wages range from $24 to $63 per month, which is way below the estimated Poverty Datum Line of $110 per month.[78]

Chevron Regent**

This is a consortium of Chevron (Standard Oil of California) and Regent Petroleum, a subsidiary of Texaco. In January 1971 they were granted exploration rights for oil in a new 4,000 square mile offshore concession.[79] They later withdrew and were granted another concession further out to sea, as a sublease from the Marine Diamond Corporation (a subsidiary of de Beers), which had a pre-1966 concession.[80]

Aracca Exploration,** Phillips Petroleum,** Milford Argosy Corporation,** Getty Oil Company,** Continental Oil**

These companies were granted oil-prospecting concessions for offshore operations.[81] Phillips applied for, and received, an offshore exploration concession from the illegal occupying power in 1972. It took over a concession which had been abandoned by other foreign investors, presumably for political and legal reasons. Milford Argosy also started active exploration offshore.

Getty Oil owns a 46 percent interest in Tidal Diamonds SWA (Pty), Ltd. through its subsidiary, Tidewater Oil Company. Tidal Diamonds retrieves high-quality gem diamonds from an offshore concession area.[82]

Getty Oil also was involved through Getty Minerals SWA (Pty), Ltd., which obtained oil-prospecting concessions off the coast of Namibia in June 1972. Continental Overseas Oil was the first to announce its withdrawal from Namibia, clearly as a result of stockholder challenges.[84] This led to the withdrawal of Continental Oil, Aracca Exploration, Getty Oil, and Phillips Petroleum.

Brilund Mines, Ltd.

Although incorporated in Ontario, Canada, in 1952, the official address of this company does not exist in Toronto; a law office acts there as a front for executive offices, which are listed as located in New York and Dallas. Brilund Mines is associated with Syracuse Oils of the United States. A Canadian government report in reply to a U.N. Security Council request for information on national corporations active in Namibia indicated that "while the headquarters of Brilund Mines Ltd. is in Toronto, Canada, its executive offices are in Mount Vernon, New York. It is a holding company only and obtained 100 percent interest in Etosha Petroleum Co. in 1966." Etosha Petroleum is a wholly owned subsidiary in Namibia.

Etosha has exploration rights over an area of 116,000 square miles from the Atlantic Ocean to the Botswana border, and from the Angolan border to the 20th parallel. In December 1970 Etosha announced that it had discovered eleven "very favorable" potential oil structures, the immediate drilling sites for the next phase of its R5.4 million ($7.6 million) exploration program. Since then, however, there has been no further news, and it appears that Etosha Petroleum has sold much of its equipment in Namibia and begun to move all the heavy equipment into Angola, where it was reportedly leased to another oil company.[85] In 1971, the *New York Times* reported that Etosha had found a major zinc deposit in northeast Namibia, although other reports state that "heavy involvement in the search for minerals was abandoned late in 1970." The reasons for such sketchy and contradictory information is perhaps best summed up by its managing director and controlling shareholder of the company, Mr. Rosenblat: "It was in the interest of the country to say as little as possible."[86]

Arthur G. McKee**

The Western Knapp Engineering Division of this company has won a contract for the development of the Anglo-French-South African Govern-

ment Rossing uranium mine. The contract will involve engineering, procurement design, and construction work.

This mine has been the subject of great controversy in the United Kingdom, especially as it has been made possible by a large purchase contract
with the U.K. Atomic Energy Authority, and now also with the French
Government. It is alleged that this will make the British and French nuclear weapons programs largely dependent on the goodwill of the South
African occupation regime in Namibia. The mine is due to enter production in 1977, and South Africa's position as a major supplier of uranium
is greatly enhanced by it.

THE NATURE OF AMERICAN
INVOLVEMENT IN NAMIBIA

The number of American interests in Namibia is extensive, given the limited nature of the territory's economy, and there is probably much more of
it than has been ascertained to date, particularly with the over 300 U.S. companies operating in South Africa that have direct or indirect operations in
Namibia. A list of those known is in Appendix II. It is in fact difficult for
a company to have a substantial investment in South Africa and not have
at least a distribution outlet in Namibia; the products of the major investors such as GM, Ford, and Chrysler are certainly sold in Namibia. Even
if a company were to make every effort to avoid investing in Namibia or
dealing directly or indirectly with the illegal occupying regime there, if it
has a sizeable operation in South Africa it is unlikely that it will be able to
achieve this.

It must be placed on record that, apparently as a result of the special
legal and political character of the Namibian situation, some foreign investors have decided to withdraw their involvement there. A spokesman
of the State Department has said that, in response to a letter from the department to companies operating in Namibia informing them of the policy to discourage such investments, some companies had replied that U.S.
policy had been a factor in their decision not to invest in Namibia; however, for reasons of commercial confidentiality, their names could not be
disclosed.[87] It is unlikely that such a decision, especially if it involves re-
fraining from a new commitment, would become known unless the com-

pany concerned made a point of announcing it. A stake in South Africa, for example, might make a company reluctant to announce any move that would risk antagonizing the South African government.

Among the cases that are known, there is that of Phelps Dodge, the second biggest copper producer in the United States. It had applied in 1971 for a concession over a vast tract of land in the north of Namibia.[88] When contacted by researchers in December 1972, Mr. Arnold Godduhn, a lawyer in the company's International Department, said that the company had withdrawn from Namibia in 1972; "The political considerations made it imprudent to stay there." Phelps Dodge is however planning to invest heavily in mining in South Africa.

A number of foreign companies also withdrew from Namibia at about the time of the ICJ's advisory opinion. They include Anglovaal of South Africa, and Kewanee, H.M. Mining, Gulf Oil Corporation, Syracuse Oil, and Woodford Oil and Gas, all U.S. companies involved in oil exploration consortia.

The most recent and clear-cut case of withdrawal is that of the five U.S. oil companies which had been prospecting for oil in Namibia. At the end of 1974 and beginning of 1975, following sustained challenges to their involvement there, on legal grounds, by churches and other stockholders, they all announced their withdrawal. The five involved are Continental Oil Co. (CONOCO), Aracca, Standard Oil of California (Chevron), Getty Oil, and Phillips Petroleum.[89]

Some Additional Considerations Relating to U.S. Investment in Namibia

There is no question that the Namibian economy under illegal occupation is flourishing. Gross domestic product (GDP) per capita is the second highest in Africa, after Libya, and one of the fifteen highest in the world.[90] GDP rose by an average of 10.23 percent per annum between 1963 and 1969.[91] The nature of the economic activity fueling these impressive figures, however, and the distribution of the income, demonstrates a complete disregard for the stated purposes of the mandate under which South Africa purports to rule.

It can be instructive to refer to South Africa's claims and compare them

with the facts of its occupation policy and practice. In his statement to th
almost empty General Assembly on October 5, 1973, in an attempt to defend his country's illegal occupation, the South African foreign minister
claimed:

> . . . we believe we have a duty to continue to assist in the development
> South West Africa in all spheres: economic, social and political. We der
> no financial or economic advantage whatsoever from our presence in th
> Territory. Every cent which accrues from taxation levied on income de
> rived within the Territory, including profits on foreign investments and
> operations in the Territory, is re-invested in South West Africa for the
> benefit of all its inhabitants. In addition, South African taxpayers con-
> tribute to the Territory's advancement on current account alone—that
> is, excluding payments to finance capital projects—funds which in the
> last few years have varied between $60 million and $80 million per
> annum.[92]

This claim cannot be independently verified, for the simple reason that
the complete accounts relating to South Africa's income from, and expenditure in, Namibia are not published and are becoming increasingly difficult to trace through the deliberate obscurantism of the occupying regime
Most revenues from Namibia, in particular the major source of income,
taxes on white income-earners and companies, are paid directly to the Sou
African government in Pretoria, in line with the advanced stage of South
Africa's annexation of Namibia. Despite South Africa's claims that the
Class "C" mandate empowered it to administer Namibia as an integral par
of the Republic, the International Court is firmly on record as stating, in
1950, that "it is clear that the Union [of South Africa] has no competenc
to modify unilaterally the international status of the Territory."[93]

The incorporation of all financial activities of the previous South West
Africa administration into the operations of the South African governmer
without even recording the payments relating to Namibian activities separately, is one of the major elements in the process of annexation and clear
modifies unilaterally the international status of the territory. Pretoria now
controls directly the taxation on all mining income, company tax (35 percent), undistributed profits tax, diamond export duty and diamond profit
tax, stamp duty and marketable securities tax, transfer duties, film duties,

customs and excise taxes, posts and telegraphs, and fire-arms licenses. Total revenue is divided between Pretoria and Windhoek on a certain formula,
which has nothing to do with the actual amount received from Namibia.
Much of the money passing to projects in Namibia is in the form of repay-
able loans.[94] Furthermore, only 18 percent of the "direct" expenditure
in the 1970-1971 budget for Namibia went to the African 84 percent of
the population, whose well-being South Africa claims to promote. Eighty-
two percent goes to the white settlers.[95]

The system of accounting is such as to obscure completely the question
of whether South Africa profits from Namibia, and by how much. Revenue
from a South African-based company that contains some element derived
from Namibian operations would not be susceptible to analysis, even if
there were a determined effort to separate the two items. Diamonds, for
example, are actually the major export from Namibia, but are counted as
South African exports and marketed along with some South African diamonds. The trend is toward less, rather than more, effort to set the record
straight. There are now no less than three budgets published by official
South African sources that relate wholly or in part to Namibia. They overlap, fail to distinguish consistently between South Africa and Namibia,
and together present a hopelessly confused picture. The inference must be
that they are designed to conceal the profit and loss situation for South
Africa's occupation.

Finally, all the indications are that Namibia is in fact highly profitable
to South Africa and that the participation of foreign companies contributes toward a situation of blatant exploitation. To quote the findings of
the South African *Financial Mail:*

Published information tends to be rather one-sided, showing in the main
how favourably South Africa's economic management of the territory has
reflected on the welfare and prosperity of its inhabitants.

What is not disclosed, however, is the extent to which the gap between
GDP and GNP has increased since the last published information in 1962.
Then, GNP at R104 million was about 30 percent less than GDP.

And it is reasonable to assume that the process, in which one third of GDP
accrued to foreign capital and labour, has continued and that the gap has
stretched considerably in the intervening years. As has the gap between

the *per capita* income of Whites in the Police Zone and Blacks in the Homelands.[96]

The extreme maldistribution of the benefits of economic activity can be seen from figures published before the flow of information was halted. In 1966 the average GDP per capita was $651,[97] and estimated distribution was as shown in Table 2.

TABLE 2 GDP PER CAPITA (RANDS)

Total population	360
Whites only	1,602
"Nonwhites," northern sector (i. e., Africans)	61
"Nonwhites," police zone (including Coloureds, who would tend to raise the average)	229

Assuming a constant distribution of GDP, this would mean that by 1970 the figures would be:

Total population	467
Whites only	2,078
"Nonwhites," northern sector	79
"Nonwhites," police zone	312

Source: U.S. State Department, *Area Handbook for the Republic of South Africa* (Washington, D.C.: Government Printing Office, 1971).

Thus in 1969, over thirty of the forty-one independent African countries had a higher GDP per capita than the northern sector of Namibia, which is where one-half the Namibians live. This area accounted for only 3.5 percent of Namibia's national GDP in 1951.[98]

Figures for GDP per capita are a guide, but they are misleading in that they may conceal extreme poverty if profits are being removed by those other than the producers. The latest available figures show estimated income per capita in 1956 was only R17 ($23) outside the white "Police Zone"—below even the figure for South African reserves, and possibly the lowest in the whole of Africa.[99] This compares with per capita income for all groups in the white sector of Namibia of R342 (almost $480) per annum, indicating an income ratio of over 20:1 in favor of the police zone. The incomes of whites only is not stated, but must be far higher. The gap between white and black incomes is substantially wider even than the outstandingly unequal ratio of South Africa itself, which stands at around 13:1.[100]

This unprecedented inequality in distributing the benefits of the territory's wealth by explicit racial discrimination is in blatant violation of Article 22 of the Covenant of the League of Nations, which established the mandate system on the understanding that: "There should be applied the principle that the well-being and development of such peoples form a sacred trust of civilization." The use of the territory and its inhabitants for the benefit of the occupying power and various other foreign interests is also in clear contradiction to Articles 2 and 3 of the mandate for South West Africa:

> The Mandatory shall promote to the utmost the material and moral well-being and the social progress of the inhabitants of the Territory subject to the present Mandate [Article 2].

> The Mandatory shall see that the slave trade is prohibited and that no forced labour is permitted [Article 3].

The exploitation of the territory's natural and human resources has been growing since the inception of the mandate, but particularly after World War II, which is when most of the American investment occurred. In 1946, before the expansion of the mining sector in which foreign interests predominate, the proportion of the territory's GDP accruing to foreign capital was 8 percent; by 1962, it had risen to 31.7 percent.[101] The South African Commission of Enquiry on South West Africa, known as the Odendaal Commission, reported in 1964, "It is therefore a feature of the economy of South West Africa that with the development of mining the ratio of the gross national income to the GDP has diminished considerably.[102] The Odendaal Commission stressed the prime importance—to South Africa's interests—of "the rapid development of known and determinable resources." This recommendation has certainly been carried out enthusiastically: in 1966 the total value of mineral sales reached $177.9 million, over one-half the territory's GDP, and in 1970-1971 this reached $182 million. Base minerals, as opposed to diamonds, are of increasing importance in the total mineral production: they rose from 33.8 percent in 1966 to 46 percent in 1970-1971.[103] This means that American-dominated activity increased in this proportion relative to the South African diamond operations. In 1970 over 100 prospecting grants were purportedly issued by the illegal regime, and the South African Department of Mines reported a jump in prospecting fees from $63,000 in 1966 to $700,000 four years later. Much of this, of course, was from American-dominated interests. The South African *Financial Gazette* commented: "Mineral development and exploration in South West Africa is booming as never before. With 18 companies engaged in mining production and a further 44 or so prospecting . . . there is a possibility of a bonanza that will alter the whole structure and future of the area."[104]

The advantage of rapid exploitation of natural resources for the South African occupation regime is obvious. The Tsumeb Corporation, for example, pays 30.26 percent of its gross "rent" direct to the South African occupation regime and only 6.39 percent in the form of wages to Africans in the territory. Dividends remitted abroad were the major item and accounted for 45.98 percent.[105] It could be said, then, that in this case American interests benefit even more from the current illegal situation than the occupation regime itself.

The South African occupation regime purports to control all mineral rights in Namibia, on which it collects royalties and prospecting fees as well as taxes. This arises from a questionable interpretation of the original mandate—which authorized South Africa to administer the territory as it was—as a license to expropriate land and mineral rights, which the original German colonial regime had vested in a number of companies, individual settlers, or the Africans in certain areas. The result of South Africa's economic policies is that 60 percent of the land, including all the best farming land, diamond areas, other mineral-rich areas, ports and other assets of the territory as a whole are assigned to the 16 percent of the population that is made up of white settlers. The distribution of oil rights may be equally as dubious; prospecting concessions were sold in 1968 by an agency of the "administration" of Namibia, SWAKOR, a subsidiary of the

South African Government's agency, SOEKOR. A condition of all concessions purportedly granted is that any company striking oil must transfer 10 percent of its shares to SOEKOR, while royalties are paid to SWAKOR.

The integration of the economic life of Namibia into that of South Africa since 1966, a major step toward total annexation of the territory, has been greatly facilitated by the fact that most of the foreign interests involved have operations in both areas, and administer them together. A step in the direction of total annexation was the South West Africa Affairs Act, No. 25 of 1969, which made all taxation other than individual income tax payable to the central government in Pretoria; mining legislation was also to be administered direct from there.[106] U.S. interests in Namibia are therefore in the forefront of the move to treat Namibia as part of South Africa and in addition are paying taxes, royalties, and other items directly into the occupation regime's Treasury, which clearly increases the degree of control exercised over Namibia by the regime.

One particular area in which collusion with the illegal regime is particularly obvious is the project to develop the Kunene River on the frontier between Namibia and Angola, and extending well into Angola. This network of dams, hydroelectric plants, and irrigation works will be of great benefit to the illegal regime in Namibia, supplying scarce water and energy to the booming mineral exploitation, starting with Tsumeb, and the "white" towns including the capital, Windhoek. The original, advertised plans to irrigate parts of Ovamboland have been dropped in the implementation of the plan, which started with a major dam project at Gove, inside Angola. The most striking feature of this project from the point of view of a foreign investor is that the entire scheme using Kunene River waters is based on a purported bilateral treaty between South Africa (for Namibia) and Portugal (for Angola) of 1969; the International Court of Justice has pronounced such treaties to be illegal and invalid. Therefore any contracts or financing arrangement for the Kunene scheme based on this treaty are themselves illegal and invalid.[107] South Africa's armed intervention in Angola started with the occupation of the Angolan areas of the Kunene project.

Considerations such as these tend to be dismissed by some investors—notably those with a large vested interest in the illegal occupation—as purely academic and irrelevant to "realistic" investment decisions. It may be worth pointing out, therefore, that of all the stockholder resolutions presented on southern African issues during 1972, those calling for disclosure by Newmont and Amax with regard to the operation of the Tsume Corporation in Namibia obtained the highest percentages (2.93 percent for Amax, 2.68 percent for Newmont). In the case of Amax there was overwhelming abstention by institutional investors; among those stockholders reporting to the Africa Policy Information Center of the African-American Institute, 67,527 shares were voted for management, and 191,500 (almost three times as many) abstained. This is very unusual, perhaps unprecedente in the recent experience of church-sponsored stockholder resolutions. In 1973, resolutions concerning Namibia were filed with four companies (Am Newmont, Continental Oil, and Phillips Petroleum); in the case of the latte two, the oil companies starting new operations in Namibia were asked to te minate their operations. The votes were unusually high, 5.2 percent for the resolution in the case of Continental Oil and 4.2 percent in the case of Phillips Petroleum, enabling the sponsors of the resolution to reintroduce it in 1974. Two more companies operating in Namibia were added to the list of challenges for 1974: Getty Oil and Standard Oil of California, both involved in offshore oil exploration. The five oil companies withdrew, star ing at the end of 1974. Namibia is one of the major issues currently being focused on by the corporate challengers and also the most successful in attracting support and widespread abstentions from institutional stockholde who normally vote automatically with management.[108]

The question of Namibia, therefore, is a serious one, and an issue wher U.S. policy is unequivocal: to discourage investment. A sense of urgency is felt by those most closely concerned because of the heavy concentration of investment in extractive industries. This concern has been expressed by the United Nations: "The country runs the risk of finding itself, in the not too distant future, without the raw materials that now provide the main support for the money economy."[109] This is also a valid concern of the United States and other governments which, given the international responsibility repeatedly stressed by them at the United Nations, are likely to find themselves having to give "aid" to a newly independent Namibia, after it has lost the irreplaceable mineral resources with which it would be able to build up self-sustaining growth for the benefit of the whole region (including Botswana in particular) and its own inhabitants. Such national leaders as are allowed to speak have protested violently at the exploitation of Namibia's natural resources; Chief Kapuuo, elected chief of the Herero people, has written:

This country, which is our country, is being exploited by greedy entrepreneurs, stripped of its wealth, and rendered barren for the future, Our fear is that when freedom finally comes to this land, it will be returned to us with no minerals left. Thus you will see the one wonderful asset which we have for developing the land for the well-being of all its people will have been taken away from us.[110]

Bishop Winter has voiced the obvious question arising from the notorious reputation of American employers in the long-term perspective: "When freedom comes to Namibia, as it surely will, what of the future of American investments in my land after independence comes?"[111]

NOTES

1. Company responses to questionnaire from Congressman Charles C. Diggs, Jr., 1962-3; in U.S. Congress, House of Representatives, committee on Foreign Affairs, Subcommittee on Africa, *U.S. Business Involvement in Southern Africa*, Part III (Washington, D.C.: Government Printing Office, 1973), appendix 81,82 and 83, pp. 978-1067.
2. William P. Rogers, speech to the U.N. General Assembly, 4 October, 1971; U.N. Document A/PV. 1950, p. 2.
3. Testimony by Hon. David Newsom on March 27, 1973, before the House Subcommittee on Africa, ibid., p. 12.
4. Testimony by Hon. Robert S. Smith on March 28, 1972, in ibid., p. 56. Substantially repeated in a letter to Congressman Diggs from John R. Stevenson, The Legal Advisory, Department of State, October 10, 1972, in ibid., appendix 66, pp. 911-2.
5. Testimony by Hon. Robert S. Smith, March 28, 1972, in ibid., p. 58.
6. Written statement subsequent to request for data in testimony by Hon. R. Smith, March 28, 1973, in ibid., p. 58.

7. Letter from Congressman Diggs to the chairman of the SEC, Augus 15, 1973, in ibid., appendix 61, pp. 899-900.

8. Letter to companies operating in Namibia from Willis C. Armstrong assistant secretary for Economic Affairs, State Department; enclosure to letter to Congressman Diggs from David Abshire, assistant secretary for Congressional Relations, December 4, 1972.

9. Hon. R. Smith, testimony of March 28, 1973, in *Business Involvement in Southern Africa*, Part III, p. 71.

10. State Department memorandum submitted for the record in ibid., p. 71.

11. Statement by Toivo ja Toivo in the Supreme Court of South Africa Transvaal Provincial Division, Pretoria, February 1, 1968.

12. Guy Arnold in Gemini News Service article, August 23, 1973.

13. Report of the United Nations Council for Namibia, U.N. Doc. A/9(October 12, 1973.

14. Bishop Colin Winter, Anglican Bishop of Damaraland, in testimony the Subcommittee on Africa, March 28, 1973, in *Business Involvement in Southern Africa*, Part III, p. 55.

15. Ibid., p. 62.

16. For a fuller description, *see* Marcelle Kooy, "The Contract Labor System and the Ovambo Crisis of 1971 in South West Africa," *African Studies Review* 16, 1, (April 1973): pp. 83-105.

17. John Kane-Berman, "Contract Labour in South West Africa" (Pape read at the 43rd Annual Council Meeting, South African Institute of Race Relations, Johannesburg, January 16-19, 1973. RR. 10/73).

18. Quoted in David Hemson, "The Ovambo Workers' Strike," *NUSAS Press Digest* 2/72, National Union of South African Students, Cape Town mimeographed, p. 1.

19. Interviews by the author in Ovamboland, July 1971.

20. *NUSAS Press Digest* 2/72, p. 22.

21. Ibid.

22. "[Republic] Regulations for the Establishment of Employment Br reaus in the Territory of South West Africa," Proclamation No. R. 83/72, April 4, 1972; summarized in a memorandum on Labor Regulations for Namibia by Michael Davis, June 1972 (mimeo).

23. The "Labour Enactment for Owambo [Enactment 6 of 1972]," enacted by the "Owambo Legislative Council" in terms of the "Development of Self-Government for Native Nations in South West Africa Act, 1968," gazetted by the South African State President on August 18, 197:

24. The term "desertion" for attempting to change or terminate emplc

ment is that used by the occupation administration itself: for example, the statement from the Department of Bantu Administration, Pretoria: "Any employee who illegally deserts from his service can be considered to be in a particular area without permission. He may be persecuted [sic] and removed from the area." (Quoted in the *Financial Mail* (Johannesburg), 7 April 1972.)

25. "Labour Enactment of Owambo."

26. John Kane-Berman, "The Ovambo Strike," (Paper delivered to a meeting of the Progressive party in Houghton, Johannesburg, February 1972), p. 1-2.

27. *Financial Mail*, special supplement: "South West Africa—Desert Deadlock," 2 March 1972.

28. Quoted by Kane-Berman in "Ovambo Strike."

29. Ibid.

30. Rauha Voipio in a study published by the Christian Institute, Johannesburg, quoted in Kane-Berman, "Ovambo Strike."

31. *Financial Mail*, 11 February 1972.

32. Rauha Voipio, in *Race Relations News* (Johannesburg), February 1973.

33. South African press, quoted in Council for Namibia Conference Room Paper, U.N. Doc. SCI/72/8.

34. Kane-Berman, "Ovambo Strike."

35. *Financial Mail*, special supplement.

36. Ibid.

37. Mr. Smith, State Department, March 27, 1973; *Business Involvement in Southern Africa*, p. 63.

38. *Church Investments, Corporations and Southern Africa* (New York: Corporate Information Center, National Council of Churches, 1973), p. 36.

39. *Annual Report*, Newmont Mining Corporation, 1971.

40. *Annual Report*, American Metal Climax, 1971.

41. U.N. Doc. A/8423/Add. 3 (Part I).

42. U.N. Doc., Conference Room Paper SCI/72/8.

43. Annual Report, Newmont Mining Corporation, 1971.

44. Interview with Herbert Drechsler, Columbia School of Mines, former employee of Tsumeb, May 3, 1972; quoted in Terence M. Strong, "Newmont Mining Corporation, Southern Africa Operations," (M.A. thesis, Columbia University Business School B9501, May 15, 1972).

45. *Annual Report*, Newmont Mining Corporation, 1971.

46. G. Sohnge, *Tsumeb: A Historical Sketch* (Windhoek: South West Africa Association, 1967).

47. 1922 Report of the Administrator of South West Africa, quoted in U.N. Doc. A/AC.109/L 154, October 16, 1965.

48. *See* Strong, "Newmont Mining Corporation."

49. *Annual Report,* Newmont Mining Corporation, 1947 and 1971.

50. Ibid., 1971.

51. Calculated by Strong "Newmont Mining Corporation," from the *Annual Reports,* Newmont Mining Corporation, 1947 and 1971.

53. *Annual Report* Tsumeb Corporation, Ltd., 1970.

54. *Financial Gazette* (Johannesburg), 18 June 1971.

55. Tsumeb Corporation advertisement in *Wall Street Journal,* 5 September 1969.

56. Ibid.

57. U.N. Doc. A/8398/Add. 1, December 6, 1971; also Tsumeb Corporation advertisement.

58. Interview at Tsumeb, March 9, 1971; Tami Hultman and Reed Kramer, "Overseas Mining Firms Continue to Snub UN," *Sunday Nation* (Nairobi), 3 October 1971.

59. Kane-Berman, "Ovambo Strike."

60. T. Strong, "Newmont Mining Corporation."

61. Calculated from figures given in ibid.

62. Tsumeb Corporation advertisement in *Sunday Times* (Johannesburg), 26 September 1971.

63. Hultman and Kramer, *Sunday Nation.*

64. *Annual Report,* Newmont Mining Corporation, 1971.

65. Unofficial transcript of the Annual General Meeting of Rio Tinto-Zinc, May 17, 1972, in London.

66. Interviews by the author in Ovamboland, July 1971.

67. Bishop Colin Winter in testimony of March 28, 1973, in *U.S. Business Involvement in Southern Africa,* Part III, pp. 52 and 54.

68. *Annual Report,* Zapata Norness, 1969.

69. U.N. Doc., Conference Room Paper SCI/72/8, July 5, 1972.

70. U.N. Doc. A/8423/Add. 3 (Part I), September 27, 1971; Conference Room Paper SCI/72/8.

71. Ibid.

72. *The Star* (Johannesburg), 14 November 1970.

73. U.N. Soc., Conference Room Paper SCI/72/8.

74. *Wall Street Journal* (New York) 4 November 1971.

75. *Financial Mail,* 4 August 1972.

76. *Financial Gazette,* 3 August 1973; *The Star,* 4 August 1973.

77. Winifred Courtney and Jennifer Davis, *Namibia: U.S. Corporate*

Involvement (New York: The Africa Fund, together with the World Council of Churches, March 1972), p. 23.

78. "Falconbridge," mimeographed briefing paper by the Development Education Centre, Toronto, Canada, 1973.

79. *Financial Gazette*, 29 January, 1971.

80. U.N. Doc., Conference Room Paper SCI/72/8.

81. *The Oil and Gas Journal* (3 July 1972).

82. *Financial Gazette*, 29 January 1971.

83. Information supplied by the Department of Commerce in *U.S. Business Involvement in Southern Africa*, Part I, p. 269; also the *Windhoek Advertiser*, 22 June 1972.

84. *Wall Street Journal*, 1 November 1974.

85. U.N. Doc., Conference Room paper SCI/72/8; also Courtney and Davis, *Namibia*, pp. 25-6.

86. "Falconbridge."

87. Letter to Congressman Diggs from the State Department, August 21, 1970, *U.S. Business Involvement in Southern Africa*, Part II, p. 68.

88. *Financial Gazette*, 9 October 1971.

89. *The Star*, week of 1 February 1975, and press releases by the companies.

90. U.N., Economic Commission for Africa, *Economic Indicators 1968*.

91. G.M. E. Leistner, "South West Africa's Economic Bonds with South Africa" in Anthony Lejeune, ed., *The Case for South West Africa* (London: South African Embassy, Tom Stacey, 1971), p. 213.

92. Mr. H. Muller, Speech to the U.N. General Assembly, 5 October 1973; U.N. Document A/PV. 2141, pp. 48-9.

93. "International Status of South West Africa, 1950," *I.C.J. Reports*, pp. 131-143.

94. *Financial Mail*, special supplement on South West Africa, March 2, 1973.

95. Information from the Department of Commerce, submitted to House Subcommittee on Africa; *U.S. Business Involvement in Southern Africa*, Part III, p. 269; also *Windhoek Advertiser*, 22 June 1972.

96. *Financial Mail* supplement, p. 42.

97. U.N. Doc., Conference Room Paper SCI/72/8.

98. U.S. State Department, *Area Handbook for the Republic of South Africa* (Washington D.C.: Government Printing Office, 1971).

99. D.C. Krogh, "The National Income and Expenditure of South West Africa (1920-1956)," *South African Journal of Economics*, 28, 1 (March 1960), p. 16.

100. Kane-Berman, "Ovambo Strike," p. 3.

101. Roger Murray, "Namibia: An Initial Survey of the Pattern of Expropriation of the Mineral Resources of Namibia by the South African Government and Overseas Companies" (Paper for the Namibia International Conference and Overseas Companies, Brussels, May 26-28, 1972).

102. Republic of South Africa, *Report of the Commission of Enquiry into South-West-African Affairs, 1962-1963,* R.P. No. 12/1974 (Pretoria: Government Printer, 1964), p. 327.

103. U.N. Doc. A/8148/Add. 1, November 30, 1970; also Murray, "Namibia."

104. *Financial Gazette,* 13, March 1970.

105. T. Strong, "Newmont Mining Corporation," calculated from 1970 figures.

106. Murray, "Namibia."

107. For details of the Kunene scheme, see *Cunene Dam Scheme* (Geneva: World Council of Churches, December 1971).

108. *Update* (African Policy Information Center, African-American Institute) Special Report of Namibia, March 1973, and December 1973; also *Corporate Challenges 1974,* mimeographed, Corporate Information Center, National Council of Churches, New York, 1974.

109. U.N. Doc. A/AC. 109/L. 154, October 16, 1964.

110. Letter of September 3, 1971, from Chief Clemens Kapuuo to his lawyers in London, reproduced in a press statement by the Africa Bureau, London.

111. Testimony to the Subcommittee on Africa, March 28, 1973, in *U.S. Business Involvement in Southern Africa,* Part III, p. 52.

chapter 6 _____

SOUTHERN RHODESIA

The question of investment in Southern Rhodesia in present circumstances is a very simple one: it is illegal in terms of U.S. law. Following an affirmative vote by the U.S. representative for Security Council Resolution, No. 253, which was presented by the British government, Executive Order, No. 11419 was issued on July 29, 1968, "relating to trade and other transactions involving Southern Rhodesia." The Executive Order reads, in part:

The following are prohibited effective immediately, notwithstanding any contracts entered into or licenses granted before the date of this Order:

. . . (d) Sale or supply by any person subject to the jurisdiction of the United States . . . to any person or body in Southern Rhodesia or to any person or body for the purposes of any business carried on in or operated from Southern Rhodesia of any commodities or products.

. . . (f) Transfer by any person subject to the jurisdiction of the Uni-

ted States directly or indirectly to any person or body in Southern
Rhodesia of any funds or other financial or economic resources.

It should be emphasized that the sanctions were not imposed on the
United States by the United Nations; the United States possesses a veto
power in the Security Council, which it has in fact used to prevent the passage of resolutions on Rhodesia that it does not favor. In light of fairly
prevalent misconceptions about the political situation of Southern Rhodesia, it should also be emphasized that comparisions with the Declaration of Independence are spurious. American democracy and independence were predicated on the will of the majority of the electorate, freely
expressed. In the case of Southern Rhodesia, this is legally a British colony that was to have been brought to independence under a participatory
democracy—i.e., majority rule such as large numbers of former British
colonies in Africa and Asia have acquired in the last twenty years. The tran-
sition to independence and democracy was forestalled by what amounted
to a coup d'état by a small minority unwilling to allow the transfer of powe
to the people of the colony. This very small minority of white settlers—virtually all of them first-generation immigrants of fairly recent date—seized
power in November 1965 in an illegal declaration of independence that was
in fact a parody of the American declaration since it forestalled the attempt
to give independence to the inhabitants of Southern Rhodesia, over 95 percent of whom are indigenous Africans.

These Africans are now condemned to a very severe form of colonial-
type repression and deprivation of democratic freedoms. The vote is
available only to a very small minority of the Africans, far fewer even
than the small white electorate. The franchise is tied to a certain income
level, and since, increasingly along the lines of South African apartheid,
the wealth of the country has been appropriated by the white settlers,
with the gap between them and the dispossessed Africans apparently
growing, it is virtually automatic that the white minority will retain
power under the present structure. Although it had been widely
assumed that Rhodesian Africans were accepting this with relatively little
protest, a Commission of Inquiry sent to Southern Rhodesia under Lord
Pearce to test African reactions to a settlement proposal that would have
offered no guarantee of the balance of power being reversed in the fore-

seeable future reported an overwhelming rejection by the Africans in both urban and rural areas. The monopoly of power and wealth by the illegal regime, under Ian Smith, has become so entrenched politically that the Africans have been forced to wage their own war of independence—independence from the settler junta. The guerrilla war has been a constant problem for the regime, and a drain on its resources of capital and armed forces.

SANCTIONS AND INVESTMENTS

A major reason why this legislation and the international sanctions have been so openly flouted is that U.S. and other foreign companies operating in South Africa deal openly with Rhodesia, either by trade, franchises or, fairly commonly, investment transactions. A number of the companies replying to the Diggs questionnnaire on investment in South Africa stated that they had ancillary operations in Rhodesia, Namibia, and elsewhere. This is clearly illegal, even though the law is not enforced. In some cases, the presence of these companies has enabled the illegal regime to benefit from sanctions by taking them over under "emergency powers" legislation and by utilizing their productive capacity for the promotion of import substitution under the siege economy created by sanctions. The benefits have been considerable, with the companies providing a kind of guarantee against international sanctions; however, the limits to the import substitution program were reached within a few years. It is now over eight years since the Unilateral Declaration of Independence (UDI) by the illegal regime, and sanctions are becoming a major burden.

Just as this was becoming evident, despite the tight censorship imposed by the regime, foreign investors came to the rescue again—this time through the determined promotion by the U.S. mineral companies Union Carbide and Foote Mineral, which mobilized their considerable political lobbies in Washington to work with the Liberty Lobby, the Rhodesian Information Office, and other proregime elements for the passage of the so-called Byrd Amendment, Section 503 of the Military Procurement Act of 1971, allowing commodities on the "strategic and critical materials" list to be imported from Southern Rhodesia. This has resulted in a major boost for the Rhodesian regime at a difficult time, with exports to the U.S. of chrome, ferrochrome, asbestos and other materials, amounting to $13 million in 1972 and $30 million in 1973. The latter figure represented a tripling of Rhodesian exports in 1965.[1]

The extent to which the foreign investors have supported the illegal regime—under compulsion as a result of their presence there at the time of UDI, but in many cases involving an enthusiastic degree of cooperation that indicates an identity of interests with the regime—is an indication of what could be expected in the event of an emergency in South Africa or elsewhere in southern Africa generally. It should be pointed out that of the foreign companies in Rhodesia that can be identified, there are more U.S. investors than South African (fifty-six and forty-seven, respectively), and that the U.S. stake is second only to the British.[2] This is the same balance, in fact, as in South Africa itself.

The economic and political structure inside Southern Rhodesia is also very similar to that in South Africa; the white minority monopolizes the modern sector, including cash farming, mining, and industry; foreign investment is allied with the minority, predominantly in mining and industry. Although the complete legislative structure of apartheid is only now beginning to be imposed in Southern Rhodesia, the basic balance of power between various white interests is sufficient to provide for educational expenditure to go mainly to whites; the best jobs go to whites, although there is no formal "job reservation"; housing is segregated; and the whole country is being partitioned on an imitation of the "Bantustan" system in South Africa. Africans are crowded into "tribal trust lands" under the control of white civil servants, while the best land goes to white farmers or, more recently, commercial plantations. The gap between white and African incomes is large (eleven to one), and growing; 90 percent of African workers earn less than the Poverty Datum Line.[3] The *Rhodesia Herald* has reported that the earnings of employed Africans have not kept up with inflation.[4] Opportunities for employment are dwindling, largely because the companies are obliged by the regime to create what amounts to sheltered employment for whites who would otherwise be out of work from sanctions. Africans are therefore being fired to subsidize the cost of employing redundant whites. Between 1963 and 1971, the proportion of Africans in employment fell from 15.93 percent to 15.03 percent.[5]

The successive white regimes in Southern Rhodesia—starting with outright company rule up to 1923—have always encouraged foreign investment as a contributor to the division of the territory's economy into a European sector and provide it with labor on white farms and in mines and industry. The foreign companies were to keep the white population of the territory fully employed at wages that provide relatively high standards of living, which the regime was then to use to attract new white immigrants and boost the growth of the European minority and its hold over the territory's resources. As already noted, most of the white population is of very recent origin, attracted by employment and high standards of living since World War II. Since 1963 there has been full employment for immigrants,[6] almost one-half of it in the manufacturing and distributing sectors, where foreign investment is concentrated. White workers in Rhodesia have one of the highest living standards in the world.[7] As in South Africa, then, the proceeds of the economy go to foreign investors, in alliance with the local white minority.

The Africans, on the other hand, while deprived of the freedom to develop their own resources of land, minerals, and human and other potential, do not even receive any substantial employment spin-off from foreign investment. The increase in European employment each year between 1963 and 1973 has been proportionately higher than that of African employment. Almost one-half of Africans employed worked on white farms, where there is little foreign investment.[8] The proportion of Africans employed by foreign companies is, by comparison, negligible, especially by comparison with the problem of unemployment among Africans in Southern Rhodesia, including educated Africans (many of them trained at mission schools). Unofficial estimates are that two-thirds of the Africans working in the colony are Malawians, deliberately brought in by the whites as easier to discipline than those Africans living in the country.

Apart from being basic to the structure of this two-tier economy that supports white minority rule, foreign companies have also played a major role in collaborating openly with the illegal regime to break international sanctions. They provide an elaborate international mechanism for large-scale evasions by reason of their own international business connections or in many cases, especially for U.S. subsidiaries, associated or related companies in many countries of the world. By definition, any mining company with investments in Southern Rhodesia that continues to operate has to be breaking sanctions, since the territory exports virtually 100 percent of its mining production. Union Carbide is a classic case of a huge, multina-

tional corporation with contracts in both producer and consumer countrie
This enables business deals to be done entirely with the company itself,
which makes detection almost impossible under present enforcement procedures.

To set the record straight, it should not be assumed that the collaboration of foreign companies and their successful lobbying on behalf of the
Smith regime have resulted in sanctions being a complete failure. The clain
that this is the case has in fact been a major argument by the pro-Rhodesia
lobby that has been trying hard (contradicting their own argument about
the ineffectiveness of sanctions) to have them lifted altogether. So long as
there is a formal ban on foreign investment, the regime is unable to acquire
the funds it needs for the kind of expansion that would guarantee the futu
of white rule. At the beginning of 1973 a South African newspaper, which
would not be inclined to seek out these problems where they did not exist
summed up the situation as one of

> uncertainty, uneasiness and frustration born of continued isolation and
> the inability to shape her own destiny free from the fetters of powerful
> outside influences.
>
> . . . White Rhodesia may put up a brave and defiant face, but it is clear
> that the years of economic warfare and isolation are taking their toll. Th
> desire for a settlement and the more secure future it would bring has ne
> been stronger.
>
> . . . The foreign exchange position is desperate (the reason that luxuries
> like Scotch whisky are disappearing from shop windows) and it is this
> factor which is causing a number of residents to ponder on whether it is
> worth sinking their roots deeper into Rhodesian soil.[9]

The trend toward white emigration from Southern Rhodesia overtaking
immigration is the most significant indication of the success of sanctions—
and in itself may be a healthy sign that the territory will eventually achieve
independence under majority rule. The net gain in population due to immigration for 1973 was only 1,680, the lowest figure since 1966. The second
half of the year showed a net outflow of 270 persons. While new arrivals
fell by 32.5 percent, the outflow rose by more than 50 percent.[10] A spoke
man for the regime has said that emigration is causing a shortage of skilled

artisans in most trades.[11] Apart from the sense of there being no economic future in the territory for the settlers, a major impetus to the new trend is a very serious situation facing the regime militarily. There is tight censorship on this, but travelers returning from the territory report that many areas, including those close to centers of European settlement, have been closed off as unsafe.[12] There have been reports of mutiny in the ranks of African units organized by the regime.[13]

In the increasingly desperate attempt to regain control, the regime has resorted to what the London *Guardian* has called "counterterror."[14] Collective punishments have been imposed on whole areas where the liberation movements are operating. Spreading "rumours likely to cause alarm and despondency" can now lead to seven years' jail. Wholesale deportations of Africans were started in May 1973 in the contested areas, together with a "scorched earth" policy for the Northeast and seizure of property that could be used by guerrillas.[15] By January 1974, nearly 10,000 African villagers had been forcibly deported, and the program of "strategic hamlets" was well on the way.[16] The methods involved on the side of the regime and the South African intervention force that is fighting openly in the territory have been reported to be ruthless where civilians are concerned; many civilians were killed in the hunt for "terrorists" and reprisals carried out for successful operations by the guerrillas, including in one case the reported reprisal raid by South Africans that included the slitting of a baby's throat.

Escalating military confrontation is imposing very heavy strains on the already thin manpower at the disposal of the regime, and with frequent reserve call-ups even for men well above normal military age, this is adding to the exodus of white settlers. The regime has launched a last-ditch "Settlers 74" campaign to boost immigration of whites into the territory; this has been heavily criticized by Catholic spokesmen and others as "a notable example of insensitivity to the feeling of the African people who deeply resent it." Bishop Muzorewa of the United Methodist Church, the leader of the moderate African National Council, added, "The 'Settlers 74' campaign is destroying all the goodwill we have been building up among the Africans."[17] Muzorewa has appealed for sanctions to be continued and strengthened to bring a merciful end to the regime which is constantly adding new burdens to the African population of 5.5 million: "The Africans accept sanctions as a price for their freedom and declare as our enemy any person who claims on our behalf that sanctions should be withdrawn. . . . The African National Congress [sic] calls upon the Security Council and the States which support the cause of human freedon to intensify sanctions."[18]

U.S. INVESTMENT IN SOUTHERN RHODESIA

Almost all the major U.S. investment in Southern Rhodesia is in the mining sector, which is in turn completely dominated by foreign companie Since the imposition of sanctions reduced the significance of tobacco and sugar as foreign exchange earners, the importance of minerals to the government's economy has greatly increased; it is now the major source of vital foreign exchange. The mining companies are all large, international con cerns that obviously play an active part in the marketing of production by their Southern Rhodesian subsidiaries, even though they publicly deny any specific allegations. In arguing that Japan, France, and other countries wer breaking sanctions (supposedly an argument for the United States to follov suit), Union Carbide and the other lobbyists neglected to mention what steps they had taken to provide the evidence of such violations to the appropriate authorities for enforcement action. Since they were themselves involved in some of the transactions, this is perhaps not surprising.

About 70-80 percent of the $57 million in American investment in Southern Rhodesia consists of the Union Carbide operation, which has approximately $40-45 million invested in four subsidiaries: African Chrom Mines, Ltd.; Rhodesian Chrome Mines, Ltd.; Union Carbide Rhomet (Private), Ltd.; and Mitimba Estates.[19] Union Carbide began operating in Southern Rhodesia in 1923, only seven years after the company was incorporated in New York, and the Rhodesian operation has become a major part of the company since then. Mitimba Forests supplies timber for mine supports. Rhodesian Chrome Mines and its wholly owned subsidiary African Chrome Mines produce most of the country's chrome ore. In 1963, the last year for published figures, their combined output was 78 percent of the total. Rhodesian Chrome was awarded several prospecting concessions in 1968, not only for chrome but also for nickel, platinoids, and copper. Union Carbide Rhomet operates a ferroalloy plant near Que Que, with a production capacity of at least 40,000 tons of ferrochrom an iron alloy used to make stainless and specialty steel as well as other alloys. This new ferrochrome capacity, combined with the enlarged capacity in South Africa that is dependent on Rhodesian chrome ore, is posing a major threat to the U.S. ferrochrome industry, partly as a result of the differential in labor costs between southern African blacks and American workers (many of them Afro-Americans).

Following the imposition of sanctions, according to a company official:

> On February 8, 1966, the de facto Rhodesian government [sic] directed our local management, pursuant to emergency power regulations, to continue to produce, sell, and export chrome and appointed the individual then serving as managing director of both companies its agent to effect this purpose. As a result, the local management of our Rhodesian affiliates continued to operate the mines and ship ore to ports in Mozambique.[20]

Later, the regime directed the company to sell all its chrome to a state trading corporation.

Union Carbide played a special role in the erosion of U.S. sanctions, starting even before they were decided on. A special U.N. report on sanctions maneuvering by foreign companies just before the sanctions came officially into force commented: "In this connection special mention must be made of the Union Carbide Company of the U.S., which was reported to have imported significant amounts of chrome from its stockpile of an estimated 140,000 tons in Mozambique."[21] Apart from stockpiling in Mozambique, the company took other precautions in 1966 in case the threatened sanctions were imposed. In November, the U.S. headquarters transferred $2 million to a South African subsidiary, Ruighoek Chrome Mines. On December 16, the day the United Nations adopted mandatory sanctions, it sent another $1 million to Ruighoek; and five days later Ruighoek forwarded $2,680,000 to Rhodesian Chrome Mines as advance payment for chrome ore. Later, the company applied to the U.S. government for permission to import 150,000 long tons on the grounds that it was purchased before the United States enacted sanctions.[22]

This transparent maneuver was rejected by administration officials under President Johnson, but in September 1970, the Nixon administration allowed the importation of the 150,000 tons of chrome; this is now seen as the beginning of a series of erosions of sanctions. There have been reports that Keneth Rush, a former president of Union Carbide and a major adviser in the Nixon and the Ford administrations, influenced the decision while serving a ambassador to West Germany. During confirmation hearings in the Senate for Rush's previous post in the State Department, some senators suggested that Rush had a conflict of interest arising out of his large holding of Union Carbide stock and the fact that his pension from the company would be lar er than his salary from the State Department. Union Carbide continues to be heavily involved in the lobbying effort to prevent Congress from repealing the Byrd Amendment and restoring compliance with its treaty obligations. This is a vital issue for the regime in both psychological and economi terms. The London *Sunday Times,* commenting on the effect of the Byrd Amendment on attempts by the British government to achieve an honorable settlement in Southern Rhodesia, observed: "Coming as it did just four days before Sir Alex Douglas-Home left to negotiate with Ian Smith, [the 'Byrd Amendment'] was the death knell of Britain's non-violent 'solution' of the Rhodesian problem."[23] Bishop Muzorewa, while visiting the United States, expressed dismay at the lobbying by Union Carbide and its allies: "Many people are dismayed that the U.S. has *failed* them through its decision to relax sanctions and allow the importation of chrome ore from Rhodesia. . . . Sanctions must remain. Sanctions are the only weapon we have."[24]

Another U.S. company with chrome interests in Southern Rhodesia was Foote Mineral (one-third owned by the Newmont Mining Corporation), which has also been very actively lobbying for the violation of international sanctions by the U.S. government. Ironically, the Byrd Amendment, allowing in cheap Rhodesian and South African ferrochrome, helped to put Foote's U.S. ferrochrome plants out of business. Foote has now sold its sub sidiary, the Rhodesian Vanadium Corporation, to the Anglo-American Corporation of South Africa, and has dropped out of the lobbying on behalf of the Smith regime.

American Metal Climax has an interest in Southern Rhodesia through its subsidiary, Roan Selection Trust, which holds a 50 percent interest in Bikita Minerals, producing lithium near Fort Victoria.[25]

The other aspects of U.S. involvement are not well known, due to the secrecy involved in Southern Rhodesia's economy. Several U.S. oil companies appear to be operating, and supply oil openly under their brand names, presumably supplied by their refineries in South Africa. Caltex (Texaco and Standard Oil of California) has equity interests in two Rhodesian companies, a marketing and refining company. A U.N. document stated in November 1967 that Caltex had extended its storage facilities to help the regime prepare for international embargoes.[26] The company has made public statements opposing sanctions on Southern Rhodesia. For example, a Texaco official has written: "the imposition of these sanctions during the past five years has not brought about a change."[27] He neglects to mention that the evasion of sanctions by companies on a widespread international scale has been largely responsible for their slowness in bringing effective pressure to bear. Mobil Oil also seems to be very active in Southern Rhodesia, although it maintains an official silence; a Rhodesian publication recently showed a photograph of a Mobil tanker refuelling Air Rhodesia aircraft.[28]

Almost all the other known American investment in Rhodesia is a by-product of South African operations. The Ford Motor Company, for example, has an assembly plant in Southern Rhodesia. ITT is heavily involved, through the Supersonic Radio Manufacturing Company, which even exports telecommunications equipment, radio, televisions, and similar items to South Africa and Namibia. Under Emergency Powers Regulations, the regime has appointed Supersonic's managing director as its "agent" and ordered him to continue production. STC officials in South Africa have indicated that there is contact between them and the Southern Rhodesian operation.[29]

Other U.S. household names with interests in Southern Rhodesia are the Chase Manhattan Bank, through its interest in the Standard Bank, IBM, Kodak, Dun and Bradstreet, Pepsi-Cola, and many others. A complete list of U.S. companies in Southern Rhodesia, according to available information, is at Appendix III.

NOTES

1. *Rhodesia Herald* (Salisbury), 25 January 1974.
2. U.N., Special Committee on Decolonization, *Working Paper on Investment in Southern Rhodesia,* April, 1974.

3. Research study quoted in *The Star* (Johannesburg), week of 28 September, 1974.

4. *Rhodesia Herald,* 7 April 1973.

5. *Financial Mail* (Johannesburg), 17 May 1974.

6. "Government of Rhodesia, Ministry of Finance," *Economic Survey of Rhodesia 1972* (Salisbury: Government Printer, 1973), p. 5.

7. G. Arrighi, *The Political Economy of Rhodesia* (The Hague: Mouton, 1967), p. 49.

8. U.N., *Working Paper.*

9. *The Star* week of 30 December 1972.

10. *Financial Times* (London), 30 January 1974.

11. *The Guardian* (London), 16 November 1973.

12. *Rhodesia Herald,* 2 February 1974.

13. *Africa Confidential* (London), 18 January 1974.

14. *The Guardian,* 7 April 1973.

15. *The Star,* week of 7 September 1974.

16. *Daily Telegraph* (London), 14 January 1974. *The Star,* week of 19 May 1973.

17. *Rhodesia Herald,* 21 January 1974.

18. Speech to the U.N. Security Council, 16 February, 1972: U.N. Document S/PV. 1640, pp. 15-16.

19. U.S. government estimates and calculations in Corporate Information Center, National Council of Churches, *Church Investments, Corporations and Southern Africa* (New York: Friendship Press, 1973), pp. 140-1, note 8.

20. J. Clayton Stephenson, president of the Mining and Metals Division, Union Carbide, in testimony to the House Foreign Affairs Subcommittee on Africa, October 31, 1969; quoted in U.S. Congress, House of Representative Committee on Foreign Affairs, Subcommittee on Africa, *Rhodesia and United States Foreign Policy* (Washington, D.C.: Government Printing Office, 1969), p. 30.

21.U.N., Special Committee on Decolonization, *Foreign Economic Interests and Decolonisation* (New York: United Nations, 1969).

22. Stephenson testimony.

23. Tony Geraghty, "Why the U.S. gave Smith a chromium polish," *Sunday Times,* 30 January 1972.

24. Information from Congressional sources and *Church Investments* pp. 132-41.

25. *Mining International Year Book, 1975* (London: Financial Times, Ltd., 1975): 83-4, 502.

26. U.N. Doc. A/6868, November 1967.

27. Letter to Ronald L. Phillips, Research Director, Corporate Information Center, National Council of Churches, from Kerryn King, Senior Vice-President, Texaco Inc., September 8, 1972; quoted in *Church Investments*, p. 50.

28. *Rhodesian Commentary* (Salisbury, Southern Rhodesia), September 1972.

29. *Church Investments*, pp. 108-17.

chapter 7 ⎯⎯⎯⎯⎯⎯⎯⎯

FORMER PORTUGUESE COLONIES

Since the military coup d'état in Portugal on April 25, 1974, the situation in Portugal's African colonies has changed drastically. The new government rapidly negotiated independence for Guinea-Bissau in 1974, and for Mozambique, Angola, and Sao Tome e Principe in 1975. In Angola, civil war erupted shortly before independence, fueled by Soviet, U.S., South African, and other foreign intervention.

American investment in these countries, which had been growing rapidly since the 1960s in the expectation that colonial rule would continue indefinitely, has been caught up in these events and in many cases suffered serious setbacks from the economic dislocation of the transfer of power, the disruption of port and other facilities, and in the long run probably a damaging identification with the old colonial regime.

FALSE ASSUMPTIONS BY U.S. INVESTORS

The most striking lesson of the recent events is the unreliability of the white minority power structure in southern Africa. Decolonization was rapid and, in both Mozambique and Angola, involved serious racial clashes. The events belied platitudes repeated frequently by both the U.S. government and American investors prior to the Portuguese coup: that there was no serious threat from the liberation movements, no substantial liberated areas, and little support inside the colonies for the movements; that the Portuguese had the situation well in hand; and that the prospects of political and economic stability, in the alleged absence of racial friction, were excellent at least for the medium term. Following the Portuguese coup, which was prompted largely by the disastrous impact of the thirteen years of colonial wars on Portugal itself, Portuguese military spokesmen admitted that troop morale in Africa had reached a very low ebb because of their deteriorating military position and increasing support being given to the liberation movements by the African population. Right up to the coup, however, State Department spokesmen dismissed the importance of the African resistance to the colonial power, and corporations reacted accordingly. As expressed by a State Department witness at Congressional hearings: "Our position with respect to U.S. investment in South Africa: we neither encourage nor discourage such investment."[1] Official policy cannot be held entirely responsible for the calculation of risk taken by the major investors on their own account. A former State Department official, Don McHenry, has described his contacts with Gulf Oil, the major U.S. investor in the colonies:

> That first well came through in 1966. At that time it came through I happened to be in Africa representing the United States in a discussion of Portugal's African territories. . . . The Gulf issue was a major topic. It wasn't a very comfortable position. . . .
>
> When political developments were moving swiftly in the early and middle sixties, the Kennedy Administration actually thought Angola was going to blow as early as 1961. In other words, your major investment decisions were made at precisely the time when they were very much involved in a political situation . . . your major drilling started somewhere around 1960 or '61. The political revolt in the Portuguese Territories started around 1960 . . . if I had been having to make the kind of investment decisions that you had to make, I would have had many, many second thoughts. . . . At that time you had to make a decision as to whether or not you were indeed going to be politically neutral.[2]

Gulf Oil has readily conceded that its investment is seen as "transform-
ing [the] economic outlook in Angola,"[3] but maintained that this con-
stituted a "politically neutral" act.[4] However, in the final economic and
political crisis of the old Portuguese regime, arising from the absolute embargo on oil supplies there by the Arab producers, Gulf was far from neutral. The contract for Gulf's operation in the Cabinda enclave of Angola
provided for the Portuguese state to have preferential access to three-
eighths of the production, and in addition Gulf was obliged to provide
it with oil from other sources to compensate for any technical difficulties that might arise from the refining of Cabinda crude[5] —which could
in fact be used only in limited quantities in Portuguese refineries.[6] In
addition, Gulf appears to have been instrumental in a special U.S. government deal with the old regime to ensure the continuing oil supplies
so vital for the colonial war effort. As reported by a well-informed British
journalist, Bruce Loudon, citing Portuguese government sources:

> What is clear is that at about the time of the beginning of the Middle
> East crisis Gulf executives were in Lisbon. They left after a few days
> with smiles reported all around.
>
> Informed speculation is that as part of the Azores airlift deal [to sup-
> ply Israel in the 1973 war] the Cabinda oil is taken by the U.S. in
> direct exchange for crude that is more suitable for Lisbon's refinery
> needs. . . . Hence Lisbon's confidence despite the reported threat of a
> "total trade boycott" by Arab countries.[7]

Following the collapse of the old regime, Gulf Oil has apparently continued to intervene in Angolan affairs in a way that can only be described
as political. There are persistent reports that the company is financing a
group in Cabinda known as the Front for the Liberation of the Enclave
of Cabinda, or FLEC, which advocates separation of Cabinda from an independent Angola.

It is also widely assumed that the U.S. government is tacitly encouraging Gulf in this, as well as providing financial support for the National
Front for the Liberation of Angola (FNLA), a movement also backed by
the Chinese to oppose the Soviet-supplied Popular Movement for the
Liberation of Angola (MPLA). It is the massive foreign intervention and

manipulation from all the superpowers that is responsible for the escalation of conflict in Angola. The flood of press reports in the United States about Soviet intervention clearly was officially inspired as both justification and cover for increasing U.S. commitments of money, weapons, aircraft, and even personnel. This massive covert operation indicated that little had been learned from the Vietnam war in a case where U.S. investments were seen to be at stake.

Right up to the Portuguese coup, American economic commitments in Portugal and particularly the colonies were growing rapidly, some of it independently and some linked with government policy: for example, an Export-Import Bank loan of $1.8 million helped to finance the sale of U.S. goods and services required for the establishment of a General Tire factory in Mozambique,[8] and there was a range of other deals that built up the Portuguese communications and transportation networks as well as new industries in the colonies.

Trade was becoming an increasingly important factor, also backed by major Export-Import Bank commitments, which many companies took to be tacit encouragement for their participation in the colonial system. Americans were the largest foreign buyers of Angolan coffee, taking over 50 percent of its exports at some $60 million a year, and of Mozambican cashews, another $9-10 million.[9] For Angola, the United States in 1971 was the major purchaser, after Portugal, of its exports—taking 20.2 percent—and supplier of its imports—11.1 percent.[10] For Mozambique, the United States replaced South Africa in 1971 as the territory's best customer after Portugal, taking 13.5 percent of its exports and supplying 7.5 percent of its imports. In 1970 and 1971, the United States accounted for more than three-quarters of Mozambique's imports of aircraft.[11] The importance of the American connection was underlined by frequent reports of the strategic value of American imports, including herbicides, military equipment, and especially aircraft. An experienced South African reporter in Mozambique placed great emphasis on the role of the nominally civilian pilots, "without whom the increasingly desperate Portuguese effort to stem the terrorist tide here would grind to defeat."[12]

Experience of U.S. government intervention in Chile, the Dominican Republic, Portugal, Greece, Iran, and many other countries since World War II indicates that attempts to manipulate other people's political structures does not stop once they are independent; in fact, with the colonial power withdrawn there is a tendency to take over the colonial role. This is a process which led to increasingly futile involvement in Vietnam and Southeast Asia generally. Factors leading up to the initial decision to become involved include an alleged "strategic importance" of the country concerned, and the presence of natural resources of interest to U.S. companies. This is very much the case with Angola; it is seen by the U.S. and Brazil as of crucial importance to their amibitions in the South Atlantic, and possesses very important mineral resources. It also offers the prospect of rival liberation movements supported by the various superpowers. South Africa initiated the large-scale program of Western intervention and pressed the United States to follow its lead.[13]

The presence of major U.S. investment in the former Portuguese colonies, notably Angola, therefore proved to be a serious hazard to the African people there and their attempts to achieve self-determination and independence. However, given the tendency for U.S. intervention to backfire, and the hostility of many of the Africans toward any collaborators with the former colonial occupation, the situation could equally well prove to be a threat to the interests of the U.S. companies involved. Only time will tell what future they have in independent Angola, Mozambique, and Guinea-Bissau. The companies would not have committed themselves with such confidence if they had realized the fragile character of white supremacy in Portuguese Africa. Whether change in South Africa, Southern Rhodesia, and Namibia will come as suddenly is impossible to predict; if it does, it will be far too late to recoup investments. The experience of investors in Portugal and its colonies should prompt some rethinking of the political risks arising in the rest of southern Africa, particularly given the interdependent character of all the minority regimes in the regic

U.S. INVESTMENT IN THE COLONIES
AT THE TIME OF THE PORTUGUESE COUP

Gulf Oil

Estimated U.S. investment in Angola and Mozambique amounts to about $220 million, the bulk of it being the Gulf investment in Angola.[14]

Gulf's total investment there up to 1972 amounted to $209 million; in that year the corporation's net income from Angola was about $30 million.[15]

The importance of this investment to the Portuguese administration in Angola was enormous. In 1972, Cabinda Gulf paid the Portuguese at least $61 million, and total payments over the period 1958-1972 have amounted to $96.7 million; the annual payments are increasing rapidly.[16] Mainly due to Cabinda Gulf's efforts, Angolan exports of crude oil increased from 4.7 million tons in 1971 to 6.8 million tons in 1972, an increase of 43.9 percent. This brought in some $140 million in foreign exchange, equivalent to 25.4 percent of all Angola's export earnings at a time of very severe shortages of foreign exchange due to a change in the monetary arrangements with Portugal.[17] According to the corporation, it spent about $20 million a year in Angola for services and products, employed 266 people (of whom only 57, or 21 percent, were local Africans) and was expected to bring in an estimated $45 million in foreign currency during 1972, according to the Portuguese.[18]

The financial contribution of the Cabinda operation to the Portuguese was equivalent to 60 percent of the total cost of the war in Angola. Its importance to the colonial regime was even greater in the fact that the administration could take the 12.5 percent royalties in kind and had preferential access to another 37.5 percent of production. In addition, according to Gulf's *Orange Disc* magazine, "the Government has reserved the right . . . to take all production in the event of war or national emergency."[19]

In 1972, Cabinda Gulf produced 6,297,985 tons of crude oil, of which 80,790 tons were supplied to the refinery in Luanda, the capital, and the remainder exported as shown in Table 3.

TABLE 3

	Metric Tons
Canada (for U.S. market)	2,269,161
United States and Trinidad and Tobago*	1,807,647
Japan	1,327,488
Portugal	484,948

Spain	258,709
Denmark	69,272
TOTAL	6,217,195

---

*Trinidad and Tobago have stopped the importation of Cabinda oil for their refinery, but it is likely that the same amount will reach the U.S. market by another route.

Gulf's large investment in Angola had only recently started to pay off, and since the prospect of oil production increasing is not very likely, the recovery of the initial investment would require a government subject to strong U.S. influence; the capital would not be recovered at current rates of profit until about 1979, and only then would the investment begin to show a net profit. Gulf's strong interest in manipulating political events in Cabinda is therefore obvious.

There were enthusiastic statements by the Gulf directors when they started to invest in Angola. In 1967 the Portuguese government announced "a strike as big as that in Nigeria," and estimated "15 million tons by 19 (over twice the amount actually produced two years later).[20] It appears that Gulf greatly exaggerated the technical prospects; the *Petroleum Press Service* has subsequently stated that following the production of 7.3 million tons in 1973, production could start to decline within a relatively short time, since some of the older fields would start to fail. The service adds: "The company has had many disappointments in its search efforts here, and has now given up onshore, with the recently relinquished onshore acreage comprising a quarter of its total former permit area."

Gulf has claimed, along similar lines to the familiar argument about South Africa, that its investment benefitted the people living in Cabinda by, for example, creating employment. However, only fifty-seven local Africans were in fact employed, and this small spin-off effect was negligible compared to the fact that, according to the local press, Gulf's presence had led to an increased cost of living in Cabinda, making living conditions "unbearable" for those living on wages. A Gulf stockholder who visited the operation in 1973 reported that the U.S. technical personnel were "rednecks," that facilities on the drilling rigs were segregated, and that their Portuguese personnel were also racist: "It was more than awk-

ward to witness such obvious racial overtones in your Angolan office."
She was told by local officials that they had had opportunities to withdraw from Cabinda, but had not done so. She commented, "A corporation which moves into a colonial country without perceiving the inevitable conflict or trying to work for an improvement of relations with the
majority concerned is taking a narrow and dim view of democratic procedures," and concluded that Gulf had been supporting Portuguese colonialism without even attempting to make such limited local contributions
as they could under the circumstances.[21]

Other U.S. Investments in Oil

Perhaps the most important group of U.S. investors apart from Gulf
were the other oil companies involved in exploration in the colonies. Of
these, one of the most conspicuous was Esso Exploration, a subsidiary of
Standard Oil of New Jersey, or the Exxon Corporation, which held an exclusive petroleum concession in Guinea-Bissau. This was probably the only
item of foreign investment of any size in Guinea-Bissau under colonial rule.
The concession was estimated to cover some 50,000 square kilometers, comprising all the land area of the territory (even though Portugal had little control over that area).[22] Since 1966, Esso has spent 750 million escudos (over
$25 million) in the former colony and had located some potential areas for
petroleum exploitation along the coast. The terms of the concession were
apparently revised in January 1973, and the company was purportedly
granted a further exclusive concession over the continental shelf of the colony, comprising an area of some 9,700 square kilometers.

During the first three years of the 1973 contract, Esso undertook to spend
not less than 8.1 million escudos. The concession could have been extended
three times for three, two, and two years respectively. Esso undertook to
spend 93.5 million escudos during the period of each extension, bringing the
total minimum investment over the ten-year period up to 288.6 million escudos (well over $10 million). Esso also undertook to pay an annual surface
rent of 350 escudos per square kilometer during the initial period, which
corresponds to some 3.4 million escudos a year. The annual surface rent
would increase to 400 escudos per square kilometer during the first extension, 500 escudos during the second and 600 during the third. In areas

under exploitation, the surface rent would be 1,500 escudos per square kilometer.[23] It is clear that given a situation of dwindling income resulting from the loss of Portuguese administrative control over the territory and population and the build-up of alternative and more profitable sources of trading and other economic activity by the liberation movement, PAIGC, the Portuguese were in dire need of income from whatever source to cover some of the financial burden of the war. Esso's willingness to pay a flat rate for the concession purportedly granted by the colonial administration, regardless of whether the Portuguese actually controlled the areas in question, amounted to a direct prop to a shaky and financially embarrassed colonial force and helped to prolong the fighting and, therefore, the suffering of the people of Guinea-Bissau—now independent.

In addition to the concession in Guinea-Bissau, Esso also applied to the Portuguese Government for rights to explore for oil in an offshore area of Angola.[24] Esso spokesmen have said in informal meetings that they were very enthusiastic about the prospect of involvement in Angola and that they intended to commit large amounts of capital and effort to this concession— although production was not foreseen, even under the most favorable circumstances, until the 1980s.[25] Clearly, the company assumed that the Portuguese would rule in Africa for at least the next twenty years.

Many other U.S. oil companies were already involved in exploration in Angola. Texaco had a 25 percent interest in a concession held by Petrangol and Angol (the two state-run oil companies) in the basins of the Cuanza and Congo rivers, and offshore with a concession extended in May 1973. It also had an interest with Petrangol and Angol in an onshore field in Cabeç da Cobra, which had started production on a small scale.[26] In 1971, Angol conducted prospecting offshore in the Congo area through a U.S. contractor, the Western Geophysical Co., a subsidiary of Litton Industries, Inc.[27] (Litton Industries is a company heavily involved in arms production in the United States, and is known to have sympathies with the minority regimes in Africa.) Petrangol was also reported to be stepping up oil prospection offshore and inland of Ambriz and the Cuanza River estuary, in conjunction with Mobil Oil of the United States.[28]

During 1972, various U.S. companies applied to the Portuguese for petroleum concessions in Angola. The Ranger Oil Company of Cheyenne applied for a concession to prospect for and exploit petroleum deposits in an area adjacent to the Petrangol concession. The Superior Oil Company of

Houston applied for a concession for an area covering part of the continental shelf and the seabed. The Carlsberg Resources Corporation of Los Angeles applied for the concession to an area extending from Egipto Praia, north of Benguela, to the Novo Redondo area further north. The Milford Argosy Corporation of North Portland, which had also just started prospecting in Namibia, applied for a concession to an area lying between the border with Zaire and the Cabinda Gulf concession in Cabinda district. The Ocean Drilling and Exploration Company also applied for a concession,[29] as did an international consortium consisting of Tesoro Petroleum Corporation of San Antonio, General Exploration of Los Angeles, and Geotherme of Paris, France, in 1973.[30] It is ironical that the rush to conclude deals with the Portuguese in Angola came just before the coup.

Angol and Petrangol "farmed out" concession contracts to Occidental Petroleum Corporation, Continental Oil Company, Standard Oil of Indiana, Amoco Cuanza Petroleum Company, and Iberian Petroleum, Ltd. of Stamford. Another concession was to be awarded to the Sun Oil Company, Sunray D.X. of Philadelphia (Sunoco).[31] Other companies reported to be involved in the search for oil were Standard Oil of California and the Union Carbide Corporation of New York.[32] Supporting services, oil rigs, and installations were provided by Tidewater Marine Service, Inc. of New Orleans, through its Luanda subsidiary Tidex, Inc.;[33] Halliburton Company, through Halliburtons Operator, Inc. of Luanda;[34] and, according to the Department of Economic Affairs in Angola, Intercontinental Marine Drilling; Marine Services, Inc., in Cabinda; and Schlumberger, Ltd., of New York.

One concession, granted in April 1972 to the Argo Petroleum Corporation of Los Angeles, will serve as an indication of the standard arrangement for U.S. applicants for Portuguese concessions in Angola. Under the terms of the contract the corporation was required to set up a subsidiary in Portugal, Argo Petroleum Portuguesa, which was the official holder of the concession and had headquarters in Lisbon. In case of a conflict of interest, therefore, it would be subject to the commands of the Portuguese government. Its initial capital was 110 million escudos (about $4 million), and could be increased by the company by up to 500 million (about $18 million). The colonial authority received free of charge a 20 percent share of the original and any subsequent capital.

The company was granted prospecting rights over an initial period of three years, which could be extended for another seven years. It would have production rights for thirty years, extendable for two successive ten-year periods. Prior to signing the contract, Argo Petroleum was required to deposit a security of 50 million escudos with the Portuguese government as a guarantee. It also had to spend a minimum amount of prospecting in each year of the contract and make contributions to the Mining Development Fund; if production was started it then had to pay various bonuses to the colonial administration in addition to taxation amounting to 50 percent of income, plus 12.5 percent royalties. The company was required to give preference to the hiring of Portuguese personnel on a rigorous quota system and also give preference to Portuguese goods and services, particularly transport facilities.

From all this it is obvious that the company's operations were designed by the Portuguese to provide the maximum benefit and support to the metropolitan and colonial governments in a variety of ways and that the company was tightly controlled by official policy. Perhaps even more important, however, was the potential use of its resources in a time of crisis: there was a contractual provision that the Portuguese government had to be given preference in the purchase of up to 37.5 percent of output, and in case of war or "serious emergency," the total output of the company had to be placed at the disposal of the government. The colonial regime also reserved to itself the right, following demarcation of the first petroleum deposit, to form an association between a state-owned company and Argo Petroleum on a joint venture basis for the exploitation of any deposit that was discovered.[35]

Although on a lesser scale than in Angola, oil prospecting was also an important element of economic activity in Mozambique. Exploration rights were granted in December 1967 to the Hunt International Petroleum Company, a subsidiary of the Hunt Oil Company of Dallas (another of whose subsidiaries is Placid Oil). In November 1973 the company requested an extension of its prospecting license and restarted its formerly suspended activities in the mouth of the Zambezi River.[36] Texaco Petroleum (short for the Texas Corporation of the United States) received a concession in 1968 along the northern coastline.[37] Loffland Brothers, Inc., of Tulsa, Oklahoma, was involved in exploration.[38] Sunray D.X. (Sun Oil Company) was the operating partner in a subsidiary with Skelly Oil (an indirect subsidiary, via Mission Corporation, of the Getty Oil

Company) and Clark Oil and Refining Corporation. They had a 14.4-million acre concession on-and offshore since 1967 and had already spent $10 million in an unsuccessful oil search.[39] New York Kilroy, of Houston, applied for a concession along the southern coast of Mozambique and three concessions in Angola, including the area along the Namibian border.[40]

In Saō Tome e Principe, a small island colony off the African coast, independent July 12, 1975, the U.S. company Ball and Collins has been prospecting since 1970. In terms of its contract with the Portuguese government, the company formed Hicrocarbo, Hidrocarbonetos de Saō Tome e Principe, SARL (the Portuguese equivalent of Inc.). In May 1971 this subsidiary entered into a joint venture with the Texas Pacific Oil Company of Portugal, Inc., a division of Joseph E. Seagram and Sons, Inc., of the United States.[42]

Under the terms of the joint venture contract (Decree No. 219/71 of May 25, 1971) Hidrocarbo had a 62.5 percent share in the joint venture and Texas Pacific a 37.5 percent share. The latter was responsible as the operating company for all prospecting and exploitation activities, although its prospecting plans had to be approved each year by the Portuguese government. Texas Pacific was obligated to make an initial investment of $390,670. Further investments above this amount by the two partners would be in the same proportion as the original shares. The joint venture was to be supervised by a *commisaō directiva* (committee) comprising one representative of each company and a representative of the Portuguese government.[42]

The oil industry was of crucial importance to Portuguese colonial rule, by fueling the military operations and by providing taxation revenue and valuable foreign exchange to the colonial regime. In addition, the operations were closely tied in to direct state intervention at all levels—managerial, financial, and operational—and were entirely at the disposal of the regime in the event of emergency. The role of extractive industry in a colonial situation, by exploring for and removing irreplaceable natural resources before independence, is also clearly evident with the many U.S. oil companies operating in the colonies.

Not only were American companies producing crude oil and searching for new sources, but they played an extremely active part in distribution and marketing in the colonies. California Texas Oil Company (Caltex) of New York was engaged in fuel distribution in Mozambique.[43] Texaco was a large fuel distributor in Angola.[44] Bigger than either was the Mobil Oil Corporation of New York, which through local subsidiaries was engaged in distribution in both Angola and Mozambique and had also built a 15 million escudo ($500,000) plant in Luanda for oil storage and the processing of lubricating oil.[45]

Investment in Mining

Even apart from a leading role in the oil industry, U.S. economic involvement in Portugal's African colonies was overwhelmingly in the extractive industries. One of the most substantial of these was the Bethlehem Steel consortium's concession in the Tete province of Mozambique, granted in September 1972 to cover several thousand square miles with rights to a large variety of minerals. The terms of this and other mining concessions were similar to those applicable to oil concessions: a minimum expenditure on exploration, maximum benefit to local entrepreneurs, registration under Portuguese law, and payment of taxes, royalties, and other contributions, including one to the Portuguese Overseas Mining Fund. Also in Mozambique, the Continental Ore Corporation of New York was exploiting and prospecting for fluorites in Tete province with Interminas Fluorites of Mozambique.[46]

In Angola there has been much more activity. The Chromalloy American Corporation had taken over Sociedade Mineira da Huila, which had gold and other mining concessions in southern Angola and was to spend $750,000 in an exploration program.[47] Tenneco Oil of Houston, a subsidiary of Tenneco Corporation of Wilmington, Delaware, had since December 1968 held prospecting and mining rights for sulphur, gypsum, and anhydrite near Benguela. By May 1969 there were reports of rich sulphur discoveries. Portuguese officials were quoted as saying that Tenneco would spend $50-$75 million developing the sulphur deposit.[48]

There was also considerable American involvement in diamond mining in Angola, the major extractive industry. American interests, including Morgan Bank, Guaranty Trust Bank, and Guggenheim, held 40 percent of the initial capital of Diamang, the Diamond Company of Angola, which for a long time held the monopoly and made annual profits of several times the initial investment.[49] Diamang's reports for 1961 and 1962 showed direct participation by the company in financing the construction of barracks and military bases. The 1962 financial statement included an item of 88.6 million escudos ($3.5 million) for the "defense" of Angola at that critical time. Since then, in common with all other foreign-owned firms, Diamang was paying large amounts to the Portuguese for the "defense of the national heritage."[50]

Diamond Distributors, Inc., of New York had a 73 percent interest in Oestdiam (West Angolan Diamond Company) and the Portuguese government had another 10 percent; Oestdiam was granted a concession in May 1969 for diamond prospecting in a vast area right down to the Namibian border and offshore. Minimum expenditure onshore was $2 million, and offshore $1 million in the first period.[51] Another Luanda company organized for diamond prospecting in 1969 is Diamul-Companhia Ultramarina de Diamantes SARL, which was reported to involve U.S. capital.[52] In addition, Diversa, Inc., of Dallas, through Diversa Internacional do Exploracão de Diamantes SARL of Luanda, was granted diamond prospecting rights for thirty-five years, with a minimum expenditure of $17.5 million.[53] It seems also that Rockefeller interests, through Clark Canadian Exploration Company, formed part of the Companhia dos Fosfatos de Angola (COFAN), which held a phosphate concession covering most of the Cabinda district. The company started prospecting in January 1969 and before the coup it was reported to be near the start of exploitation. Early in 1973, it was reported that the Companhia dos Asfaltos de Angola had signed a contract with Riverwood Corporation of Midland, Texas, for exploitation of rock asphalt.[54]

Allis-Chalmers of Wisconsin, which was reported to have nine branches in Angola, had a contract to process iron concentrates.[55] Two other mineral ventures were also being sought: U.S. Steel had applied for a concession in Angola for all minerals except diamonds,[56] and in May 1972 the Great Lakes Carbon Corporation of New York applied for a concession to prospect for and exploit copper deposits and a range of other minerals in another area of Angola.[57]

Other Areas of U.S. Investment

Even U.S. interests not involved in mineral exploitation did in some cases develop such connections. For example, General Electric was associated with Krupp of West Germany, the Portuguese government, and other foreign interests in developing the rich iron mines at Cassinga, near the major Kunene project on the Namibian border; in 1967 GE provided the consortium with a credit loan of $1.2 million, at the same time as an Export-Import Bank loan of $7.8 million, for the purchase of thirty diesel locomotives to remove the extracted ore for export. A subsequent deal was made between the Export-Import Bank and the Chase Manhattan Bank of New York for the financing of twelve more diesel locomotives from GE for Angola.[58]

On the other side of the continent, the controversial Cabora Bassa Dam in Tete province, Mozambique, involved another U.S. firm, Caterpillar Tractor Company. The dam was the focus of major protests in Europe, and a number of European companies had withdrawn from the scheme because of its overtly political character. General Electric, of the United States, was refused Export-Import Bank backing for its proposed involvement in the scheme and withdrew also. The State Department appears to have adopted a policy of discouraging U.S. participation in this as well as the Kunene River dam scheme and other major Portuguese projects; the Assistant Secretary for Africa, in a prepared statement, said: "Despite the obvious losses to U.S. exporters, we have not encouraged involvement in major projects in these [Portuguese] territories."[59]

Caterpillar Tractor was therefore the exception, and a key participant in the Cabora Bassa scheme, having been selling construction equipment to the Zamco consortium there since 1970 through its agent, Steia. This included eighteen 769B trucks, ten wheel loaders, eight track-type tractors, two 14E motor graders, and three industrial engines. The company also supplied skilled personnel to service and install the equipment and airlifted spare parts in "extreme emergencies," in particular the periodic attacks by FRELIMO on the dam site's transportation links, which greatly hampered development work and added considerably to costs.[60] The main backers of Cabora Bassa now face major losses as a result.

Some U.S. agribusiness interests have also been involved in the colonies, taking advantage of the deportation of the Africans to "second-class" areas. Arbor Acres Farm, Inc., a subsidiary of the Rockefeller-backed International Basic Economy Corporation (IBEC) of Glastonbury, Connecticut, invested 6 million escudos through its subsidiary in Angola, the Companhia de Produtos Agricolas-COPA, SARL. This was part of a group of companies covering a broad range of agricultural activities, the Companhia União de Cervejas Angola (CUCA). Other members of the group included local subsidiaries of Crown Cork and Seal Company, Inc., of Philadelphia (a major investor in metropolitan Portugal), and International Protein Corporation of Fairfield, New Jersey.[61] An even more important interest was the subsidiary of Universal Tobacco, SETA (Sociedade Exportadora de Tobacos de Angola), which held a marketing monopoly over the output of the main tobacco grower cooperatives in Angola. The obligation on Africans to grow cash crops at fixed prices instead of food crops for export was a major element in their impoverishment and malnutrition under colonial rule.

U.S. interests were becoming involved in the provision of electronic communications systems, which had obvious military applications. The Angolan administration signed a contract with the Boeing Aerosystems Corporation for a study of the remodelling of the Angolan air traffic control and navigational aids structure, with priority for the airports at Luanda, Nova Lisboa, Cabinda, Luso, Sa da Bandeira, Moçamedes, and the new Lobito-Benguela airport at Catumbela.[62] Since these airports were used to varying degrees by military aircraft, such a study was a direct contribution to the aerial warfare against villagers and their crops in liberated or contested areas. As a direct aid to communication between Lisbon and Luanda, ITA Space Communications together with the Portuguese Marconi company were spending over 100 million escudos ($4 million) on the ground satellite communications center at Boane, near Lourenço Marques.[63] A subsidiary of ITT, Standard Electric, had a plant manufacturing transistors, electronic components, and radio receivers at Cascais, near Lisbon, since 1968. According to press reports, the company had already invested over $6 million and would invest a further $36 million in Portugal and the colonies during the Third Development Plan period. Already it had a large contract to supply equipment for expanding the communications system in Lourenço Marques and Beira, in Mozambique.[64]

Another area where American concerns were becoming increasingly involved was finance: for example, the Inter-American Capital Corporation of New York provided in 1966 a $2.5 million loan for a new textile factory and $4.5 million for a hydroelectric power station and other projects in Angola, including road and airport construction.[65] The Chase Manhattan Bank in New York, in addition to itself financing GE locomotive exports, is also a shareholder in the Standard Bank, which was associated with Banco Totta Alianca of Portugal, and operated in Angola through Banco Totta-Standard do Angola SARL, and in Mozambique through Banco Standard-Totta do Mozambique SARL.[66] The First National City Bank of New York joined with Lisbon's Banco Espirito Santo e Comercial to form a new commercial bank in Angola, the Banco Interunido, to specialize in the provision of medium and long-term capital to meet the growing demands caused by Angola's rapid economic expansion. It was also intending to provide all normal commercial banking facilities. Citibank subscribed about $3.25 million to the issued share capital, which attracted commercial attention because this in effect was the first time that one of the major international banking corporations had taken a direct interest in the colonies.[67]

The tourist industry in the colonies also received its share of American investment. Playboy Clubs negotiated the purchase of the Paradise Islands, a well-known tourist resort off Mozambique for South Africans, for about $60 million.[68] Holiday Inns sold a franchise to the Amalgamated Hotels group in South Africa, which was planning a series of motels in Mozambique.[69] And ITT, through the Sheraton Corporation, was planning a 380-room hotel to be built in Luanda at a cost of 275 million escudos (about $10 million).[70]

American interests were also heavily involved in tire production—a field which was obviously related to military capacity. The General Tire and Ruber Company of Akron, Ohio, had a 10 percent interest in Mabor, a Portuguese company whose factory had been producing tires and air compressors since 1968. It aimed to produce all the tires required in Angola, and had been granted a 10-year monopoly by the Portuguese Government.[71] In January 1972 Mabor Angolana (short for Manufactura Angola de Borracha) applied for a license to set up a rolled steel plant in Angola with a production capacity of 60,000 tons a year.[72] Mabor was also planning to open a tire plant in Lourenço Marques, Mozambique; of the total investment of 350,000 contos ($14 million), 50,000 contos, or $2 million, was being lent by the Export-Import Bank to finance American equipment purchases.[73] Meanwhile the Firestone Tire and Rubber Company, also of Akron, Ohio, was planning to invest 150 million escudos ($5.25 million) in a tire factory in Mozambique.[74]

The other American interests covered miscellaneous activities. IBM had sales and service facilities, supplied from their South African headquarters, in Angola and Mozambique.[75] Operations in Guinea-Bissau as well as Angola and Mozambique were carried on by 3M and Ascinter-Otis (in which Otis Elevator Company holds a majority interest).[76] NCR, Inc. (formerly the National Cash Register Company) of Dayton, Ohio, also operated in Angola, making sophisticated electronic machinery, including computers, and expertise, widely available in the colonies from a variety of sources.[77] Pharmaceutical products were provided by Charles Pfizer and Company of New York,[78] Abbott Laboratories, and Eli Lilly,[79] in both Angola and Mozambique. The Chicago Bridge and Iron Company had a construction contract in Mozambique.[80] American Cyanamid Company of Wayne, New Jersey, operated in Angola, as did Fort Dodge Laboratory of Ford Dodge, Iowa.[81] A variety of other American concerns had distribution networks in the colonies, linked with their South African operations.

NOTES

1. R. Smith, State Department, in testimony to the House Subcommittee on Africa, March 29, 1974, in U.S. Congress, House of Representatives, Committee on Foreign Affairs, Subcommittee on Africa, *U.S. Business Involvement in Southern Africa,* Part III (Washington, D.C.: Government Printing Office, 1973), pp. 94-6.

2. Charles Powers, ed., *People Profits: The Ethics of Investment* (New York: CRIA, 1972), pp. 178-83.

3. *New York Times,* 7 July 1968.

4. "Gulf Statement to Trustees," read at the Ohio Conference, The United Church of Christ, Columbus, Ohio, September 10, 1970.

5. Angola, *Report from Portuguese Africa* (Luanda: Administration of Angola, 26 October 1973).

6. *Journal of Commerce,* New York, 1 November 1973.

7. *Financial Times,* London, 28 November 1973.

8. Export-Import Bank press release, Washington, D.C., 4 October, 1973.

9. U.S., Department of the Census, *Statistical Abstract of the United States, 1971,* 92nd edition (Washington, D.C.: Government Printing Office, 1971), pp. 769-70.

10. *Angola,* U.N. Doc. A/AC. 109/L. 842, February 28, 1973, p. 21.

11. *Mozambique,* U.N. Doc. A/AC. 109/L. 843, March 6, 1973, p. 23.

12. Wilf Nussey in *The Star* (Johannesburg), week of 6 April 1974.

13. *See* Barbara Rogers, "U.S. Involvement in the Portuguese Colonial Policy" (Paper delivered to the Annual Convention of the African Studies Association, Chicago, Ill., October 30-November 2, 1974); also, *The Guardian* (London), week of 7 December 1975.

14. No detailed breakdown is available; *see* Smith testimony in *U.S. Business Involvement in Southern Africa*, p. 101.

15. U.N. Doc. A/9023 (Part III) Annex, paras. 21-2.

16. Ibid.

17. Mario Sampaio, "Cabinda Gulf Oil," *African Development* (November 1973), p. 11.

18. *See* "Fact sheet on Cabinda Gulf Oil Co.," distributed by the Gulf Oil Corporation, U.S., and the statement by the Portuguese Overseas Minister in the National Assembly, Lisbon, cited in *Economic Conditions in Angola*, U.N. Special Committee on Decolonisation, Conference Room Paper SCI/72/6, June 15, 1972.

19. *Orange Disc* (Pittsburg), May-June 1972, p. 14

20. Quoted by Sampaio in *African Development* (November 1973), p. 1?

21. Mrs. E. Jackman, letter to Mr. B.R. Dorsey, Chairman of the Gulf Oil Corporation, July 20, 1973.

22. U.N. Doc. A/6700/Rev. 1, chapter V, paras. 342-352.

23. *Guinea (Bissau) and Cape Verde*, U.N. Doc. A/AC. 109/L. 844, May 24, 1973, paras. 76-79.

24. Correspondence with Congressman Diggs; letter from Exxon, October 26, 1972.

25. Interview by the author with a senior Exxon executive.

26. *Petroleum Press Service*, London, November 1972.

27. U.N. Doc. A/9023 (Part III) Annex, para. 28.

28. *The Star*, week of 17 November 1973.

29. *Actualidade Economica* (October 16, 1969).

30. *Diario de Noticias* (Lisbon), 16 October 1973.

31. *Marchés Tropicaux* (Paris) 8 February 1974; Angola, *Report from Portuguese Africa*, 1 February 1974; *Wall Street Journal*, 29 March 1974.

32. *Wall Street Journal*, 5 January 1970.

33. *Moody's Transportation Manual;* also Angola Department of Econom? Affairs, quoted in Jennifer Davis, "U.S. Economic Involvement," *Africa To? day*, 17.4. (July-August 1970), p. 13.

34. *Moody's Industrial Manual, 1969;* Angola Department of Economic Affairs; "Oil," *Standard and Poor's Industry Surveys*, January 29, 1970.

35. U.N. Doc. A/9023 (Part III), Annex, paras. 33-40.

36. *Provincia* (Angola), 9 November 1973; *Daily News* (Tanzania), 11 N? vember 1973.

37. *Diario de Lisbõa*, January 1969; *Marchés Tropicaux*, 2 November 1973.

38. J.L. Angel, *Directory of American Firms Operating in Foreign Countries*, 7th edition, (New York: Simon and Schuster, 1969), p. 725.

39. *Wall Street Journal*, (New York), 25 September 1969; *The Star*, 17 January 1970; Clark Oil and Refining Corp., *Annual Report, 1969;* Angola, *Report from Portuguese Africa*, 1 February 1974.

40. *Daily News*, 11 November 1973.

41. *Territories under Portuguese Administration*, U.N. Doc. A/8723/Add. 3; September 1, 1972, p. 212, para. 10.

42. Ibid., para. 11.

43. *Directory of American Firms.*

44. *Diario de Lisbõa*, January 1969.

45. *Bank of Portugal Information* (Lisbon: Government Printer), February 1969.

46. U.N. Doc. A/8423/Rev. 1/Add. 1, Annex, appendix IIB, paras. 30-2.

47. *Report from Portuguese Africa*, 9 November 1973.

48. *Diario de Lisbõa*, 10 January 1969; *Financial Mail*, Johannesburg, 15 August 1969; *Standard Bank Review*, May 1969; *Wall Street Journal*, 1 January 1970.

49. Perry Anderson, *Le Portugal et la fin de l'ultra-colonialisme* (Paris: François Maspero, 1963), pp. 95-6.

50. U.N. Soc. cited in Eduardo de Sousa Ferreira, *Portuguese Colonialism* (Freiburg: Aktion Dritte Welt, 1972), p. 54. For a list of Diamang contributions to the colonial war, *see* J. Martins, *Angola, L'intensificazione dello sfruttamento imperialistico nel settore minerario* (Rome, 1970), p. 21.

51. *Portuguese Government Gazette*, Lisbon, 2 May 1969.

52. *Diario de Luanda*, 22 June 1969; Angola, Department of Economic Affairs, quoted by Davis in *Africa Today*, p. 9.

53. *Financial Mail*, 5 August 1969; *New York Times*, 8 June 1969.

54. U.N. Docs., quoted in Paul Irish, "Memo on Recent U. S. Investments in Mozambique and Angola," mimeographed (New York: Interfaith Committee on Social Responsibility in Investments, National Council of Churches, 1973).

55. U.N. Doc. A/6868/Add.

56. *Diario de Noticias*, 20 February 1973.

57. *Economic Conditions in Angola*, U.N. Special Committee on Decolonisation, Conference Room Paper SCI/72/6; June 15, 1972, para. 60.

58. *Provincia* (Angola), 31 January 1974.

59. Statement by Mr. David Newsom, State Department, to the House Subcommittee on Africa, March 27, 1973; *U.S. Business Involvement*, Part III, p. 13.

60. *The Dealer,* Caterpillar Tractor Co., April 1972.

61. U.N. Docs., cited in Paul Irish, "Memo".

62. *Diario* (Mozambique), 24 January 1974.

63. *Noticias* (Mozambique), 30 January 1974.

64. *Primeiro de Janeiro,* 27 June 1968; *Diario de Lisbõa,* 26 June 1968.

65. U.N. Doc. A/6300/Rev. 1.

66. *Multi-National Banking Directory,* Chase Manhattan Bank, January 1970.

67. *Journal of Commerce* (February 7, 1973).

68. *The Star,* week of 24 March 1973.

69. *Financial Mail,* various dates.

70. Paul Irish, "Memo".

71. *Financial Mail,* 15 August 1969; *Primeiro de Janeiro,* 14 July 1968; D. Abshire and M. Samuels, eds., *Portuguese Africa: A Handbook* (New York: Praeger, 1969), pp. 305-6.

72. *Economic Conditions in Angola,* para. 83.

73. *Portugal,* Portugal, December 1973.

74. U.N. Doc. A/6868, 1967,

75. Reply to questionnaire from Congressman Diggs; *U.S. Business Involvement,* Part III, appendix 82, pp. 981-1058.

76. Ibid.

77. Angola, Department of Economic Affairs, quoted by Davis in *African Development,* p. 11.

78. *Directory of American Firms.*

79. *Economic Conditions in Angola.*

80. Ibid.

81. *Directory of American Firms.*

chapter 8 _____

THE PROSPECT OF INTERNATIONAL BOYCOTTS

Starting in the early 1960s, there has been constant talk of mounting an international trade boycott, or more recently action against investment, in southern Africa. Because of the gap between rhetoric and action, the prospect of serious action has been largely discounted. It would be well to remember, however, that a full-scale program of international sanctions has been instituted since 1968 against the illegal regime in Southern Rhodesia. There has been discussion of certain steps along these lines in the case of Namibia. There has been sporadic activity, originally at the time of Sharpeville and reemerging at the present time, to boycott specific goods from South Africa and, until recently, Portugal and its colonies. A highly successful campaign was launched in Holland against the sale of Angolan coffee, resulting in a total boycott; the campaign was later transferred to Canada and Britain. Boycotts of fruit, wines, and other goods have emerged from time to time, with a number of local boycott victories in various countries.

In the United States, legal action seems to offer the most serious prospects. For example, a suit aimed at stopping Commerce Department contacts in the South African government over the importing of seal skins from Namibia resulted in the decision by the department not to allow the import of these skins despite strong political pressures from the importer, the Fouke Company.[1] Subsequently, the decision was reversed.

The more recent phenomenon of action against companies that invest in southern Africa has yet to run its course. Activities that range from putting resolutions at stockholder meetings to a full-scale boycott campaign in the case of the Gulf Oil Company have spread from the United States to Canada, Holland, Britain, and elsewhere and are beginning to be noted in Africa. It is here of course that adverse publicity can have a substantive effect: it seems that British companies, for example, were placed in an unfavorable position when competing for major contracts from African governments at the time that Britain was selling arms to South Africa, and that the awarding of contracts for the Kafue Dam, in Zambia, was one example of this.

Certain American business concerns have become aware of a lack of enthusiasm toward them since the passage of the Byrd Amendment made the U.S. government the only state in the world to violate sanctions against Rhodesia publicly. Peugeot cars, with 49 percent of the market, have been banned in Tanzania apparently as a result of strong opposition to French arms sales to South Africa.[2] Tanzania also withdrew the crucial import license from the Zephyr group following its conviction in a Dutch court for breaking Rhodesian sanctions. A British company participating in the Cabora Bassa Dam scheme, the United Transport Company, was nationalized in Zambia when this became known to the government. Carreras Rothmans cigarettes have been banned from sale in the Sudan, where they previously had a virtual monopoly, because of the company's links with southern Africa. Amoco was obliged to abandon its prospecting for oil in Mozambique to bid successfully for an exploration concession in Tanzania.[3] While erratic and partial, such actions seem to be gaining ground as time goes on, and on the initiative of the Sudan, the Organization of African Unity in 1972 passed a resolution calling for all African states to ban companies that operated in Southern Rhodesia and elsewhere in southern Africa. In 1974, the OAU Secretariat started to compile a blacklist of these companies. There have been suggestions that the Arab boycott of Israel be linked to the African boycott of South Africa.

Not only governments, of course, but international organizations and national nongovernmental organizations have taken up positions in support of trade boycotts and investment embargoes or action against investors in southern Africa. The World Council of Churches has taken the lead in this, selling off all its stock in corporations doing business in southern Africa and banks providing major loans, and calling on member-churches and national Councils of Churches to do the same. It is no accident that most of the pressure on U.S. corporations on any sustained basis has come from the National Council of Churches, with individual denominations also taking a strong line in many cases. Some of them have sold all their stocks in companies involved in the region, while others prefer to retain them for the time being to attempt to influence management. In October 1974 the first case of withdrawal in response to church stockholder action took place. Continental Oil Company (CONOCO) announced the withdrawal of its participation in oil exploration off the coast of Namibia, following challenges by the United Church of Christ in 1973-1974.[4] Conoco was followed by the withdrawal of four other oil companies from Namibia, some of which also faced stockholder challenges.

Equally interesting is the attitude of foreign trade unions and the International Labor Organization. British and Australian trade unions have shown a particularly vivid interest in labor conditions in South Africa; in 1973 Australian unions launched a one-week blockade of imports from southern Africa, while the British Trade Union Congress has recommended opposing British investment in South Africa unless companies recognize African trade unions; and raising money overseas for the same purpose. In reply the secretary of the white Confederation of Labor in South Africa, Mr. C. Grobler, reiterated the confederation's opposition to African unions.[5]

In the United States, trade union interest is more recent, but has had considerable impact. Such unions as the Steelworkers' Union, Union of Automobile Workers (UAW), and Oil, Chemical and Atomic Workers' Union (OCAW) have lobbied for repeal of the Byrd Amendment and restoration of economic sanctions against Southern Rhodesia. Dock workers, backed by the International Longshoremen's Association (ILA), have refused to unload cargoes from Southern Rhodesia, which are imported under the Byrd Amendment at Baltimore, Philadelphia, New York, and some southern ports. In some cases the ban has been extended to South African cargoes as well.

In a major action prompted by the United Mine Workers Union (UMW), the attorney general of Alabama in August 1974 asked the U.S. customs commissioner to prohibit electricity producers from importing South

African coal. He invoked a statute of 1880 in arguing that South African coal is mined by "forced labor."[6] A court case brought by the UMW and the attorney general of Alabama to the same end produced an immediate reaction in South Africa: the repeal of all the penal provisions of the Masters and Servants Act and forty-one other pieces of labor legislation.[7] At the same time, coal miners temporarily blocked the unloading of South African coal at Mobile, Alabama. A union spokesman said, "The alternatives to buying South African coal are readily available; it's just cheaper to buy the African coal produced with cheap forced labor."[8]

Mr. J. A. Grobbelaar, the general secretary of the other main trade union organization in South Africa, TUCSA (Trade Union Council of South Africa), has written that the emerging attitudes of foreign trade unions represent a major threat to South Africa. He points in particular to the resolution adopted by the Workers' Group of the ILO, which alleged that contract and migrant labor systems were a disguised form of modern slavery and condemned South African and foreign employers and investors for being a source of direct or indirect support for the policy of apartheid. It called on the unions in all countries to boycott the loading and unloading of goods to and from South Africa and Namibia; to boycott South African ships and aircraft; and among other things, to bring pressure to bear on their governments to take specific action against South Africa. Grobbelaar comments:

> It would be exceedingly foolish . . . for anybody to reach the too tempting conclusion that [the resolution] can be safely ignored. Experienced opinion knows that it will not be *easily* implemented but, by the same token, it is necessary to recognize that the degree of determination for seeing such action introduced has increased immeasurably over the last few years. *It is completely realistic to opine that the noose is tightening on South Africa.* [Emphasis in the original.]

> ... It needs to be indicated that if the resolution is implemented to any meaningful degree, then the economic collapse of South Africa is inevitable. The Rhodesian experience [of being able to evade sanctions] must not be seen in the same context as the problem facing South Africa; there is no com-

> parison. . . . Concerted [British] Labour Party government
> action supported by the TUC, undoubtedly would be totally
> effective. . . .[9]

A substantial and increasing number of Western countries are exper-
iencing challenges to investment in southern Africa, either by their
governments or bodies such as churches and other pressure groups. In
Canada, for example, the government was instrumental in the decision
by the Polymer Corporation, a Government-owned firm, to dispose of
its assets in South Africa. Comprehensive reports on Canadian investment
in southern Africa have been drawn up by the YWCA[11] and more specialized pressure groups, and fairly wide press publicity has resulted. The
Canadian government's Department of Industry, Trade, and Commerce
reports that at least $70 million is invested in South Africa, involving
twelve Canadian companies—most of them, like Alcan Aluminium Ltd.,
being linked with U.S. investment.

Meanwhile, in Europe there has been strong controversy involving
several governments over the question of "starvation wages" being paid
in South Africa by subsidiaries of their companies. In West Germany, a
list of twenty-four companies that are alleged to be paying their African
workers below subsistence level has been published, and questions are
being raised in the Bundestag.[12] The government of Denmark has ordered
an investigation of the wages paid by South African subsidiaries of Danish
companies, especially East Asiatic and Christiani and Nielsen.[13] The managing director of the latter's subsidiary has been called home to a "storm of
public protest" over reports of labor conditions there.[14] There have also
been parliamentary questions in Switzerland, arising out of a report in
1972 that about fifty Swiss firms have invested or loaned almost $500
million to South Africa, making Switzerland the fourth largest source of
foreign capital after Britain, the United States, and West Germany as well
as providing more loans in the period 1947-1971 than any other country.
The report also stated that many of the employees of Swiss concerns
were paid below subsistence levels.[15] The raising of these issues in Europe
was largely the result of the major press exposé of starvation wages
paid by British-owned firms in South Africa in the London *Guardian*, and
the special parliamentary investigation that resulted.[16]

Aside from the question of private investment, various other official
actions against labor exploitation in southern Africa are being taken or

being contemplated by governments. The Dutch government, for example, has announced the termination of its financial aid for emigration to South Africa and the stiffening of U.N. embargoes against Rhodesia.[17] Finland has considered breaking diplomatic relations with South Africa, as has Sweden.[18] Australia has terminated all official promotion of trade and investment with South Africa, and announced that it would participate in international economic sanctions.[19] In another major policy move, Australia notified the International Monetary Fund that from September 1974 it will no longer caucus with South Africa in the election of a regional director of the fund and the World Bank.[20] As a result, with no other state willing to represent its interests, South Africa has lost its participation on the boards of the International Monetary Fund (IMF) and the World Bank (IBRD), which is seen in these circles as a "disaster," "an awful defeat," and "a humiliation."[21] Australia's more conservative neighbor, New Zealand, has gone even further by revoking its tariff preference for South Africa as from the end of 1973.[22] The Republic of Ireland has terminated all promotional campaigns in South Africa, and following controversy about starvation wages in South Africa, it instructed the Industrial Development Authority of Ireland to halt all contacts there.[23] Japan, which already bans direct capital investment in South Africa, has intervened to halt loans from the London-based Japan International Bank, Ltd. to interests in South Africa.[24] The foreign minister of Japan agreed in a visit to Africa to limit Japanese trade with South Africa. Following strong criticism in the Organization of African Unity, Japan is tightening up its enforcement of Rhodesian sanctions.[25]

All these actions and policies are very recent: they represent a new trend in Western Europe and Japan rather than established fact of general opposition to economic links with southern Africa. Perhaps the most comprehensive is the British Labour party's policy. The party had, prior to winning office in 1974, been involved at the local level in the withdrawal of municipal and other accounts from banks and companies with a stake in southern Africa. Its official policy now states:

South Africa could be suspended from GATT (the General Agreement on Tariffs and Trade) and the EEC could refuse all preferences and trading concessions to South Africa. . . .

With the distinct possibility of a future conflagration in South Africa these firms (with investments there) could well find themselves opposing the liberation movements and asking the British Government for support.

For these reasons Labour believes that Britain's economic involvement in Southern Africa should be reduced. . . . We would accept and enforce United Nations mandatory economic sanctions on South Africa if it were clear that they could be effectively introduced and policed.

We have asked the Executive Working Party . . . to examine other areas where it might be possible for Britain to take independent action to bring to an end Britain's dangerous and unhealthy involvement in Southern Africa, an involvement which by its very nature, means Britain benefits from the fruits of Apartheid.

We have asked the Working Party to investigate and evaluate the following possibilities as lines of action to be followed by the next Labour Government:
i) the termination of all export credits, loans and guarantees to South Africa;
ii) the ending of the policy of exchanging trade missions;
iii)the terminating of the Ottawa Agreement (which allows South Africa vital "Commonwealth Preferences");
iv) the ending of banking links which enable South Africa to raise money on the London market;
v) machinery to prevent further British investment in South Africa;
vi) the ending of cover under the Overseas Investment and Export Guarantee Act;
vii) the withdrawal of all or part of existing British investment in South Africa.

The policy Labour develops on investment and trade with South Africa will also apply to Namibia. We will immediately review all treaties with South Africa (including double-taxation agreements) to seek to exclude Namibia from all provisions. . . . Labour will terminate the atomic-energy contract with Rio Tinto Zinc for uranium in Namibia.[26]

With the Labour party now in power, there is a continuing debate about implementation of this policy. Western European policies do not necessarily have a direct impact on those of the United States government, but the trend away from official support for trade and investment with southern Africa emphasizes the isolation of a U.S. policy founded on "communication," which in practice involves extending government subsidies and facilities to U.S. traders and investors. The broad trend toward concentration on economic issues in southern Africa, observable in many countries recently, could well find an echo within the Democratic party in the United States. A study on Africa prepared for Democratic candidates in the 1974 elections called for an end to "U.S. Government commercial or financial support of apartheid."[27] It is therefore useful to keep under observation the movement toward exerting pressure on economic interests in southern Africa.

A few small examples will suffice to illustrate new approaches to the southern African issues. In the United States companies that lobby in support of government help to the minority regimes are becoming more conspicuous, the main one so far being Union Carbide, which lobbies in favor of violating international sanctions on Southern Rhodesia by the so-called Byrd Amendment. However, the corporation has also tried to build up a good image in the United States with respect to minorities and was awarded the Frederick Douglas Award by the New York Urban League in early 1973. There were immediate protests from African-Americans because of Union Carbide's deep involvement in southern Africa, including one from Congressman Charles Diggs, concluding: "Any award to Union Carbide would . . . be an insult to the memory of both Jackie Robinson and Frederick Douglas, who fought all their lives against racial discrimination and exploitation such as Union Carbide practices." As a result, the unprecedented step was taken of withdrawing the award.[28]

Municipal action has been slower in the United States than in Europe, but questions have been raised in various places, including the District of Columbia, about municipal contracts with companies or banks doing business with companies investing in southern Africa. The City Council of Dayton, Ohio, decided to terminate municipal contracts with Gulf Oil because of its involvement in Angola. The Berkeley (California) City Council has passed a resolution by a large margin, calling for a full investigation of its contracts with companies "giving direct or indirect aid or support to the racist government or the economy of South Africa."[29]

In 1975 the City Council of Gary, Indiana, voted to terminate all contracts with IBM and other companies operating in South Africa.

The major legislative effort is Congressman Diggs' bill, introduced under various numbers, including 522 and 269. It is designed to protect U.S. domestic and foreign policy interests by making fair employment practices in the South African and Namibian enterprises of U.S. firms a criterion for eligibility for government contracts. The rationale is that the bill should influence U.S. businesses by conditioning eligibility for U.S. government contracts on the provision of equal employment opportunity in their South African enterprises on a similar basis to that used to promote equal employment opportunity in the United States.[30] This legislation is likely to be the subject of recurring efforts in the Congress. Meanwhile, of course, there are grounds for legal action against some companies in terms of existing equal employment legislation: Black employees of multinational corporations could claim that by being denied postings to the South African subsidiaries (often seen as a stepping-stone up the corporate ladder) they are being denied their full promotion prospects. A variety of approaches that have been suggested have yet to be elaborated and implemented, whether in Congress or through the courts.

SANCTIONS AGAINST SOUTHERN AFRICA: A CASE STUDY IN OIL

It should be noted that trade embargoes and sanctions are no novelty for South Africa itself; they are a recognized part of the arsenal with which the Republic asserts its own dominance in the region. This probably arises out of the historical importance of boycotts and embargoes as practiced by the Afrikaner people since the Boer War, to gain economic and political influence at the expense of the ruling English-speakers. Internally, political and ethnic considerations dominate the granting of government contracts and the implementation of regulatory legislation in favor of Afrikaner capital and the state corporations with which it is often linked.

Internationally, economic leverage is used more discreetly. A government directive was reported in 1972 that emphasized the source of imports of certain commodities so as to favor those African states that were cooperating with the policy of "dialogue" at that time. Thus, for example, 18 percent of the country's coffee was to come from Madagascar and 25 percent from Angola; 7 percent of tea imports were allocated to Malawi, 11 percent to Mauritius, and 11 percent to Rhodesia.[31] Following the lead taken by the Mauritian ambassador to the United Nations in the 1973 challenge to South Africa's credentials, a boycott of Mauritian tea was launched. The government attributed the boycott to the S.A. Tea, Coffee, and Chicory Association, but it was widely reported to have official backing.[32]

The outrage with which South Africans react to boycotts and embargoes against them may therefore be seen in part as fear of serious pressure based on their own use of such pressure against their weaker neighbors. The most concerted embargo so far, and also the one involving South Africa's weakest spot, is the oil embargo imposed by the oil-producing Arab states at the end of 1973. Apart from being a demonstration of the realistic possibility of serious economic action being adopted by Third World states, the embargo was in itself of considerable significance to the interlocking economic, political, and military structures of power in southern Africa. The government of South Africa in particular has always recognized its vulnerability to an oil embargo: it has found no oil in its own territory or in Namibia; the use of oil has been rising steeply in line with economic growth, and it could not easily be replaced with alternate forms of energy for the vital transportation and other sectors.

One result of the threat of an oil embargo was the lavishing of very large sums that would otherwise have gone to other government priorities (such as defense, the implementation of segregation policies, overseas public relations, and so on) on a fruitless search for oil, and the construction of refineries, pipelines, special offshore terminals, and extensive oil reserves in tank farms and disused coal mines. These reserves represent a heavy financial burden by tying up scarce capital resources in unproductive fixed assets, which are dwindling fast in terms of the proportion of demand that they can cover. Although grossly exaggerated estimates of the duration of these reserves are in currency, it is very unlikely that they would cover anything more than a year, and most responsible estimates put the stocks at something like six months of normal consumption.[33]

In 1973, 75 percent of South Africa's oil imports came from the Middle East, with the remaining 25 percent from Iran. The latter is establishing

increasing cooperation with South Africa, including participation in the
National Refinery at Sasolburg (Natref) and increased military collaboration.
The collaboration of Iran was critical in enabling South Africa to withstand
the Arab oil embargo, although with some difficulties; the price was almost
total dependence on a single source, which is not guaranteed to cover South
Africa's growing demand for oil. The Republic is now about 90 percent dependent on Iran for its oil imports, and allegedly obtains the rest from
Iraq's Basrah fields and from Indonesia. Official sources in Iran have made
it clear that the country cannot support increments in South African demand indefinitely, because the reserves are not large to start with; most of
current production is tied up in bilateral government deals with the main
consuming countries; increasing amounts of oil are required for industrialization in Iran; and finally, "South Africa is a bit of a political embarrassment, more so because of her Rhodesian connection." Iran is therefore understood to have imposed a ceiling on South African supplies, although it
is not known what the figure involved is.[34]

The international oil companies were crucial to South Africa from the
beginning of the embargo, when the *Financial Mail* reported that "only
expert and artful juggling by international oil companies is keeping some
refineries going."[35] "Chiefs of South Africa's major oil companies . . . have
been advising Government and their head office on how best to conserve
and utilise supplies."[36] The chairman of BP, during a visit to South Africa,
confirmed that all the international oil companies had "intentionally set
out to thwart Arab attempts at enforcing oil embargoes on countries like
South Africa. . . ."[37] Among the most prominent of these companies are
Mobil, with 23 percent of sales of all petroleum products in South Africa,
Caltex with 18 percent, and Esso (Exxon) with 2 percent. Shell and BP of
the United Kingdom have 23 percent and 14 percent respectively.[38]

Despite the assistance from Iran and the international oil companies,
the supply of oil in South Africa was seriously curtailed as a result of the
Arab embargo. The severe restrictions on oil use, originating with the
worldwide shortages at the end of 1973, were continued long after all other
Western countries had returned to normal. The minister of Economic Affairs stated in September 1974 that strategic reserves had been depleted,
and the situation required a continuation of the restrictions.[39] For South
Africa, alternative sources of supply to the Middle East such as Nigeria,
Venezuela, and to a large extent Indonesia are committed elsewhere and
for various reasons are unlikely to provide a solution to the supply prob-

lem. There have been various suggestions that Angola can become a major crude oil source; however, there are serious technical difficulties involved in using this for South African refineries. Most of the output is currently going to Portugal and the United States, and the general disruption in Angola is a serious threat to the industry. The prolonged shortage of oil in South Africa had severe repercussions for the economy as a whole.

Although oil accounts for only 25 percent of the total energy needs, 85 percent of this is for the vital transport industry and such important sectors as automobiles and related industries are directly affected by this, as well as practically every other kind of concern that depends on internal transportation for supplies and deliveries. Substantial numbers of workers, mainly in the motor assembly plants, were being laid off within weeks of the embargo.

At the end of November 1973, at the time of the embargo decision, there was a complete failure of fuel supplies for light aircraft, due to the breakdown of a tanker heading for South Africa.[40] This points up the connection between oil supplies and military strength, since South African refineries do not produce this kind of fuel, and the thousands of privately owned light aircraft, organized under the Air Commando system, are a vital element in the government's "countersubversion" plans.

Marine diesel and marine fuel oil became in particularly short supply at the beginning of the embargo, and ships without a priority listing had to avoid South Africa altogether. This obviously affected the country's external trade, on which it is strongly dependent; since then there have been frequent freight increases, which make exports less competitive in major overseas markets. These are all located at great distances as a result of the almost total failure, for political reasons, to develop large-scale markets in Africa. In addition, the essential imports of capital equipment and machinery to keep industrial growth moving are made more expensive by freight increases.

As is the case internationally, the rising price of oil in South Africa exacerbates domestic inflation. There is the related possibility of even greater labor unrest as the cost of living moves further ahead of African wage increases. Strikes and riots in the coal mines, which have become increasingly important as a source of fuel, have been a major problem. In fact these mines are now notorious for their labor problems, involving the firing of hundreds of workers.

It is in the most modern, capital-intensive industries, such as petro-chemicals and the motor industry, that the oil embargo was felt most strongly; and it is here that recent foreign investment, especially from the United States, is concentrated. A senior executive of General Motors was recently asked at a seminar, where he had claimed GM's South African operation to be motivated by concern for their black employees, how long they would stay if they were making a loss. He pointed out that if the oil embargo reached a certain level of effectivness, they would make a loss; and that in that case they would close down their operation in South Africa immediately.[41]

The oil situation in South Africa has been emphasized because its economy is so crucial to that of the whole region. South Africa also supplies oil to some other countries in the region directly. Southern Rhodesia, for example, was receiving only 6,000 barrels per day from the Mozambique refinery's spare capacity under the Portuguese regime, as compared to consumption of 17,000 bpd; the rest came from South Africa. Since the Portuguese coup and Mozambique's progress toward independence, oil supplies to Southern Rhodesia have dwindled. Consumption of over 20,000 bpd is now supplied from South Africa. Again, the attitudes of the international oil companies are crucial, involving deliberate evasion of international economic sanctions. Caltex, Mobil, and Shell have been named as suppliers to Southern Rhodesia. The colony had suffered from gasoline rationing previously, following the illegal Declaration of Independence, but its economy then was far more resilient than after the cumulative effect of many years of partial sanctions, and especially the unhealthy state of its railroad network. The stronger guerrilla challenge is also a weakening factor, and the gas shortage clearly affects South Africa's willingness to become too involved in the operations there. High level military conferences were held immediately following the announcement of an oil embargo on southern Africa between South African and Rhodesian staffs and it is from this time that South Africa has shown a strong determination to impose a settlement on the minority regime.

It is possible that the Arab oil embargo on Portugal and the colonies was a contributing factor in the coup d'état and the collapse of the colonial war effort. A report presented to the Portuguese government on October 10, 1973 (before the embargo) by the general director for combustibles in the Ministry of Economics is quoted as warning:

We are on the eve of a serious and unexpected crisis: our petroleum reserves are limited to three months at most. The stability of the regime and the security of its African provinces could be in question if effective and urgent measures are not taken in case the Arab countries should decide to place a sudden embargo on the supply of "crude" to this country.[42]

According to the South African press, the oil situation in Mozambique deteriorated sharply in the month following the embargo, and shortages remained severe, despite consultations with "oil company officials of South Africa and Mozambique.[43] The grim long-term outlook for the colonies just before the coup was indicated by the indefinite postponement of the project to build a 1 million ton per year refinery at Nacala, because of the uncertain crude-oil supply situation; the group of companies involved included Mobil, Caltex, Shell, and BP.[44]

The rapid liberation of the Portuguese colonies, and the precarious economic and military situation of the illegal regime in Southern Rhodesia after the loss of its Mozambique buffer, have given a new perspective to the future of southern Africa. The number of targets falls, and pressure is concentrated on the remaining areas of minority rule—in particular on Southern Rhodesia and Namibia. In the case of the former, the economic sanctions that were largely discounted at the time of their introduction by the United Nations in 1968 are now being taken seriously by even the most militant opponents of the Smith regime as a major support for the domestic struggle for liberation.

In all cases, boycotts and embargoes are part of the pressure being exerted on white minority rule. They also assist the liberation movements by restricting the access of minority regimes to arms, equipment, and financial support. The prospect of further economic pressure on South Africa and Southern Rhodesia is an element that, however it is assessed, clearly needs to be included in any calculation of the risks involved in a stake in that region.

NOTES

    1. *Washington Star-News* 28 August 1974; *New York Times,* 29 August 1974.

2. *Le Monde* (Paris), 4 August 1973.

3. *Afrique-Asie* (Paris), 4 March 1974.

4. *Wall Street Journal* (New York), 1 November 1974.

5. *The Star* (Johannesburg), 15 December 1973.

6. *New York Amsterdam News,* 24 August 1974.

7. *The Star,* week of 9 November 1974.

8. *Christian Science Monitor* (Boston) 22 August 1974.

9. J.A. Grobbelaar, "The International Labour Organization and South Africa," *South Africa International,* 4, 2 (October 1973), p. 100.

10. *The Star,* week of 17 March 1973.

11. *Investment in Oppression* (Toronto: Y.W.C.A., May 1973).

12. *The Guardian* (London), 28 April 1973; *The Star,* week of 31 March and 21 April 1973.

13. *The Star,* week of 31 March 1973 and 2 February 1974.

14. Ibid., week of 26 January 1974.

15. *The Guardian,* week of 15 September 1973; *The Star,* week of 11 August and 15 September 1973.

16. *The Guardian,* 12 March 1975, and subsequent articles; also *Wages and Conditions of African Workers Employed by British Firms in South Africa,* 5th Report from the Expenditure Committee, House of Commons, Session 1973-74 (London: HMSO, 1974), and *Minutes of Evidence,* Vols. I-III, Trade and Industry Sub-committee (London: HMSO, 1973).

17. *The Star,* week of 2 June 1973.

18. Ibid., week of 24 November 1973.

19. Ibid., week of 28 September 1974.

20. Ibid., week of 29 September 1974.

21. Ibid., week of 5 October 1974.

22. Ibid., week of 29 September 1973.

23. Press statement of the Hon. Administrative Secretary, Irish Anti-apartheid Movement, quoting the Minister for Industry and Commerce.

24. *The Star,* week of 14 September 1974.

25. Ibid., week of 16 November 1974.

26. Labour party policy on southern Africa as adopted by the Party Conference in September 1973.

27. *New York Amsterdam News,* 16 August 1974.

28. Ibid., March 24, 1973; and other sources.

29. City Council of Berkeley, Calif. Resolution No. 45,358, N.S. (Resolution regarding the Republic of South Africa), reproduced in the *Congressional Record,* November 2, 1972, p. E 9012.

30. For full hearings on the bill, *see U.S. Business Involvement in Southern Africa,* Parts I, II, and III, and hearings before the Subcommittee IV

of the House Judiciary Committee on the bill (in preparation), in particular the statement by Congressman Diggs of September 20, 1973.

31. *Rand Daily Mail* (Johannesburg), July 20, 1972.

32. *Financial Gazette* (Johannesburg), November 30, 1973.

33. The South African press is guessing at six months. A major embassy in Pretoria estimates just over six months, including both coal mines and surface tank farms. During previous research by the author, the figure most commonly guessed at by South African commentators prior to the crisis was around nine months at the most. This would still make the reserves proportionately larger than any other country's, as far as these are known or estimated, and in relative terms a heavy financial burden.

34. *Financial Mail* (Johannesburg), 18 April 1975.

35. *Financial Mail*, 14 December 1973.

36. Ibid., 16 November 1973.

37. Sir Eric Drake, chairman of BP, quoted in *Anti-Apartheid News,* (London), September 1974.

38..*Financial Mail,* 16 November 1973.

39. *The Star,* week of 14 September 1974.

40. Interviews by the author in South Africa, November 1973.

41. Interview with Mr. Walter H. Gussenhoven, General Motors Overseas Corporation, in Addis Ababa, December 6, 1973.

42. Quoted by Aquino de Bragança in *Afrique-Asie,* 26 November 1973

43. *Financial Mail,* 14 December 1973.

44. *Platts Oilgram News Service,* December 17, 1973.

chapter 9 _____
SUMMARY

In the Republic of South Africa, the government is trying to rationalize its official policy of white supremacy, or apartheid by promoting the idea of "homelands" for the African majority. These areas cover only 12 percent of the land area, most of it very poor and badly eroded. In fact the old "native reserve" policy is a basic element in the history of white invasion and domination of South Africa, with Africans being increasingly pushed back into the poorest areas and later forced out of them to work on the mines by the imposition of taxes and further impoverishment of the "reserves." The reserves offer no basis for subsistence; agricultural production is declining, and millions of "unproductive" Africans are being forcibly deported to the "homelands" from the areas of economic activity known as "white areas" where they have settled.

The deportations are matched by shifting of boundaries in the interests of local whites and by large-scale reshuffling of the population inside the "homelands," making them areas of extreme insecurity and violence, and contributing to impoverishment. Increasing numbers of people are landless and confined to camps where conditions are sometimes desperate.

Official plans have indicated the need for creating industrial employment in "border areas" and more recently, inside the "homelands" to compensate for agricultural deterioration. However, the development corporations are badly managed, have no African representation, tend to increase the influence of the whites with vested interests, and have proved incapable of promoting overall "development." Border and "homeland" industries offer negligible new employment since investment, which in any case is usually capital-intensive, is very slow to enter. The only attraction that the "homeland governments" can offer is the removal of any restrictions of minimum wages for Africans, while the proposal to scrap the color bar has been abandoned. Industrial growth points may also contribute to the overall economic decline of the "homelands."

U.S. investors are showing interest in "homeland" investment, mainly for public relations purposes. However, conditions for Africans there are even worse than in the urban areas.

South Africa as a whole is very rich, growth being encouraged by government policy through direct intervention and state corporations. A recent priority has been the promotion of automation and capital-intensive production. Africans in South Africa, however, are worse off than those in much poorer independent states, and the "homelands" are among the poorest areas of the continent. African poverty is also increasing, slipping further behind even the lowest subsistence estimates. The deterioration in African living standards has taken place in both urban and rural areas, owing to the relatively rapid rise of the cost of living for Africans, which is higher than that for whites. High growth rates are associated with a widening gap between white and African incomes, already uniquely unequal, together with a faster decline in African real incomes.

Under industrialization, Africans form an increasing proportion of the labor force, and their productivity is rising much faster than their cash wages. The trend toward job fragmentation is very hard on African incomes since the negotiations with the white unions often include immediate cuts in African rates to compensate for increased white salaries, and the general inflationary impact of white salary increases, the main feature of job fragmentation, is depressing African incomes generally. Africans are therefore increasingly used by the economy, while suffering increasing deprivation. The power structure that brings this about has demonstrated considerable flexibility in adapting white supremacy techniques to changing economic patterns and has turned each modification into a means of strengthening white privilege.

Government policy is that Africans should be treated solely as units of labor. There is therefore complete government control over African movement and employment to deprive work-seekers of any freedom of choice and to give employers absolute power over them during the period of the contract or even beyond. The system of migratory labor that is associated with the color bar is being forcibly advanced with full-scale deportation of nonproductive Africans to the "homelands" and construction of "hostels," which further destroy African family and social life.

The slogan of "rate for the job" has been a device used by white unions to preserve their members' privileged status. Moves to organize any Africans who might compete with them are also protectionist of white privilege. There is almost total opposition from the white interest groups to Africans registering their own unions.

South Africa has a national system of forced labor, in violation of internationally recognized labor standards and in blatant disregard for the principles of the Universal Declaration of Human Rights.

All white interest groups—labor, local and foreign investors, farmers, and the government—benefit from some of the aspects of apartheid, and there is a trade-off process between them that results in the deteriorating situation of the African majority. Employers are heavily responsible for African poverty since they take full advantage of the powers given them by the government, although more attention has been focused on their nagging complaints at the privileges accorded to white workers. The impression is created that they are therefore against apartheid.

In reality, apartheid is a product of urbanization and industrialization, not a traditional rural-based ideology as it is often portrayed. Although extreme inequality of opportunity and reward results in inefficiency, it is in none of the white groups' interest to challenge the structure that brings them all such economic, political, and social benefits. Efficiency and economic redistribution is a response to the acquisition of trade union and political power by workers, which has been lost rather than gained by Africans in South Africa.

Profit margins depend on keeping African labor costs down, by government and employers reinforcing each other's power. The Oppenheimer thesis—that "economic growth will break down apartheid"—is based on a fundamental misunderstanding of the nature of the apartheid power structure. Yet, it is at the basis of U.S. companies' arguments for investing in South Africa. In fact, economic growth is managed by the white interest groups that benefit from it and that use economic and political power to maintain and reinforce white supremacy, by force where necessary. Repression of African efforts at participation in the structure has been most ruthless during the decade of the economic boom in the 1960s.

There is therefore an essential compatibility of white economic interests that appear—through white party politics and limited criticism by the English press and tiny liberal groups—to be in conflict. However, conflict is over the distribution of benefits among the whites, not over the structure of white minority rule as such. The apparent lack of friction with Africans is a result of their being excluded from bargaining. Any ideological considerations are readily discarded where questions of mutual interest to all white groups, such as migrant labor, are concerned. This may give an impression of apartheid as an ideology breaking down only if there is a false concept of the nature of white supremacy and apartheid.

African bargaining power is now virtually destroyed, although it was previously a factor in some aspects of South African political life. Growing African unemployment and poverty is being recognized as a major threat to white security, especially as violence increases in South Africa and strikes break out not for specific demands but apparently out of desperation, with no spokesmen coming forward to negotiate.

At this point the South African economy is suffering from erratic growth, the balance of payments outlook is uncertain, and inflation is soaring. This seems to be the result of a structural imbalance that is becoming apparent, a fundamental element of the apartheid system and one that is not conducive to normal corrective measures. The extent to which the special privilege of the ruling minority is locked into the whole structure of the Republic, however, has eliminated any political machinery for fundamental readjustment. There are no easy answers about the future of South Africa—least of all further investment in the structure of white privilege.

Foreign capital has been essential to every stage of economic growth in South Africa, and is becoming increasingly vital at the present time. It has always conformed to local discriminatory patterns and was crucial to the establishment of the centralized African recruitment system for the gold mines. The state has also played a major role in channeling foreign capital to further its own policy objectives and to promote local white interests closely allied to it.

The trend of foreign investment is now to high technology, capital-intensive sectors where U.S. capital in particular is focused and where its financial and technical power has been crucial in this priority objective of the South African government. A continuing inflow of foreign capital is crucial to the apartheid economy; exchange control has been used to make investors increase their stake, which they have done apparently without reservations. Loan finance for the government and its agencies has also been important recently. The balance of payments is dependent, and increasingly so, on continuing capital inflows to cover the structural trade imbalance, and to finance essential imports. After the economic crisis following the Sharpeville massacre, U.S. financiers raised large sums to promote a recovery of business confidence.

Foreign investment is vital in building up South Africa's military-industrial complex, undermining the arms embargo policy of the United States and most other Western countries. Many companies are undoubtedly involved in direct military contracts for the government, although there is strict censorship on these deals. In an emergency the automobile, chemical, and other industries could immediately be turned over to military production, and the presence of numerous U.S. companies operating in these fields would be crucial, any ritual expression of opposition to apartheid policy meaningless. Foreign investment is also associated with further European immigration. U.S. companies have recruited actively in Europe, intensifying the basic problem of South African blacks.

Claims by investors that Africans support their presence are self-serving. Heavy penalties can be and have been imposed on those representing the African, Asian, and Coloured communities who have spoken out against foreign investors.

Businessmen with a genuine social conscience have tended to avoid any involvement with South Africa on moral grounds. However, increasingly there are considerations of economic and political risk that militate against a commitment. Just as economic growth, foreign investment, and white immigration are mutually reinforcing, any hesitancy operates in the same way. Immigrants are fewer, and not putting down roots; investors are showing concern about exchange control, which would make withdrawal almost impossible in the event of a crisis. Arbitrary government action against foreign shareholdings in banks and rumors of a plan to take over "strategic" industries have caused great concern while capital inflows as a whole have fallen away. Decisions by U.S. companies to refrain from increasing investment in South Africa would tend to increase the hesitancy among other nations' investors. U.S. subsidiaries are irreplaceable with their technical and financial power and prestige.

U.S. investment is the second largest in South Africa, after Britain's, and has been the fastest growing during the 1960s. It now amounts to over $1 billion, focused in areas of rapid growth that depend on technical and managerial skills and personnel as well as financial resources. These are are much more profitable than other sectors, and expansion results largely from reinvestment of local earnings, which could otherwise have been repatriated without limit. U.S. investment is unique in being mainly direct involvement by subsidiaries of U.S.-based multinational corporations.

While of crucial importance to South Africa, this stake is only 1.1 percent of total U.S. investment abroad, and its relative size has not grown. U.S. investment in independent African countries is almost double this amount, and is more profitable than South African investments. However, the companies with a commitment to South Africa devote a disproportionate amount of their political clout to promoting the regime's interests in Washington.

U.S. private investment in South Africa, during a time of unprecedented repression of the population, has been in conflict with official U.S. government expressions of distaste for apartheid; a pattern that is analogous to the racial policies of Nazi Germany in the 1930s. Three-quarters of it is concentrated in the hands of only twelve major corporations, which operate in strategic sectors such as oil, automobiles, construction equipment, electronics and computers, and rubber. Although they are unwilling to disclose information, it is clear that most cooperate closely with the government and depend on government contracts; that they provide irreplaceable expertise and equipment, especially in computers and electronics; and that they provide a reserve of military capacity arising from massive defense contracting in the United States.

These companies are very capital-intensive, often importing highly skilled whites, and their employment of Africans is negligible. Those that they have are paid less than the Minimum Effective Level. They are investing heavily in projects which are priorities for the South African government, such as local content production and moves to "border areas." Many of them are providing the means by which South African employers can automate work that previously provided large-scale employment for

Africans. They show a spontaneous enthusiasm for the South African government and its policy objectives.

In the United States, the companies have spent large amounts on projecting an image that is vastly different from this reality, one as major and benevolent employers of Africans who are trying to "break down apartheid." In fact it is apparent from numerous sources that U.S. subsidiaries, especially where an American is in charge, do nothing to improve their employment record where they readily could and care very little about the issue.

Claims that the companies can be persuaded to operate as charitable institutions are naive in the extreme. It is not in the interests of the companies to do so; and in the face of their refusal to provide relevant information on a regular basis, this cannot be satisfactorily enforced by well-meaning reformers outside the company's decision-making structure. The major British parliamentary inquiry into subsidiaries of British companies in South Africa concluded that without exposure and compulsory monitoring, companies can be expected to allow gross abuses in their South African subsidiaries. In many cases, U.S. companies may be defending their operations there in good faith on the basis of false information supplied by their South African subsidiaries.

The most determined attempt so far to "reform" the South African operation of a U.S. concern, that of NASA with its tracking station, merely highlighted the gap between "above-average" South African employment practices and the minimum standards of U.S. legislation. As a result, NASA decided to phase out its operation there.

U.S. businessmen use job fragmentation widely, in collusion with white workers and at the expense of Africans. They enter fully into the trade-off system with the white unions, to their mutual advantage, and then use this in the United States to claim they are "breaking down" the system of white privilege, which is reinforced by these bargains. Their claims to favor the dispossessed majority are further belied by their universal hostility to black trade unions in their plants.

U.S. investors help to finance the South African public relations machine, which establishes a strong although misleading image of the well-being of all races in South Africa and the benefits of foreign investment. The prevalence of this misinformation about South Africa is one of the major problems in this field. The South Africa Foundation, financed largely by major foreign investors in South Africa, has been a very potent force in deflecting U.S. government pressure on South Africa, and individual companies also lobby in Washington on behalf of their South African commitments.

The increasing use of foreign loans by the South African government has provoked strong opposition leading to the termination of some major loans from U.S. banks; this is now tending to draw further attention to the question of direct investment by U.S. companies in South Africa.

Other southern African issues tend to revolve around investment in South Africa. This is most obvious in the case of Namibia, formerly South West Africa, which is illegally occupied by the Republic of South Africa as determined by the United Nations, backed by the International Court of Justice in an advisory opinion accepted by the United States government. Namibia' status is a major issue in international law. Official U.S. policy is to discoura investment in Namibia; the government will refuse to protect such U.S. inve ment from future lawful governments in Namibia and has stated that severa companies have in fact been deterred by this. However, many U.S. compani are operating in Namibia as part of their South African operations.

Various questions concerning investment arise out of the legal situation, such as South Africa's invalid claim to represent Namibia in international o ganizations including those of technical, scientific, or economic importance U.S. bilateral treaties with South Africa are not invoked in the case of Nam bia. Since all purported South African laws and concessions are invalid, this puts into question the basis on which U.S. companies in Namibia are operat ing and will affect SEC rulings on share issues relating to Namibia. The U.S. government has tried to persuade companies already involved in Namibia at least to implement the Universal Declaration of Human Rights, which none them are doing at present.

Namibian Africans have shown determined resistance to South African c cupation, especially since the decisive 1971 opinion that South Africa is legally obliged to withdraw from the territory. A general strike was held December 1971-February 1972. Organized armed resistance under SWAPO ha been going since 1966, tying up South African troops in the north of the territory. Many Africans feel that political repression gives them no practical alternative.

A state of emergency is in force in the north, and there have been hundreds of arrests, detention without trial, and public floggings of members of SWAPO and other opposition parties. The extent of popular opposition was indicated by the overwhelming boycott of elections for the South African-imposed "Bantustan" in the north.

Contract labor in Namibia involves 86 percent of all African workers, who are forcibly separated from their families to work on the mines and white farms. Employers can order certain categories of workers, including children, and they are then dispatched with no right of refusal. The system has been condemned from many quarters as "akin to slavery." Workers are subject to the complete control of employers, including severe physical abuse. The general strike of 1971-1972 was directed against the whole contract labor system.

The system has been revised, but remains fundamentally the same as before. The movement and employment of African workers is strictly controlled by the government network, and workers have no independent grievance procedure or the right to terminate a contract unilaterally. An African can be forced to work, wherever he is living. Criminal penalties can be invoked to enforce the obligation to work wherever the occupation regime sends him.

Conditions in the compounds where African workers are confined have been described as "disgusting." In the rural areas, migratory labor has caused widespread social destruction and the associated personal problems, as in South Africa but on an even more extensive scale.

Responsibility rests largely on the employers—especially the American-owned Tsumeb Corporation, the largest employer of contract labor in Namibia and a party to the agreement forming the new contract system. Tsumeb pays much lower wages than the South African-owned diamond mines. The employers have made deals to keep wages down and eliminate the theoretical right to change jobs that was to have been a concession resulting from the strike.

The United States has the largest foreign stake in Namibia, after South Africa. Probably 90 percent of this is the investment by American Metal Climax and Newmont Mining in the Tsumeb Corporation, which operates what may be the richest mine in the world. Many other U.S. corporations are involved in mineral exploration and mining and oil prospecting—many of them since the decision by the U.S. government to discourage investment in Namibia. However, some shareholders are tending to withdraw their traditional support of management over challenges to their Namibian ventures.

While South Africa claims to be developing Namibia for no profit, it is suppressing any data that could be used to substantiate this, and the claim is not regarded as credible. South Africa is increasingly annexing the international territory; revenue from these territories goes directly to Pretoria. The fact that the major investors operate in both South Africa and Namibia facilitates this process. At least one-third of GDP apparently leaves Namibia in dividends to foreign investors. The gap between white and African incomes is huge, and Africans live in extreme poverty, even worse than in South Africa, although Namibia is an extremely wealthy territory. Its mineral assets are all in U.S. and other foreign hands. This expropriation of Namibia's assets is a serious violation of South Africa's original mandate from the League of Nations. Namibians and the United Nations have expressed great concern that Namibia will be gutted of all its natural resources before it reaches independence.

Investment in Southern Rhodesia has been illegal under U.S. law since 1968, following an affirmative U.S. vote in the U.N. Security Council to impose mandatory economic sanctions against the illegal minority regime. The regime seized power to preempt independence under democratic majority rule. The African population, over 95 percent of the total, has expressed the overwhelming wish for self-determination.

The presence of foreign companies in Southern Rhodesia has greatly helped the regime to survive, and initially to take advantage of sanctions by expropriating them. They are concerned in mining, where their technical contribution and international marketing connections are invaluable in the evasion of sanctions. Union Carbide accounts for 70-80 percent of U.S. investment in Southern Rhodesia, and has led the field in political support for the regime.

Many of the companies—of which the second largest group is U.S.-owned—deal illegally with their South African associates, and use their international connections to evade sanctions. Union Carbide and other companies have successfully used their political lobbies in Washington to break down the U.S. government's commitment to sanctions, to the benefit of their own special interests in opposition to the U.S. national interest in observing this treaty commitment. The political support for the regime offered by so many U.S. companies in Southern Rhodesia is an indication of the massive support they would probably mobilize for South Africa, in the event of a crisis in which the U.S. national interest would demand neutrality.

As in South Africa, the white minority in Southern Rhodesia, allied with foreign investment, monopolizes the modern sector of the economy, the best jobs, land, education, and other benefits. The vote is tied to "white" income levels, resulting in a negligible number of African voters. The gap between white and African incomes is increasing and most Africans live in great and increasing poverty. Foreign investment has not even provided them with any substantial employment opportunities; rather it has helped to attract European immigrants, most of the white people in Southern Rhodesia being Europeans of very recent origin. Moderate Africans have appealed for sanctions to be continued and denounced the regime's drive for more immigrants.

Five years of mandatory economic sanctions have begun to have a crippling effect on the economy, especially noticeable in the dwindling immigration and rising emigration statistics for whites. This trend is also prompted by the greatly increased effectiveness of the African liberation movements, which are imposing a severe strain on white manpower resources. Aid that previously went to movements in the Portuguese colonies is now being channeled to those in Southern Rhodesia. At the same time, ease of access to the sea is greatly complicated by the departure of Portuguese collaborators from Mozambique.

The situation in the former Portuguese colonies has been radically reversed by the Portuguese coup of April 25, 1974, and the negotiation of independence with the liberation movements. U.S. investment, which was based on the assumption that colonial rule would continue indefinitely, has been seriously affected by the dislocation and subsequent transfer of power to independent governments. Although the U.S. government itself failed to realize the imminence of decolonization, large corporations such as Gulf Oil were responsible for their own calculations as to the political risks involved in investments in Angola, Mozambique, and Guinea-Bissau; in this they badly miscalculated. Their decision to invest involved substantial support for the Portuguese colonial regime, and there are continuing reports that the U.S. government and some companies are intervening in the political struggles in Angola. Superpower intervention here is similar to that in the postcolonial era in Southeast Asia. The unexpected collapse of the Portuguese colonial policy and the chaos in Angola should provoke some rethinking of political risks in the rest of southern Africa.

By the time of the 1974 coup, the United States was the dominant foreign economic power in Angola and Mozambique. U.S. investment there was estimated to amount to about $220 million, almost all of it the Gulf Oil investment in Angola. This was crucial to colonial Angola's balance of payments situation and provided enough income in taxes and royalties to cover 60 percent of the cost of the war there.

Other major U.S. investments were concentrated in oil as well as other extractive industries; among these was the Esso operation in Guinea-Bissau. They all operated on terms designed to give the Portuguese colonial regimes maximum control and financial advantage, including the power to take over operations in an emergency. Other U.S. investors were involved in transportation, strategic industries, finance, and agribusiness.

Although the prospect of serious boycotts of southern Africa appeared remote to investors in the 1960s, it has always been taken very seriously by South Africans. The tendency has been to focus increasingly on direct investors in southern Africa, such as Gulf Oil, and banks making loans to South Africa.

African countries are beginning to take note of companies' involvement with the minority regimes, and in some cases they have been penalized as a result. Many international organizations, such as the ILO and the World Council of Churches, have taken a strong stand against economic involvement in southern Africa, and American unions are beginning to be involved.

Western governments—including Canada, Australia, and several West European countries—have recently begun to take certain steps against economic involvement in southern Africa following widespread public concern about exploitation by their companies there. Although the U.S. government has not so far shown any sign of following this trend, there have been significant private initiatives, such as Congressman Diggs' bill on fair employment practices in South Africa, and questions raised in various local governments. And there is a possibility of government opposition to U.S. investments in southern Africa becoming a plank in the Democratic party's platform. South Africans have always used boycotts themselves; Afrikaner Nationalists used them as a weapon against the dominant English-speaking community and then imposed import quotas and embargoes on weaker neighboring countries.

The most significant move against the southern African regimes so far has been the Arab oil embargo imposed at the end of 1973. South Africa is particularly vulnerable to oil shortages, and its economy reacted adversely to the embargo. Some industries, especially those where U.S. investment is concentrated, had to cut back; inflation was aggravated; and rising freight rates still pose a problem for South Africa's external trade. Oil reserves held back for military contingencies were depleted. South Africa came to depend largely on Iran for oil supplies, and on the major international oil companies, three of them American, operating in the country. Oil shortages, especially of fuel for light aircraft, are a potential problem for military operations in Southern Rhodesia and Namibia, as well as possible future emergencies in South Africa arising out of further unofficial strikes, for example, The oil embargo on Portugal may have been a factor in the coup d'état there and the ending of the colonial wars. The imposition of the oil embargo after much skepticism and the increasing seriousness of sanctions against Southern Rhodesia are indications of the increasingly serious threat of economic pressure against southern Africa's minority regimes.

chapter 10 _____

CONCLUSIONS

In arguing the case for participation in the South African economy, the advocates of investment tend to provide a multiplicity of rationalizations that verge on self-contradiction. For example, they argue that the activities of U.S. companies in South Africa are not a major support to the economic system as a whole and cannot be held responsible for apartheid to any significant degree. At the same time they heavily emphasize the adjustments made in the pay and conditions of their more favored black workers, as evidence that an "enlightened" foreign presence can radically reverse the discrimination against them in employment generally and thus undermine apartheid itself.

While claiming to provide skills and general training that constitute a major economic asset for blacks in the South African job market, they warn repeatedly that any decision to withdraw from South Africa would amount to condemnation of "their" workers to unemployment. Almost in the same breath, it is added that in any case withdrawal would be completely ineffective since other foreign investors would come in as they withdraw.

In an echo of the official South African government line, companies frequently claim that even with apartheid Africans in South Africa are better off than any other Africans on the continent. However, they also insist that they should invest in South Africa to provide economic assistance to the Africans there. If indeed the motive for investment is to assist the most disadvantaged people in Africa, the logic of the South African claim is that investment should go anywhere but South Africa, to the poorest of the independent countries. In fact, of course, the welfare of Africans is not the prime motivation behind the initial decision to invest; in fact any improvements in African welfare have come about only since the issue has become somewhat embarrassing for companies facing criticism back home, including demands for withdrawal. The major factor remains the overriding necessity of maximizing profit for the parent company. This is not compatible, as has been shown, with any attempt to reduce the privileged position of white workers in South Africa relative to blacks; it is also not compatible with raising black wages to levels where all employees can keep their families above the absolute poverty level. No American company or subsidiary in South Africa pays a minimum wage above the Minimum Effective Level.

However, to a considerable extent, the issue of U.S. investment in southern Africa has been obscured by posing the questions in an unhelpful way. The issue is usually debated in terms of whether U.S. companies should remain or withdraw. In fact that is not the kind of decision that faces company management. It assumes a static situation, which is not the case in southern Africa. The economic and political structure is dynamic, and economic growth is essential to preserve the structure of white power, maintain balance of payments equilibrium, encourage immigration from Europe (bearing in mind that the African population is increasing rapidly), expand the economy to remain competitive with other areas of international investment, and encourage major new industries vital for the increasing defense needs of the white regimes. For an individual U.S. company the competitive nature of the South African economy and the need to cultivate government favor to retain competitiveness dictate constantly increasing inputs of fresh capital, either from retained profits that would otherwise have returned to the United States or by fresh inputs of foreign exchange from the United States European subsidiaries, or the Eurodollar market. Perhaps equally vital are the supply of high level technical and managerial personnel, new licenses and patents, and the entire range of services that only a multinational corporation can provide. While this is most obviously applicable to the few giant corporations that domin-

ate the U.S. stake in southern Africa, it also applies to smaller operations and distributorships, which may depend on the input of new franchises and technical assistance. The technical and personnel input may
well be worth more than the cash input.

The question is more likely, then, to be in terms of making fresh commitments to southern Africa. In many cases, they would be required just
to maintain the current level of operation and would not produce any
more profits—for example, relocating in a "border area," or investing
in automation to replace much cheaper African workers, or fulfilling
local-content norms. A board of directors may see this as sending good
money after bad. Or it may find some way to refrain from new investment while continuing to operate. Each decision would differ according
to the circumstances. While exchange control makes repatriation of capital complicated and involves some loss of interest, it is a viable option
provided there are not too many applications at the same time. Therefore, if there is to be a withdrawal, the sooner it is done, the less loss involved to the company.

As a matter of practice, it is no problem for multinational corporations to move into and out of countries almost regardless of national legislation—which is in fact one of the major complaints of many developing countries. In particular, financial transfers can be effected by juggling accounts between different national subsidiaries. It is also quite normal for these corporations to consider closing down a subsidiary if the
problems of operation become too great—as GM and other U.S. companies
did in Chile, for example, when the Allende government was voted into
office.

With the elaborate rationale for "reform from within," however insig-
nificant one's voice within the decision-making structure, the old Wall Street
rule has been deliberately forgotten, but seems perfectly suitable to the present case: if you do not support the policies of management, sell your stock.
Experience with banks that have been persuaded to cut off their financial
involvement with the white regimes indicates that the most successful way
to change the policies of an institution is to remove one's money, making
sure that management understands the reasons for this. Once the policy
has changed satisfactorily, there is no reason why one cannot repurchase
the stock, or reopen an account.

The questions relating to investment in southern Africa, although generally argued on moral grounds, are not in fact confined to the moral issues. This is just one more way in which the debate has become unreal, and the questions posed unhelpful. The focus on moral issues should prompt companies and their stockholders to examine rigorously the economic prospects of southern Africa. The calculation would involve up-to-date information on inflation, reduced growth, and the impact of oil and other raw material shortages in the region, and the prospects for the immediate as well as the long-term future. Political risk should be assessed much more seriously than it seems to be at present. Factors that should be taken into consideration include: the fact that two illegal regimes (Namibia and Southern Rhodesia) are involved; the independence of Guinea—Bissau and Mozambique, and the uncertain future of Angola; the apparent withdrawal of South African support from Southern Rhodesia; the increasing unofficial strikes and violence in South Africa; and the expressed opposition to white rule by the African majority, as seen from time to time through, for example, the general strike in Namibia and the overwhelming "No" vote on the Rhodesian settlement proposals as reported by the Pearce Commission. Also relevant to the question of political risk are the emerging hostility of African states to companies with a stake in the minority regimes; the opposition of a fairly wide range of organizations in the United States, including black Americans and the churches; and the increasing controversy over the issue of U.S. government intervention in the military conflicts in southern Africa. It may be taken into consideration that any crisis in the region, especially in South Africa, is likely to be sudden and without warning. It will then be too late to start thinking of retrieving one's investment.

A few comments are in order on what may generally be termed the ethical aspect to investment in southern Africa. Certain analogies with U.S. legal concepts suggest that such investment amounts to direct complicity with white minority rule, regardless of the size or the significance of the amount invested. Apartheid and colonialism are widely regarded in international bodies as crimes against humanity. Gross violations of the Universal Declaration of Human Rights are openly perpetrated in southern Africa by systematic racial discrimination on a national scale. Numerous international conventions on human rights and abolition of forced labor are directly violated. The activities of the minority regimes, such as forced deportation and victimization of civilians and the whole network of repressive and discriminatory legislation in these territories, are analogous to the actions of the Nazis before and during World War II against people they thought of as racially inferior. The Nuremberg Tribunal, which introduced the concept of crimes against humanity into international law, ruled that participation in any of the Nazi crimes, even on superior orders carried out as a "good German," was itself criminal. Failure to oppose the regime (even though opposition would entail the most serious personal risks) was tantamount to being an accomplice in its crimes.

This concept of an accomplice—one who provides money, technical assistance, moral support, or other help to someone he knows to be committing a crime—is applicable to investors in the minority regimes, who provide the same kinds of support in the full knowledge of the nature of the regimes in southern Africa. Similarly, receiving the proceeds of a criminal act is in law regarded as criminal. Thus, receiving profits arising out of forced labor is ethically on a par with organizing the system of forced labor in the first place. Even if one takes pains to remain ignorant of the details of the crime, any person who pays for, and receives a benefit from, a crime against another person is criminally liable. It is here that the question of partnership comes in. Would any honest businessman go into partnership with a known criminal because he hopes to reform him? Would he commit his own funds to such a partnership, knowing that he could not retrieve them if any conflict arose? And would he do so in circumstances where he was very much the junior partner, subject to the dictates of the other? Finally, would he do so on the basis of what could only be seen as a system of unconscionable contracts or regulations?

It seems to the author appropriate to compare the issue of American investment in southern Africa with that of slavery in America. This is based not merely on the fact that most of Africans in southern Africa are forced to work for whites, with no freedom of choice and no alternative means of subsistence. It refers also to the present state of international opinion about human rights, which rightly or wrongly has reached the stage where it will no longer tolerate colonialism and racial oppression as found in southern Africa. There are innumerable other human rights issues, whose time it is hoped will come. Just as the time had come in the second half of the nineteenth century for the abolition of African slavery in America, the time is coming for the abolition of white supremacy in Africa.

In both cases, vested economic interests in trade and investment made the initial protests on grounds of humanity appear "unrealistic." It has been argued that slavery was finally abolished because the system itself was becoming a liability, keeping large numbers of potential workers from a changing, industrializing world. This was the last straw that, together with abolitionist pressure, brought an end to slavery. In the same way, white supremacy in southern Africa seems to have passed through its most profitable period. Faced with strong moral opposition, investors may examine more carefully the economic prospects for a commitment to white minority rule in the 1970s and 1980s, increasingly deprived of the huge income provided by gold sales.

To put this into perspective, another major question should be posed, which is currently overlooked: taking the stated objectives of investors at their face value (i.e., they want to help Africans, provide employment, etc.), how does investment in the minority-ruled countries compare with that in independent Africa? If it is a question of assisting African self-determination, both economic and political, then there is a whole continent of 350 million people in over forty independent states to choose from, almost all of which would welcome any U.S. company that genuinely had these objectives in mind. The major problem with U.S. investment in Africa is that the companies have appeared unconcerned about generating employment, contributing to the national economy, following national priorities, and reinvesting earnings from their operations there. (It should be added that expropriation of companies, when it occurs, is usually provoked by the obvious lack of interest by the company in African self-determination and development.)

If investment is seen as a form of "aid" to the Africans, as many companies involved in South Africa have depicted it, then it should be remembered that rational "aid" policies are based largely on judgements about a country's ability and willingness to administer development finance efficiently and to distribute its benefits to the maximum number of people. While the economic problems of African countries only recently independent after decades of colonial rule cannot be disregarded in this connection, they are not comparable to the deliberate monopolization of economic benefits by the non-African minority in South Africa, Namibia, and Southern Rhodesia and in the former Portuguese colonies.

Even if it is a question of providing employment specifically for Africans in South Africa, there is a much more effective way of doing this than the extremely capital-intensive investment in South Africa, which provides mainly non-African employment. By investing in the neighboring countries

of Botswana, Lesotho, and Swaziland instead of South Africa, two Africans
will benefit from the creation of each job. There would be jobs for local Africans in the country concerned; and by removing them from the supply of
labor for the South African mines, where they are given preference under
South African policy, this would create job openings for unemployed Africans in South Africa. An increasing proportion of South African Africans in
the mines would also increase their scope for labor organization.

Although this study has focused on private investors' partnership with
the white minority regimes, it is important to point out in conclusion that
in the U.S. political system the commitments of major corporations cannot be separated from the policy of the U.S. government, which can in-
timately affect the lives of the people. While only GM would continue to
maintain that "what's good for GM is good for America," the overwhelming political influence of this and the other giant corporations on both
Congress and the Executive branch is a basic feature of the present political structure. In southern Africa, private U.S. investment is very closely
linked with state corporations and the policy of the regimes themselves.
U.S. companies have already proved more than willing to exercise their
political influence in favor of these regimes in Washington, the classic
case being what might be described as the "Union Carbide Rhodesian
Amendment," although most of the influence is exercised more discreetly
and at the highest level.

There is already a very strong element within U.S. government circles
urging political, and even military intervention on the side of the white
minority regimes. A National Security Council Memorandum, NSSM 39,
stressed the investment of some 300 U.S. companies in South Africa and
the rest of the region and advocated protecting "economic, scientific
and strategic interests and opportunities in the region" by means of a
"partial relaxation" of relations with the white minority regimes, including the encouragement of trade and loosening of the arms embargo.

A strong vested interest in the continuation of white power on the
part of corporations at the heart of the U.S. military-industrial complex
would add considerable weight to these pressures for military intervention
in a highly charged situation. Intervention in southern Africa, however
gradually or secretly it began, would obviously involve U.S. forces that
rely increasingly on African-Americans. Intervention could have disastrous consequences for race relations in the United States.

Foreign policy cannot be seen in isolation from domestic issues in the United States. The well-organized Jewish lobby for Israel is the most obvious example of an American group influencing policy. Another is the Greek-American protest at U.S. aid to Turkey during the Cyprus issue. African-Americans are taking an increasing interest in policy toward Africa and were a major factor in the American commitment to assistance in the Sahel drought area, putting effective pressure on the Congress and the Executive in the summer of 1973. As interest and awareness of African issues grow, helped by black studies programs, there is abundant evidence of growing interest in issues of U.S. foreign policy toward Africa although as yet there is a lack of effective organization in mobilizing effective pressure.

It is probable therefore that in a crisis situation where the United States seemed about to become involved in supporting the South African minority regime, African-Americans would react even more strongly than in the case of the Sahel disaster. In that case, they would find themselves in confrontation with those major American corporations with a vested interest in white minority rule.

Southern Africa is an unpredictable region. After centuries of Portuguese rule in the colonies, and the belief by most Westerners that their colonial rule was secure despite the liberation movements, the Portuguese were revealed as having lost the colonial wars and going through a serious national crisis as a result. American investors had cheerfully committed their resources in the colonies, backed by the assurances of the U.S. and Portuguese governments that there was no prospect of independence under the liberation movements. The future of these investments is now in the balance. So is that of U.S. companies in Southern Rhodesia, where it is widely assumed that independence under African rule is simply a matter of time. Under these circumstances, it would be a rash observer who would now assert that an investment in South Africa itself, still less Namibia, is secure for the foreseeable future. All that can be predicted is that when white minority rule is challenged, the solution will not be a peaceful one. And those involved in the present situation are likely to be involved in the ultimate conflict.

APPENDIX I

*U.S. Corporations with
Operations in South Africa*

Abbott Laboratories
Abelman Agencies Ltd.
Addressograph-Multigraph Corp.
AFAMAL-Quadrant (The Inter-
   public Group of Companies,
   Inc.)
AFIA (American Foreign In-
   surance Association, Aetna)
Alcan Aluminum
Allied Chemical Corp.
Allis Chalmers
Amalgamated Packaging In-
   dustries, Ltd. (National Amal-
   gamated Packaging, Ltd.)
American Abrasives, Inc.
American Bank Note
American Bureau of Shipping

American Celanese Co.
American Chicle
American Cyanamid Co.
American Express Co.
American Home Products
American Insurance Co.
American International Under-
   writers
American Metal Climax Inc.
   (AMAX)
American Motors Corp.
American Pacific
American South Africa In-
   vestment
American Steel Foundries
Ampex Corp.
Amrho International

Amrho International Under-
 writers
Arthur Andersen & Co.
Anderson, Clayton & Co.
Anikem (Nalco Chemical Co.)
Applied Power Industries
ARCO (Atlantic Richfield Co.)
Argus Africa Ltd.
Argus Oil
Armco Steel Corp.
Armour-Africa Ltd. (Inter-
 national Packers Ltd.)
Armstrong Cork Co.
Artnell International (Artnell
 Exploration Co. & Mono
 Containers)
Ashland Oil and Refining Co.
 (Valvoline Oil Co. Ltd.)
Audco Rockwell (Rockwell
Ault and Wiborg (Inmont Corp.)
Automated Bulding Components
Avco
Avis Rent-a-Car
Ayerst Laboratories (American
 Ethicals, Ltd.)
Azolplate Corp.
Badger Co., Inc.
Balkind Agencies, Ltd.
Bankers Trust Co.
Barlow Oshkosh (Oshkosh
 Motor Truck Co.)
Baxter Laboratories
Bechtel Corp.
Beckman Instruments, Inc.
Bedaux, Charles and Associates
Beech-Nut Life Savers, Inc.
Bellows, W.S. Contruction Co.
Berkshire International Corp.
 (Berkshire Knitting Mills)
Bethlehem Steel

Bethlehem Steel Export Corp.
Big Dutchman, Inc. (United
 States Industries)
Black Clawson Co.
Black and Decker Manu-
 facturing Co.
Boeing Corp.
Borden, Inc.
Borg-Warner Corp.
Born Africa (Born Engineering)
Boyles Drilling Co.
Braun Transworld Co.
 (C.F. Braun & Co.)
Bristol-Myers Co.
Buckner Industries, Inc.
Bucyrus-Erie
Budd
Bundy
Burlington Industries
Burroughs Machines, Ltd.
 (Burroughs Corp.)
Butterick Publishing Co., Ltd.
 (Butterick Co., Inc.)
Calabran Co. Inc. of New York
California Packing Corp.
Caltex (Standard Oil of Califor-
 nia and Texaco, Inc.)
Canada Dry International, Inc.
Carbone Corp.
Carborundum Co.
Carlane Corp.
Carnation Co.
Carrier Corp. (Airco Engineer-
 ing, Ltd.)
Carrier International
Carter Products Division
J. I. Case Co.
Caterpillar Tractor Co.
Celanese Corp. (Buffalo Paints,
 Ltd.)

APPENDIX I

291

Champion Spark Plug Co.
Charter Consolidated
Chase Manhattan Bank
Chemical Bank New York
  Trust Co.
Chemical Construction Corp.
Cheseborough-Pond's Inc.
Chicago Bridge & Iron Co.
Chicago Pneumatic Tool Co.
Christiani & Nielsen Corp.
Chrysler Corp.
Cities Service
Clark Equipment
Coca-Cola Export Corp.
Colgate-Palmolive Inter-
  national, Inc.
P. F. Collier, Inc.
Collier-Macmillan, Ltd. (The
  Macmillan Co.)
Collins Radio Co.
Colloids, Inc.
Columbia Broadcasting System
Columbus McKinnon Corp.
  (McKinnon Chain, Ltd.)
Combustion Engineering
Computer Science (Computer
  Services Corp.)
Connell Bros. Co., Ltd.
Consolidated Equipment & Mfg.
  Co. (Clipper Mfg. Co.)
Consultant Systemation
Continental Grain Co.
Continental Illinois National
  Bank and Trust
Continental Insurance Co.
Control Data Corp.
Corn Products Co. (Robertsons
  Ltd.)
Crane-Glenfield, Ltd. (Crane Co.)
Crown Cork & Seal Co., Inc.

Cutler Hammer International
Cyanamid International
Dana
Dean Export International, Ltd.
Deere & Co. (John Deere & Co.)
De Leuw, Cather & Co. Inter-
  national Investments
Del Monte Corp. (South Africa
  Preserving Co., Ltd.)
Denver Equipment Co. (Joy Mfg.
  Co., Inc.)
Derby & Co., Ltd. (Engelhard
  Minerals & Chemical Corp.)
Diamond H. Switches, Ltd. (Oak
  Electronetics Corp.)
Diner's Club International, Ltd.
Dodge & Seymour, Ltd.
Dolein Corp.
Donaldson Co., Inc.
Doughboy Industries, Inc.
Dow Chemical Co.
DuBois-Dearborn-Vestol Chem-
  ical Co.
Dunn & Bradstreet Co.
Dunlop
Du Pont Chemical Co.
Duroplastic Penta Industries
  (Engelhard Hanovia, Inc.)
E. C. DeWitt & Co.
East Newark Industrial Center
Eastern Stainless Steel Corp.
Eastman Kodak Co.
Eimco Corp.
Electric Storage Battery
Electro-Nite Co.
Eltra Co.
Emery Air Freight Corp.
Encyclopedia Brittanica, Inc.
Engelhard Hanovia
Engelhard Minerals and Chemicals
Corp.

Endo Drug Corp.
Ernst & Ernst (Whitney, Ernst &
   Ernst)
ESB Incorporated
Essex Corp. of America
ESSO Standard Ltd. (Standard
   Oil of New Jersey)
Eutectic Welding Alloys Corp.
Ewing, McDonald & Co.
Max Factor & Co.
Fairbanks, Morse & Co.
Farrell Lines, Inc.
Ferro Enamels, Ltd.
Fiberglass, Ltd. (Owens Corning
   Fiberglass Corp.)
Firder, Inc.
Firestone Tire & Rubber Co.
First Consolidated Leasing Corp.,
   Ltd. (First National City Over-
   seas Investment Corp.)
First National Bank of Boston
First National Bank of Chicago
Flintkole Co.
Fluor Co.
FMC Corp.
FNCB Services Corp. (First
   National City Bank of New York)
Ford Motor Co.
Fordom Factoring, Ltd.
   (Walter E. Heller Inter-
   national Corp.)
Forsyth Udwin, Ltd.
Fram Filters Corp.
Fruehauf
George A. Fuller Co.
Gabriel International Inc., Ltd.
Galion
Gamlen Ltd. (Sybron Corp.)
Gardner-Denver Co.
Gates Rubber Co.

General Electric Co.
General Foods Corp.
General Motors Corp.
General Signal Corp.
General Tire & Rubber Co.
George Angus Co.
J. Gerber & Co., Inc.
A. J. Gerrard & Co.
Getty Oil Co.
Gilbarco Ltd. (Gilbert & Barker
   Mfg. Co.)
Gillette Co.
Gillsevey Co.
Glair and Kestler Co.
Glidden-Durkee
Goodyear Tire and Rubber Co.
W. R. Grace & Co.
Grant Advertising, Inc.
Graver Tank & Mfg. Co.
Grolier, Inc.
Gulf Oil Corp.
Harnischfeger International Corp.
Harsco
Haskins & Sells
Heinemann Electric Co.
Helena Rubinstein, Inc.
Walter E. Heller International
   Corp.
Hertz Rent-A-Car Co.
Hewitt-Robins Inc. (Litton In-
   dustries)
Hewlett Packard, Ltd.
Hochmetals Ltd. (South Amer-
   ican Minerals & Merchandise
   Corp.)
Holiday Inns of America
Home Products International, Ltd.
Honeywell Inc.
Hoover Co.
Howe Richardson Scale Co.

Hyster Co.
IBM World Trade Corp.
Industrial Chemical Products
(Amchem Products, Inc.)
Infilco Division of Fuller Co.
Ingersoll-Rand Co.
Insurance Co. of North America
Interchemical Corp.
International Banking Corp.
International Flavors and
Fragrances, Inc.
International Group of Companies
International Harvester Co.
International Latex Corp.
International Nickel
International Packers, Ltd.
International Staple & Machine
Co.
International Telephone & Tele-
graph Corp.
Irving Chute Co., Inc.
Jeffrey-Galion Mfg. Co.
(The Jeffrey Co.)
Johns-Manville International
Corp.
Johnson and Johnson
S. C. Johnson & Son, Inc.
Kellogg Co.
Kelly-Springfield Tire Co.
Kendall Co.
Kennedy Van Saun Mfg. & En-
gineering Corp.
Kewanee Overseas Oil Corp.
(Etosha Petroleum Co.)
Keystone Asbestos Corp.
Kidder, Peabody & Co., Inc.
Kimberley-Clark Corp.
Koret of California
K.R.C. Resources (King
Resources)

Lakeside Laboratories, Inc.
E. J. Lavino & Co. (International
Minerals & Chemical Corp.)
Lease Plan International Corp.
Leo Burnett Co.
A. R. Lilly & Son
Eli Lilly International Corp.
Link-Belt Co.
Litton Industries
Litwin Corp.
Loftus Engineering Co. (Western
Gear Corp.)
Lovable Co.
Lubrizol Corp.
Lykes Brothers Steamship Co.,
Inc. (Lykes Lines Agency, Inc.)
Mack Trucks Worldwide
Mahon International, Inc.
Manhattan Shirt Co.
Manufacturers Hanover Trust
Maremount Corp.
Masonite Corp.
Master Mechanics Co.
McGraw-Hill, Inc.
Mechanite Metal Corp.
Merck, Sharp & Dohme Inter-
national
Merkan Enterprises
Merrell National Laboratories
Metro-Goldwyn Mayer Inter-
national, Inc.
Meyer Mfg. Co. (George J.
Meyer Co.)
Midlands Oil
Millburg Industrial Painters
Mine Safety Appliances Co.
Minerals & Chemicals Phillipp
Corp.
Minnesota Mining & Mfg. Co.
(3M Corp.)

Mobil Oil Corp. (Socony, Ltd.)
Monarch Cinnabar
Mono Containers (J.C. Allen)
Monsanto Co.
Moore-McCormack Lines, Inc.
Morgan Guarantee & Trust
Morrison-Knudson
Motorola Inc.
MSD (Merck & Co., Inc.)
Muller & Phipps International
    Corp.
National Cash Register Co.
National Standard Co.
National Trust & Savings
    Association
Navarro Exploration Co.
Newmont Mining Corp. (O'Okiep
    Copper Co. Ltd.)
New Wellington
A. C. Nielsen Co.
Nordberg Mfg. Co.
North American Rockwell
Norton Co.
Nuclear Corp. of America
Ocean Science & Engineering
    Inc.
Olin Mathieson Chemical Corp.
Otis Elevator Co.
Owens Corning
Owens-Illinois
P. E. Consulting Group (Kurt
    Salmon Assoc. Inc.)
Robert Page & Assoc.
Palabora Mining Co. Ltd. (New-
    mont Mining Corp.)
J. J. Palmer & Co.
Pan American World Airways, Inc.
Paragon Keylite Chemicals (Key-
    lite Chemicals)
Parke, Davis & Co.

Parker Pen Co.
Pegasus International Corp.
Pepsi Cola International
Permatex Co., Inc.
Perth Products
Charles Pfizer & Co., Inc.
Phillips Petroleum Co.
Pillsbury Co.
Pipe Line Technologists, Inc.
Placid Oil
Playtex Corp.
Plough, Inc.
P. M. Products
Polaroid Corp.
Potter & Moore (DeWitt Drug
    & Beauty Products, Inc.)
Precision Spring
Preload International Corp.
Premix Asphalt Co.
Prentice-Hall Publishers, Inc.
Prestolite International
Proctor & Gamble Co.
Publicker International, Inc.
Radio Corp. of America (RCA;
    owns Hertz)
Ramsey Engineering Co.
Reader's Digest
Reichhold Chemicals, Inc.
Reliance-Toledo
Remington Rand
Revlon, Inc.
Rexall Drug & Chemical Co.
Rheem International Co.
Rheem Mfg.
Richelieu Corp., Inc.
Riker Laboratories
Ritepoint Corp.
Ritter Pfandler Corp.
River Brand Rice Mills, Inc.
R.M.B. Alloys

H. H. Robertson Co.
Rockwell International
Rockwell Standard
Rohm & Haas Co.
Royal Baking Powder, Ltd.
  (International Standard Brands)
Royal Crown Cola Co.
A. S. Ruffel, Ltd. (Smith,
  Kline & French Laboratories)
Schering Corp. (Scherag, Ltd.)
Schlesinger Organization
Scholl Mfg. Co.
W. F. Schrafft & Sons
Scripto, Inc.
G. D. Searle & Co.
Seaway Associates Inc.
Security Resources
Servac Laboratories (Miles
  Laboratories, Inc.)
Sheffield Corp.
Shell Oil Co.
Simplicity Pattern Co., Inc.
Singer Sewing Machine Co.
Skil Corp.
A. O. Smith Corp.
Southwire Co. of Georgia
  (Phalaborwa Mining & Union
  Steel Corp.)
Sperry-Rand Corp. (Vickers-West
  & DuToit Ltd.)
Squibb Beechnut Corp.
Standard Oil Co. of California
  (Caltex)
Standard Oil Co. of New Jersey
  (Exxon)
Standard Pressed Steel Co.
  (Gordon Webster & Co.)
C. V. Starr & Co.
States Marine Lines
Stauffer Chemical Co.

Stein, Hall & Co., Inc.
Steiner Co.
Sterling Drug, Inc. (Sterling
  Products & Winthrop Labs)
St. Regis Paper Co. (National
  Packaging Co., Ltd.)
D. A. Stuart Oil Co.
Symington Wayne Corp.
  (Vitreous Enamelling Corp.)
Systematics Services Pty.
Tampax, Inc.
Tedd-Hill Products
Tedd McKune Investments
Tenneco Chemicals Inc.
  (Superior Oil)
Thermo-Electric Co., Inc.
Thompson Remco (TRW, Inc.)
J. Walter Thompson Co.
Thor Power Tool Co.
Tidewater Oil Co.
Time International
Timken Roller Bearing Co.
Titan Industrial Corp. (Pantheon
  Industries, Inc.)
Tokheim Corp.
Toledo Scale Corp. of Ohio
Touche, Ross, Bailey & Smart -
  International
Transalloys Ltd. (Air Reduction
  Co., Inc.)
Trans World Airlines, Inc.
Triton Chemicals Ltd. (Rohm &
  Haas Co.)
Tuco, Ltd. (The Upjohn Co.)
Tupperware Home Parties
Twentieth Century Fox Films Corp.
Underwood (Olivetti-Underwood)
Unimark International
Union Carbide Corp. (Chrome
  Corp., Ltd.)

Uniroyal, Inc.
United Artists Corp.
United Cargo Corp.
United Shoe Machinery Corp.
United States Steel Corp.
Universal Mineral Discoveries
Valenite-Modco, Ltd. (The Valeron
   Corp.)
Valvoline Oil
Van Dusen Aircraft Supplies, Ltd.
The Vendo Co.
Vick Chemical, Inc.
Vick International (Richardson-
   Merrill, Inc.)
Wallace International (Sam P.
   Wallace Co., Inc.)
Warner Bros.-Seven Arts Corp.
Warner-Lambert Pharmaceutical Co.
J. R. Watkins Products, Inc.
Wayne Pump Co. (Symington
   Wayne Corp.)
Western International Hotels
Western Knapp Engineering Co.
   (McKee of Panama)
Westinghouse Air Brake Co.
Westinghouse Electric Inter-
   national Corp.
Weyerhaeuser Co.
Whitney Co.
Wilbur-Ellis Co.
H. B. Wilson Co.
Worldtronic, Inc.
Worthington Air Conditioning Co.
Xerox Corp.
X-Ray International, Ltd.
Arthur Young & Co.
ZOE

Source: Corporate Information Center, National Council of Churches,
Church Investments, Corporations, and Southern Africa (New York:
Friendship Press, 1973), pp. 165-9.

APPENDIX II _____

Companies with
Operations in Namibia
Linked with South African Investments

Burroughs Machines, Ltd.
Canada Dry
Firestone (S.A.) Pty, Ltd.
Galion Iron Works and Manufacturing Company
General Tire and Rubber (S.A.), Ltd.
National Cash Register S.A. (Pty), Ltd.
Royal Crown Cola
Singer South Africa (Pty), Ltd.
Caltex Oil (S.A.), Ltd.
Mobil Refining Southern Africa (Pty), Ltd. (oil marketing)
Valvoline Oil (S.A.) (Pty), Ltd.[1]
Caltex Petroleum Corp. (oil marketing)
Gemstone Miners, Ltd.[2]
Minnesota Mining & Mfg. Corporation (export sales)
Oshkosh Trucking (export sales)
Otis Elevator Company (employees)

Richardson-Merrill

IBM (installations, customer engineer services; expanded
  recently)

Automated Building Components Inc. (manufacturing engineered
  timber structures for a customer in Namibia)[3]

References

1. U.S. Congress, House of Representatives, Committee on Foreign
Affairs, Subcommittee on Africa, *U.S. Business Involvement in Southern Africa,* Part I (Washington, D.C.: Government Printing Office, 1972),
p. 269.

2. State Department listing, inserted as written memorandum in the testimony by Mr. R. Smith, 28 March, 1973 in ibid., Part III, p. 59.

3. Replies to a questionnaire by Congressman Charles C. Diggs, Jr.,
on business in southern Africa, 1973, in ibid., appendix 81, 82, and
83, pp. 978-1067.

APPENDIX III _____

U.S. Corporations with Interests in Southern Rhodesia

COMPANY	OPERATION IN SOUTHERN RHODESIA
Abbott Laboratories	"Conduct business in Rhodesia"
Affiliated Exporters, Inc., New York	Elephant Trading Company; clothing manufacturers
American Foreign Insurance Association, New York	American Foreign Insurance Association, Salisbury.
American Metal Climax, Inc., New York; and American Potash & Chemical Corp., Los Angeles	Bikita Minerals; lithium mining

Arbor Acres Farms, Inc.

Automated Building   "Customer located there"
Components, Inc.

Baker Perkins, Inc.,   Baker Perkins, Salisbury;
Saginaw, Michigan   distribution of industrial
                                      machinery

Bardahl International   Bardahl Distributors Rhodesia;
Oil Corp., Seattle,   distributor of petroleum products
Washington

Bourne & Co., Elizabeth,   Bourne & Co., Salisbury;
New Jersey   distributor of Singer sewing
                                      machines

Bristol-Myers   "Small operations"

Burroughs Corp.,   Burroughs Machines, Salisbury;
Detroit, Michigan   distributors of accounting
                                      machines

California Texas Oil   Caltex Oil (Rhodesia),
Co., New York   Salisbury; distributor of
                                      petroleum products

Canada Dry International,
Inc.

Carborundum Co., Niagara   Carborundum-Universal,
Falls, New York   Salisbury; manufacturers of
                                      coated and bonded abrasives;
                                      diamond wheels and refractors

Celanese Corporation

China American Tobacco Co.,   China American Tobacco Co. of
Rocky Mount, North Carolina   Rhodesia; Tobacco exporter

Continental Ore Corp.,   Continental Ore Africa,
New York   Salisbury; metal and mineral
                                      brokers

Christian Science Publishing
Co.

Chrysler Corp.

Dibrell Bros. Inc.,
Danville, Virginia

Dibrell Bros. of Africa,
Salisbury; and Tobacco Export
Corp. of Africa, Salisbury;
both are tobacco exporters.

Dillon Read & Co.,
New York

Merchant Bank of C.A.,
Salisbury; banking

Dun and Bradstreet,
International

Eastman Kodak Co.,
Rochester, New York

Kodak (Rhodesia) Ltd.,
Salisbury; distribution of
photographic equipment, film
processing laboratory

Electric Storage Battery
Co., Philadelphia,
Pennsylvania

Willard Africa, Southerton;
manufacturers of auto
batteries

Falls City Tobacco Co.,
Louisville, Kentucky

Falls City Tobacco Co.,
Salisbury; tobacco exporters

Foote Mineral Co.,
Exton, Pennsylvania

Rhodesian Vanadium Corp.;
chrome and manganese

Fort Dodge Laboratories

Gardner-Denver Co.,
Quincy, Illinois

Gardner-Denver Co. (Africa),
Southerton; distributors of
mining equipment

Goodyear Tire and Rubber
Co., Akron, Ohio

Goodyear Tyre and Rubber Co.,
Salisbury; manufacturers and
distributors of tires, tubes, etc.

Grant Advertising, Inc.,
New York

Grant Advertising, Salisbury;
advertising consultants, very
active in Rhodesia and in
promoting Rhodesia in the
United States

Haskins & Sells

Hewitt-Robins, Inc., Stamford, Connecticut	Robins Conveyors, Bulawayo; distribution of material handling equipment
Hoover Co.	Hoover (Rhodesia); manufactures and supplies domestic appliances
IBM, New York	IBM Central Africa, Salisbury; distributors of business machines; the company claims it is a "caretaker operation"
Ingersoll-Rand, Ltd., New York	Ingersoll–Rand Co., Bulawayo; distribution of mining machinery
Insurance Co. of North America, Philadelphia, Pennsylvania	Insurance Co. of North America, Salisbury; insurance
International Basic Economy Corp.	
International Chinchilla Headquarters, Inc., Redwood City, California	Chinchilla Headquarters of Rhodesia; distribution and sales agency for imported chinchilla
International Telephone and Telegraph Corp., New York	Standard Telephones and Cables (Rhodesia); distribution of telecommunications equipment; and Supersonic Radio Mfg. Co.; radios and televisions
The Jeffrey Co., Columbus, Ohio	Jeffrey-Galion (Rhodesia), Salisbury; distribution of roadmaking and mining machinery
J. Walter Thompson Co., New York	J. Walter Thompson, Salisbury; advertising consultants
Johnson and Johnson	Exports to Rhodesia from South Africa
Lever Bros.	Lever Bros.; manufactures food, toiletries, and detergents

Macy's New York

Macy's Consolidated (Pvt.), Ltd. brought in Sept. 1973 a R1.5m. property in Salisbury for a general retail store

Metallurg, Inc., New York

Rhodesian Cambrai Mines, Gwelo; chrome mining

Minnesota Mining and Mfg. Co., St. Paul, Minn. (3M)

Minnesota Mining and Mfg. Co., Salisbury; double coated tissue tapes, PVC, cellulose and masking tapes

National Cash Register Co., Dayton, Ohio

N.C.R., Salisbury; distribution of business machines

Oshkosh Trucking

Otis Elevator

Owens-Illinois

Has a Rhodesian subsidiary of its South African glassmaking company

Permatex Co.

Pfizer International, Inc., New York

Pfizer, Salisbury; chemicals

Phillips Petroleum

Exports of carbon black (essential for tires and auto production) from Phillips Carbon Black Co. in South Africa

Richardson-Merrill, Inc.

Exports from South Africa

Royal Crown Cola Co.

Socony-Mobil, Inc., New York

Socony Southern Africa, Salisbury; distribution of bitumens, asphalt, waxes and solvents; Mobil Oil Rhodesia, Salisbury; distribution of petroleum products

Standard Bank (Chase Manhattan)

Very wide banking services, including payments in violation of sanctions (in New York and internationally): operates through Standard Bank, Standard Finance Ltd.; 26 percent of the RIB Holdings, 13 percent of the Export Credit Insurance Corp. of Rhodesia

St. Regis Paper Co.

Trans World Airlines, Inc.

Twentieth Century-Fox, Inc., New York

African Consolidated Films, Salisbury; motion picture showing and distribution

Union Carbide Corp., New York

Chrome mining, ferrochrome production, mineral prospecting

Union Special Machine Co., Chicago, Illinois

Berzack Bros., Bulawayo; distribution of industrial sewing machines

Universal Leaf Tobacco Co., Richmond, Virginia

Rhodesian Leaf Tobacco, Salisbury, tobacco exporter

W. R. Grace & Co.

"Minor sales"

Woolworth

Chain stores in Salisbury and Bulawayo

Arthur Young & Co.

Vanadium Corp. of America

American Products Manufactured Under License in Southern Rhodesia:

Company	*Licensee*
Cheseborough-Ponds Inc., New York	Cheseborough-Ponds International Salisbury; manufacturers and distributors of toiletries

The Coca-Cola Co., New York	Salisbury Bottling Co.; bottling and distribution of soft drinks
Pepsi-Cola Co., New York	Central African Bottling Co., Salisbury; bottling and distribution of soft drinks
Scripto, Inc., Atlanta, Georgia	Scripto of Rhodesia, Salisbury; manufacturers and distributors of pens
Sterling Drug Inc., New York	Sterling Drug International, Salisbury; manufacturers and distributors of pharmaceutical products

Sources: Answers to the questionnaire from Congressman Charles C. Diggs, Jr., in U.S. Congress, House of Representatives, Committee on Foreign Affairs, Subcommittee on Africa, *U.S. Business Involvement in Southern Africa,* Part III (Washington, D.C.: Government Printing Office, 1973), appendix 82, pp. 981-1058; Corporate Information Center, National Council of Churches, *Church Investments, Corporations and Southern Africa* (New York: Friendship Press, 1973); list of U.S. companies with a stake in Southern Rhodesia as of 13 February, 1969, supplied by the U.S. Treasury Department, in U.S. Congress, House of Representatives, Committee on Foreign Affairs, Subcommittee on Africa, *Future Directions of U.S. Policy Toward Southern Rhodesia* (Washington, D.C.: Government Printing Office, 1973), pp. 97-8; United Nations, Special Committee on Decolonization, *Working Paper on Investment in Southern Rhodesia,* April, 1974.

APPENDIX IV ⸺⸺⸺

Universal Declaration of Human Rights

On December 10, 1948, the General Assembly of the United Nations adopted and proclaimed the Universal Declaration of Human Rights, the full text of which appears in the following pages. Following this historic act the Assembly called upon all Member countries to publicize the text of the Declaration and "to cause it to be disseminated, displayed, read and expounded principally in schools and other educational institutions, without distinction based on the political status of countries or territories."

[Final Authorized Text—United Nations Office of Public Information]

UNIVERSAL DECLARATION OF HUMAN RIGHTS

Preamble

Whereas recognition of the inherent dignity and of the equal and inalienable rights of all members of the human family is the foundation of freedom, justice and peace in the world,

Whereas disregard and contempt for human rights have resulted in barbarous acts which have outraged the conscience of mankind, and the advent of a world in which human beings shall enjoy freedom of speech and belief and freedom from fear and want has been proclaimed as the highest aspiration of the common people,

Whereas it is essential, if man is not to be compelled to have recourse, as a last resort, to rebellion against tyranny and oppression, that human rights should be protected by the rule of law,

Whereas it is essential to promote the development of friendly relations between nations,

Whereas the peoples of the United Nations have in the Charter reaffirmed their faith in fundamental human rights, in the dignity and worth of the human person and in the equal rights of men and women and have determined to promote social progress and better standards of life in larger freedom,

Whereas Member States have pledged themselves to achieve, in co-operation with the United Nations, the promotion of universal respect for and observance of human rights and fundamental freedoms,

Whereas a common understanding of these rights and freedoms is of the greatest importance for the full realization of this pledge,

Now, Therefore, the General Assembly proclaims this Universal Declaration of Human Rights as a common standard of achievement for all peoples and all nations, to the end that every individual and every organ of society, keeping this Declaration constantly in mind, shall strive by teaching and education to promote respect for these rights and freedoms and by progressive measures, national and international, to secure their universal and effective recognition and observance, both among the peoples of member states themselves and among the peoples of territories under their jurisdiction.

Article 1. All human beings are born free and equal in dignity and rights. They are endowed with reason and conscience and should act towards one another in a spirit of brotherhood.

Article 2. Everyone is entitled to all the rights and freedoms set forth in this Declaration, without distinction of any kind, such as race, colour, sex, language, religion, political or other opinion, national or social origin, property, birth or other status.

Furthermore, no distinction shall be made on the basis of the political, jurisdictional or international status of the country or territory to which a person belongs, whether it be independent, trust, non-self-governing or under any other limitation of sovereignty.

Article 3. Everyone has the right to life, liberty and security of person.

Article 4. No one shall be held in slavery or servitude; slavery and the slave trade shall be prohibited in all their forms.

Article 5. No one shall be subjected to torture or to cruel, inhuman or degrading treatment or punishment.

Article 6. Everyone has the right to recognition everywhere as a person before the law.

Article 7. All are equal before the law and are entitled without any discrimination to equal protection of the law. All are entitled to equal protection against any discrimination in violation of this Declaration and against any incitement to such discrimination.

Article 8. Everyone has the right to an effective remedy by the competent national tribunals for acts violating the fundamental rights granted him by the constitution or by law.

Article 9. No one shall be subjected to arbitrary arrest, detention or exile.

Article 10. Everyone is entitled in full equality to a fair and public hearing by an independent and impartial tribunal, in the determination of his rights and obligations and of any criminal charge against him.

Article 11. (1) Everyone charged with a penal offence has the right to be presumed innocent until proved guilty according to law in a public trial at which he has had all the guarantees necessary for his defence. (2) No one shall be held guilty of any penal offence on account of any act or omission which did not constitute a penal offence, under national or international law, at the time when it was committed. Nor shall a heavier penalty be imposed than the one that was applicable at the time the penal offence was committed.

Article 12. No one shall be subjected to arbitrary interference with his privacy, family, home or correspondence, nor to attacks upon his honour and reputation. Everyone has the right to the protection of the law against such interference or attacks.

Article 13. (1) Everyone has the right to freedom of movement and residence within the borders of each state. (2) Everyone has the right to leave any country, including his own, and to return to his country.

Article 14. (1) Everyone has the right to seek and to enjoy in other countries asylum from persecution. (2) This right may not be invoked in the case of prosecutions genuinely arising from non-political crimes or from acts contrary to the purposes and principles of the United Nations.

Article 15. (1) Everyone has the right to a nationality. (2) No one shall be arbitrarily deprived of his nationality nor denied the right to change his nationality.

Article 16. (1) Men and women of full age, without any limitation due to race, nationality or religion, have the right to marry and to found a family. They are entitled to equal rights as to marriage, during marriage and at its dissolution. (2) Marriage shall be entered into only with the free and full consent of the intending spouses. (3) The family is the natural and fundamental group unit of society and is entitled to protection by society and the State.

Article 17. (1) Everyone has the right to own property alone as well as in association with others. (2) No one shall be arbitrarily deprived of his property.

Article 18. Everyone has the right to freedom of thought, conscience and religion; this right includes freedom to change his religion or belief, and freedom, either alone or in community with others and in public or private, to manifest his religion or belief in teaching, practice, worship and observance.

Article 19. Everyone has the right to freedom of opinion and expression; this right includes freedom to hold opinions without interference and to seek, receive and impart information and ideas through any media and regardless of frontiers.

Article 20. (1) Everyone has the right to freedom of peaceful assembly and association. (2) No one may be compelled to belong to an association.

Article 21. (1) Everyone has the right to take part in the government of his country, directly or through freely chosen representatives. (2) Everyone has the right of equal access to public service in his country. (3) The will of the people shall be the basis of the authority of government; this will shall be expressed in periodic and genuine elections which shall be by universal and equal suffrage and shall be held by secret vote or by equivalent free voting procedures.

Article 22. Everyone, as a member of society, has the right to social security and is entitled to realization, through national effort and international co-operation and in accordance with the organization and resources of each State, of the economic, social and cultural rights indispensable for his dignity and the free development of his personality.

Article 23. (1) Everyone has the right to work, to free choice of employment, to just and favourable conditions of work and to protection against unemployment. (2) Everyone, without any discrimination, has the right to equal pay for equal work. (3) Everyone who works has the right to just and favourable remuneration ensuring for himself and his family an existence worthy of human dignity, and supplemented, if necessary, by other means of social protection. (4) Everyone has the right to form and to join trade unions for the protection of his interests.

Article 24. Everyone has the right to rest and leisure, including reasonable limitation fo working hours and periodic holidays with pay.

Article 25. (1) Everyone has the right to a standard of living adequate for the health and well-being of himself and his family, including food, clothing, housing and medical care and necessary social services, and the right to security in the event of unemployment, sickness, disability, widowhood, old age or other lack of livelihood in circumstances beyond his control. (2) Motherhood and childhood are entitled to special care and assistance. All children, whether born in or out of wedlock, shall enjoy the same social protection.

Article 26. (1) Everyone has the right to education. Education shall be free, at least in the elementary and fundamental stages. Elementary education shall be compulsory. Technical and professional education shall be made generally available and higher education shall be equally accessible to all on the basis of merit. (2) Education shall be directed to the full development of the human personality and to the strengthening of respect for human rights and fundamental freedoms. It shall promote understanding, tolerance and friendship among all nations, racial or religious groups, and shall further the activities of the United Nations for the maintenance of peace. (3) Parents have a prior right to choose the kind of education that shall be given to their children.

Article 27. (1) Everyone has the right freely to participate in the cultural life of the community, to enjoy the arts and to share in scientific advancement and its benefits. (2) Everyone has the right to the protection of the moral and material interests resulting from any scientific, literary or artistic production of which he is the author.

Article 28. Everyone is entitled to a social and international order in which the rights and freedoms set forth in this Declaration can be fully realized.

Article 29. (1) Everyone has duties to the community in which alone the free and full development of his personality is possible (2) In the exercise of his rights and freedoms, everyone shall be subject only to such limitations as are determined by law solely for the purpose of securing due recognition and respect for the rights and freedoms of others and of meeting the just requirements of morality, public order and the general welfare in a democratic society. (3) These rights and freedoms may in no case be exercised contrary to the purposes and principles of the United Nations.

Article 30. Nothing in this Declaration may be interpreted as implying for any State, group or person any right to engage in any activity or to perform any act aimed at the destruction of any of the rights and freedoms set forth herein.

INDEX

Kane-Berman, John, 191
Kapuuo, Chief Clemens, 211
Kennedy administration, 231
Kewanee, 203
Kissinger, Dr. Henry, 159
Kodak, 146; and Southern
 Rhodesia, 227
Kombat mine, 193
Koornhof, Dr., 8
Krupp, 244
Kunene dam scheme, 195,
 209, 244
Kwazulu, 11, 13, 51. *See also*
 Bantustans; Buthelezi

Laager, 63, 65. *See also*
 Afrikaners; Ideology
Labor: force, blacks in,
 72; market, domination of
 by South African govern-
 ment, 25-27; regulations of
 1968, 49; units, Africans as,
 45-47. *See also* Employment;
 Workers
Labor Bureaus, 47, 61; in
 Namibia, 186, 191
Labour party, British, 255-57
Land Bank, 56
Land tenure, 4, 56, 114; in
 Bantustans, 11, 12; in Namibia,
 208. *See also* Agriculture;
 Removals
Lange, Prof. Jan H., 77
Law. *See* International law
League of Nations, 171, 207.
 See also Mandate; United
 Nations
Legal action in U.S., 251, 259
Leon, Sonny, 110, 149-50
Lesotho workers, 79
Liberalization. *See* Apartheid;
 Reform from within; United
 States investment
Liberation movements, 231; and

boycotts, 264. *See also* ANC
 (South Africa and Zimbabwe),
 FLEC, FNLA, Frelimo, MPLA,
 PAC, PAIGC
Liberty Lobby, 160
Litton Industries, 238
Loans, foreign, to South Africa,
 114, 116, 255-57; through
 EABC, 95; importance of,
 99; and Owens-Illinois, 147;
 role of South African govern-
 ment in, 25; U.S., 102-3, 160-62
Lobbying in U.S.: and African-
 Americans, 286-87; by inves-
 tors in southern Africa, 159-60,
 258; by trade unions, 253-54;
 for Southern Rhodesian regime,
 219-20, 225-26; by U.S. Steel,
 144
Local content. *See* Auto industry
Local identification: by Exxon,
 143; by oil companies, 140-41
Loffland Bros. Inc., 240
Lombard, Prof., 17
Loudon, Bruce, 232

Mac Bride, Sean, 173
McHenry, Don H., 231
McKee, Arthur G., 201
Macrae, Norman, 69
Malawians in Southern Rhodesia,
 221
Malnutrition, 12, 30, 32, 114.
 See also Child mortality; Food
Management, 97
Mandate, 171, 203-4, 207-8
Manufacturing: African
 employment in, 39; and
 automation, 26; and foreign
 investment, 93, 221; and
 military production, 104;
 profits, 39-40; and U.S. invest-
 ment, 24, 125, 146-47; wages
 in 62-63

SOEKOR (South African state
oil corporation), 140, 209
Soil erosion, 6
South Africa Foundation, 103,
149, 159
South African Airways, 135
South African economy in
state of war, 103-4
South African government:
and African unions, 53-54;
and African wages in the
Bantustans, 18; control of
the economy, 23-27, 60-61,
94-96, 116-17; control of
foreign investment in the
Bantustans, 19; and foreign
investment in Botswana, 29;
and foreign loans, 160-61;
and job fragmentation,
41, 43; regulation of
African labor, 24, 27, 46-60;
and white farmers, 56-57; and
white workers, 60-61, 72-73
South African Productivity
and Wage Association, 30,
152
South African Railways, 41-42
South African Reserve Bank,
44, 79-80, 116-17
South Atlantic Cable Co.,
139
South-East Atlantic Fisheries
Organization, 175
Southern Africa: as drain on
South African armed forces,
114-15 See also Namibia;
Portuguese colonies, former;
Southern Rhodesia
Southern Rhodesia, x, 81, 217-
27, 283; conscription in, 115;
expropriation of companies
in, 106; and foreign investment,
219, 220, 227; and oil embargo,
263; and Portuguese colonies,

234; and South Africa, 114-
15, 180, 261, 263, 283; and
U.S. investment, 219-27, 287.
See also Lobbying in U.S.
Rhodesian Information
Office
South West Africa. See Namibia
South West Africa Affairs Act
of 1969, 209
South West Africa Co., 193
Soweto, 36, 57
Spandau, Arndt, 33-34
Sperry Rand. See Univac-Sperry
Rand
Spro-cas, 139, 153
Stallard Commission, 45
Standard Bank, 127, 147; in
Namibia, 147; in Portuguese
colonies, 246; in Southern
Rhodesia, 147, 227
Standard Electric, 245
Standard of living of whites in
Southern Rhodesia, 221.
See also Incomes
Standard Oil of California, 210,
239; and Chevron Regent, 200.
See also Caltex
Standard Oil of Indiana, 239
State corporations, 24-25,
94-95; and boycotts, 259; in
Brazil, 69; and foreign loans,
160-62; and U.S. investment,
286
State Department, U.S., 148,
158, 160, 226; and Namibia,
176, 178; and Portuguese
colonies, 231, 244. See also
Newsom; Rogers; United
States government policy
State of emergency, 13; in 1960,
74; in Ovamboland, 182
Statistics, U.S., on Namibia, 175-
76
Sterling Area, Overseas, 118

About the Author

Barbara Rogers has served as a research consultant to the United
Nations Commissioner for Namibia and to Congressman Diggs,
chairperson of the House Subcommittee on Africa. She is currently
a free-lance writer on southern Africa.